AF334538

Linguistic and Computational Techniques
in Machine Translation System Design

Studies in Computational Linguistics

Series Editor
  Harold Somers

Editorial Board:
  Joseba Abaitua, *Universidad de Deutso*
  Doug Arnold, *University of Essex*
  Paul Bennett, *UMIST*
  Bill Black, *UMIST*
  Michael Hess, *University ät Zürich*
  Rod Johnson, *Lugano*
  Jun-ichi Tsuji, *UMIST*
  Mary McGee Wood, *University of Manchester*
  Peter Whitelock, *Sharp Laboratories of Europe*
  Christoph Zähner, *UMIST*

Further titles in the series

A course in generalized phrase structure grammar Paul Bennett

Analogical natural language processing Daniel Jones

Abduction, beliefs and context: studies in computational pragmatics
  William J. Black & Harry Bunt (eds)

Linguistic and Computational Techniques in Machine Translation System Design

Second edition

Peter Whitelock
Sharp Laboratories of Europe

[†]Kieran Kilby

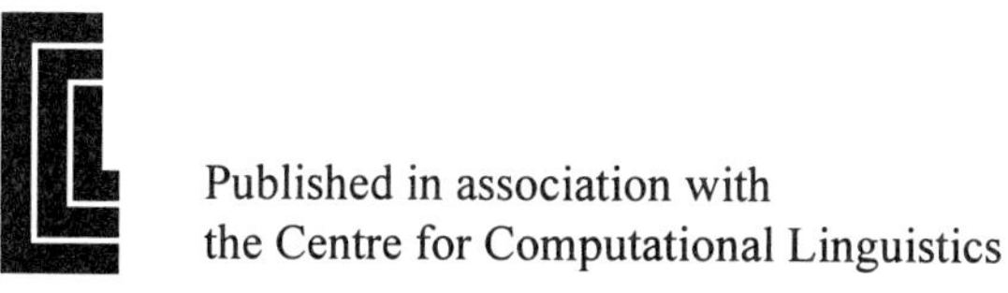

Published in association with
the Centre for Computational Linguistics

UCL
PRESS

First published in 1995 by UCL Press
Published in association with the Centre for Computational Linguistics

UCL Press Limited
University College London
Gower Street
London WC1E 6BT

The name of University College London (UCL) is a registered trade mark used by
UCL Press with the consent of the owner.

British Library Cataloguing-in-Publication Data
A CIP catalogue record for this book is available from the British Library.

Library of Congress Cataloging-in-Publication Data are available

ISBN:
1-85728-216-7 HB

Typeset in Times Roman.
Printed and bound by Page Bros (Norwich) Ltd.

Contents

Preface

It is a pleasure to launch our new *Studies in Computational Linguistics* series by issuing a second edition of "Whitelock and Kilby". Although this is a relatively old text – completed in 1983 – it is a work for which we still receive requests, and which still gets cited. At the time of writing it was the first attempt anyone had made to take a critical and objective look at the details of MT systems: until then, the only available material was of too general a nature, typically compiled by keen archivists who did not have a thorough understanding of the computational and linguistic features of the systems. What Whitelock and Kilby were able to do was to amass a huge collection of largely unpublished internal memos and semi-confidential reports, which enabled them to get a really in-depth understanding of how the systems worked.

Even in the years since that time, this effort has not yet been duplicated: certainly there has been a huge increase of interest and awareness of MT, and some splendid publications on the subject have appeared. But typically these fall into one of five categories: (a) discussions of the field in general, such as Makoto Nagao's *Machine Translation: how far can it go?* (Oxford University Press, 1989); (b) general surveys of the field, based on readily available published material, but lacking in critical discussion (e.g. John Hutchins' *Machine Translation: past, present, future*, Ellis Horwood, 1986); (c) collections of descriptions of systems by their own developers, such as Margaret King's *Machine Translation today* (Edinburgh University Press, 1987), or Jonathan Slocum's 1985 special issues of *Computational Linguistics*, later published by Cambridge University Press; (d) books entirely devoted to a single system, again written by the developers themselves; (e) proceedings of conferences on the subject of MT, where contributions tend to be more theoretical and/or speculative.

For this reason, we feel that it is not untimely to reproduce the final report of the SERC/SSRC-funded project. Naturally, there have been a lot of developments in MT since 1983, and some of them mean that a few of the observations in this book are now slightly dated, although usually only in the matter of small details. So for example a planned development never took place, or a feature of a system which was open to criticism in 1983 was later changed. And of course, a lot of the opinions expressed by Whitelock and Kilby have since been reiterated by other observers of the MT scene. However we have decided to resist the temptation to make wholesale changes to the text of this book, since this would be a major undertaking. Rather, we have added explanatory footnotes where necessary, to avoid giving the impression that we are completely out of touch with contemporary MT research!

We would like to thank Pete Whitelock and Rod Johnson for their help in preparing this second edition. A major debt of gratitude is to Debbie Sapsed, who painstakingly oversaw the transfer of the text from the somewhat primitive typescript of the first edition to the current format.

As mentioned above, this report was completed in 1983. **Pete Whitelock** went on to lead UMIST's Alvey-funded MT research programme, whose official title was "Read and write Japanese without knowing it", a title which perhaps hides the real aim of the project, which was to develop an MT system for a monolingual user. This was the ENtran system, for translating English into Japanese, which was developed between 1984 and 1986. Whitelock left UMIST in 1987 to become a lecturer in the Department of Artificial Intelligence at Edinburgh University. In 1990 he left Edinburgh to become a Senior Researcher at the newly opened Sharp Laboratories of Europe, near Oxford, where he is still working on Machine Translation.

Kieran Kilby left UMIST in 1985 to work as a research assistant in the Department of French at Leeds University. In 1986, he was appointed to a one-year temporary lectureship in French in the Department of International Studies at Leeds Polytechnic. After that, he began training as an accountant at Robson and Rhodes in Bradford. Sadly, in May 1988, he was killed in a freak accident while hill-walking, when he was struck by lightning.

Harold L. Somers
(series editor)
Manchester, December 1993

Preface to the first edition

This book represents the result of a two-year project entitled "An in-depth study of linguistic and computational techniques in Machine Translation", funded by the SERC/SSRC Joint Committee, and carried out at the Centre for Computational Linguistics, UMIST, Manchester.

The principal aims of the project were threefold:

1. To accumulate documentation pertaining to a diverse range of MT systems, thus providing a basis for Stage 2.

2. To evaluate such documentation, principally by examining each system in turn from a common viewpoint, attempting to highlight the strengths and weaknesses of each, and thereby bridging the gap that exists between:

   a. the brief introductory descriptions of such systems to be found in the Computational Linguistics literature,

    b. detailed documentation aimed principally at grammar writers, which is, of course, uncritical, and also not readily available,

    c. survey articles intended to introduce the field to workers in other disciplines, such as library and information science, or to potential users.

3. To exploit the experience gained in a variety of ways:

    a. to produce the present report, defining the scope of MT systems design, paying particular attention to the roles of its component disciplines: linguistics, computation, translation theory, Artificial Intelligence,

    b. to determine those aspects of system design which offer the greatest scope for improvement in translation quality, and thus to define areas of research to which particular attention should be paid in the future,

    c. as a sound basis for system design efforts in the Centre itself.

The results of Stage 2, detailed descriptions and evaluations of six systems, constitute Part II of this book. These were systems for which the documentation obtained covered almost all aspects of design. The Centre obtained information about other systems, though either of insufficient detail, or covering only limited design features, and thus unsuitable for similar treatment. However, relevant aspects of their design have been incorporated into the final report.

The six systems considered in depth address between them a diversity of approaches to MT, almost their only common feature being that the ideas have actually been implemented and tested. The systems examined are SYSTRAN, TAUM MÉTÉO, TAUM AVIATION, GETA ARIANE-78, LRC METAL, and Wilks's Preference Semantics system.

Authors' note

While every care has been taken, we cannot guarantee that the information presented is correct, or, in those cases where the documentation is unclear, that we have chosen the correct interpretation.

Acknowledgments

We would like to thank all those people responsible for providing documentation, the SERC/SSRC Joint Committee for financial support, and all our colleagues at the Centre for Computational Linguistics for encouragement and assistance. Without the help of any of these, the project could not even have been started.

Abbreviations

A, ADJ — adjective
ALO — allomorph
ALPAC — Automated Language Processing Advisory Committee
ART — article
ATN — Augmented Transition Network
CAT — category
CEC — Commission of the European Communities
CETA — *Centre d'Etudes pour la Traduction Automatique*
CLS — conditional limited semantics
COP — copular
cpu — central processing unit
CSIR — common-sense inference rule
det — determiner
FS — *fonction syntactique* (syntactic function)
GB — Government and Binding
GETA — *Groupe d'Etudes pour la Traduction Automatique*
GN — *groupe nominale* (NP)
GOV — governor
HLS — footnote by Somers (series editor)
indobj — indirect object
INST — instrument
IR — intermediate (or interface) representation
LDB — lexical database
LDCS — lexical data control system
LHS — left-hand side

LRC — Linguistics Research Center
LS — limited semantics
LSP — Language for Special Purposes
MAT — Machine-Aided Translation
MT — Machine Translation
N — noun
NBR — number
NP — noun phrase
NUM — number
OCR — optical character recognition
PAT — patient
PHVB — *phrase verbale* (VP)
POS — part of speech
PS — Production System (Chap. 5)
PS — Preference Semantics (Chap. 10)
PW — principal word
RHS — right-hand side
RL — *relation logique* (logical relation)
RT — root of transformation
RTN — Relational Transition Network
S — sentence
SING — singular
SL — source language
TAUM — *Traduction Automatique de l'Université de Montréal*
TG — transformational grammar
TG — topical glossary (in SYSTRAN)
TL — target language
TR — transformational rule
TS — transformational system
UL — *unité lexicale* (lexical unit)
VP — verb phrase

Part I
General discussion

1
Introduction

Translation, like other intelligent activities, is a knowledge-based process. As in many tasks involving natural language, the knowledge required is of diverse types and originates from diverse sources. These types include knowledge about individual words, their distributional properties and meanings (dictionary knowledge), about word order and other structural relations between the constituents of a sentence (syntactic knowledge), about the relations between the structure of texts and their communicative functions (pragmatic and stylistic knowledge) and about the relations which may hold between the entities and events designated by words and sentences (semantic, conceptual and "real-world" knowledge).

Thus Machine Translation (MT) system design combines elements of lexicography, generative linguistics, computational linguistics (i.e. the implementation of linguistic descriptions as algorithms), LSP (textual studies of special purpose languages, particularly those of science and technology) and the Artificial Intelligence approach to knowledge representation and organization, as embodied in a variety of Intelligent Knowledge-Based Systems.

Each of these well-established disciplines provides an extensive body of theoretical results for the MT system designer to exploit. However, a system design will also be a more or less explicit implementation of a theory of the translation task. To date, such theories either have been extremely simplistic and *ad hoc*, or have assumed that the translation task is merely the sum of the language understanding and language generation tasks. If MT quality is to improve, it must be acknowledged that translation is an expert task, and theories which make computationally realizable claims about how expert translators exploit their contrastive knowledge of source and target languages must be developed.

Chapter 2 of this book discusses the historical development of ideas about the relationship between source and target language knowledge in MT systems. The types of texts suitable for MT, and the possible relationships between human and machine, are then briefly described.

Chapter 3 gives a brief catalogue of the linguistic problems to which an MT system must address itself, including monolingual ambiguity resolution and the determination of translation equivalents.

Chapter 4 presents an overview of techniques for representing the structure of texts, of increasing degree of abstraction from the surface form. In general, the translation task will require access to information at various levels of abstraction, so the representation problem is not one of choosing between alternatives, but of integrating the descriptions of text from different viewpoints.

Chapter 5 describes how linguistic knowledge may be specified and interpreted for the purpose of building structural representations of texts.

In Part II we present an in-depth description of several MT systems. The systems examined are as follows:

- **SYSTRAN** – Though of early, and rather primitive, design, SYSTRAN is extremely successful, being the most widely used of any MT system to date. Its success is largely the result of the great effort that has been expended in incorporating expert linguistic knowledge into its procedures. Versions for various language pairs exist (including Russsian–English, English–French, French–English, English–Italian).

- **TAUM MÉTÉO** – This system is used by the Canadian Meteorological Office for translation of weather bulletins from English to French. Grammars for each stage of the translation process are expressed in the same formalism (Q-systems); MÉTÉO constitutes a paradigm case of simplicity (and generality) in design, which, for the limited domain of texts it handles, results in particular effectiveness.

- **TAUM AVIATION** – This system was designed by the same research team as MÉTÉO, but it differs considerably from it, and not always for the better. Whereas Q-systems are a declarative formalism (linguistic knowledge expressed in a form largely independent of considerations about its application), AVIATION's grammars are written in a variety of highly procedural formalisms. This seems to have resulted in some difficulties in incorporating the knowledge required for translation (of aircraft maintenance manuals from English to French).

- **GETA ARIANE-78** – Like those of AVIATION, ARIANE-78 grammars are realized in a variety of formalisms according to the phase of translation to which they are relevant. However, the style of formalism is somewhat different; a wealth of mechanisms for expression of linguistic knowledge are provided, and relatively effective grammmars have been written for the translation of technical texts between a variety of languages. Many ideas originating from GETA have been incorporated into the design of the new EC-funded project EUROTRA[1].

- The **Preference Semantics** system is largely the work of a single individual, Yorick Wilks, and has no pretensions of being directly applicable in a practical MT environment. Its importance lies in the several mechanisms it proposes for dealing with ambiguity in texts, which constitutes the central problem of MT. These ideas have been extensively reconsidered with regard to their incorporation in the EUROTRA system.

- **LRC METAL** – This is a small-scale system[2] for translation of telecommunications manuals from German to English. Based on a context-free phrase structure analysis of texts, implemented with a very efficient parsing algorithm, it is both fast and effective. It is not obvious that such a system would be equally appropriate for other language pairs; however it is an important contribution in several ways to MT design theory.

---

1. This was more or less the case in 1983. In fact, the EUROTRA system underwent several changes in design before work ended on it in 1992. What is certainly true is that the GETA design philosophy was hugely influential on all MT researchers in the 1980s, which was reflected in both the design of many systems, and the way they were described by their designers. — HLS

2. Since this was first written, METAL has progressed from a small-scale basic research system to fully fledged commercially available translation software. In making this transition, it must be said that most efforts have been put into developing the user- and developer-interfaces, while the core of the system, although extended in coverage, has remained reasonably constant. — HLS

2
Basic considerations of system design

2.1 Relationship between SL and TL knowledge

2.1.1 First-generation (direct) systems

Translation is a process of substituting a text in one language for an equivalent text in another, that is, a mapping *from* source language (SL) texts *to* target language (TL) texts. Since there is no independent standard of meaning to which appeal can be made, the appropriateness of equivalents, and hence the quality of translations, "can be determined only through the informed discussion of experts" (Newmark 1981). Correspondingly, quality can only be achieved in an MT system by incorporating expert knowledge concerning translation equivalents.

The assumption is that such knowledge is definable, but it can hardly be so *a priori*. It is thus essential that an MT system provides facilities for expression of whatever knowledge may be necessary such that it can be refined and extended, that is, tools which are both powerful and perspicuous.

Of course, it is not possible to define a mapping extensionally, i.e. by enumeration of equivalents, where the domain (the permitted values of the input) is infinite. Early workers in MT attempted, naïvely, to solve this problem by reducing translation to a mapping between finite sets, i.e. from SL lexical items (sometimes with additional,

5

limited, context) to TL lexical items, followed by some rearrangement of the target text.

The failure of this direct approach to MT was well publicized (see ALPAC 1966). However, it is arguable that the failure was due as much to the manner in which these systems were implemented as to their lack of linguistic theory. Consistent with the state of the art in programming languages at that time, linguistic knowledge (e.g. the description of context relevant for defining equivalents) was coded directly as programs in the assembly language of the host computer. This, as well as the lack of theory, made it difficult to express the knowledge needed and hence difficult to refine translation quality.

The direct approach, with its design orientation towards a specific language pair, and emphasis on a bilingual dictionary as knowledge source, is typified in SYSTRAN. That this is probably the most accurate general-purpose system available today can be attributed to the fact that, despite the inherent difficulties, a vast amount of expert linguistic knowledge has been incorporated in it over a period of 20 years.

2.1.2 Second generation (interlingual) systems

Second generation systems, starting in the 1960s, derived much of their design inspiration from the rapidly developing field of generative linguistics. The treatment of linguistic structure became more sophisticated (see Chapter 4). Moreover, the declarative nature of linguistic description encouraged the separation of algorithms and data. That is, the linguist was able to specify linguistic knowledge (grammars and dictionaries) in a formalism expressly designed for the purpose. The program for applying knowledge in this form (regardless of content), the interpreter, was not the linguist's concern. This separation greatly enhanced the extensibility of a system, and is still a fundamental approach to design.

In their approach to the relationship between monolingual and bilingual knowledge, many second-generation systems embodied the "interlingua" philosophy. In its strongest form, this can be characterized as follows. Translation is a two-stage process. A structure is assigned to an SL text, using knowledge of the source language only. This structure is a sentence in a universal language, representing the "meaning" of the text. From it can be generated an equivalent utterance in any TL, without regard for the original SL.

It is this potential for decoupling knowledge about the SL from that about the TL that is the prime motivation for interlingual MT. In a multilingual system, all-ways translation between n languages via interlingua involves $2n$ modules, i.e. analysis and synthesis for each language. This would appear to compare favourably with the number of direct systems that would be needed to give the same coverage of language pairs, $n(n - 1)$.

This apparent advantage is misleading. If a system is genuinely to decouple the knowledge specific to the languages in the system, the representation of a text may not specify values for language-specific attributes, since the values of an attribute derive a meaning only from the other values of the same attribute. Given the existence of category and level shifts in translation equivalence (see Catford 1965), such a representation would be obliged to neutralize the difference between lexical categories and even between grammar and lexicon. Given different partitioning of the conceptual space in different languages, words would have to be broken into a set of components sufficient to discriminate between any two or more concepts represented by different words in any one language. In many cases, the work involved in analysis would merely be undone in generation for an SL–TL pair in which a particular shift was inapplicable. More importantly, the criteria for defining the set of components would be very difficult to formalize (van Eynde 1983). In fact, given that translation is primarily a matter of defining equivalents, to require that they be derived in terms of a formal system with significantly different properties from any natural language would appear to add an unnecessary complication to the task.

Rather than partitioning the work of system development across independent modules, the interlingua approach ensures that the behaviour of every module is critically dependent on that of every other. Thus extensibility, both in terms of handling new languages, and incorporating expert bilingual knowledge, is drastically curtailed.

In the second generation of MT, the realization of an interlingual representation was restricted to the neutralization of syntactic categories; equivalences between (category-less) lexical stems were handled with a bilingual dictionary. Structure was represented in dependency (Vauquois 1975) or phrase structure (Lehmann and Stachowitz 1975) trees (see Chapter 4). In subsequent system designs, both these groups later abandoned even this much of the notion of interlingua. The discarding of SL-specific information necessitated by the interlingua caused problems in TL synthesis, severely hindering possible improvement of translation quality.

The interlingua approach to MT is still found in MT systems that could be considered as of the current generation (design started post-1970). By greatly restricting the class of possible input sentences and combining this with a text-type/subject area in which conceptual spaces in the different languages are partitioned very similarly (e.g. in which most items in the text are terms having standardized equivalents, with few general language items), a full interlingua can be used.

The TITUS II system (see Barnes 1983), used for storing and translating textile abstracts, appears genuinely interlingual; it is not possible to tell from the text representation the language of the original text (English, French, German or Spanish). Syntactic structures in abstracts are extremely limited, and the system imposes further restrictions. Each input sentence is manually assigned a code, determined largely by the prepositions it includes, from which is defined a one-to-one mapping onto the equivalent structures in each of the system languages. Such a mapping is also defined between other numerical codes and words or terms in each language. Although useful for compact storage of abstracts, the TITUS interlingua would be inadequate for other text types, and its analysis procedure is largely manual, so it represents a dead end with regard to MT system design.

Another trend in system design that can be considered interlingual is apparent in work on natural language processing at Yale University. Here the representation chosen is one which allows inferencing using language independent, i.e. so-called "real-world", knowledge. However, the interlingua is no longer a representation of a text, but rather a knowledge base of great detail, with slots filled in by items from the text. Analysis is therefore strongly goal driven, i.e. by knowledge of what information must be computed. However, this information is intended for use in a variety of tasks, and its primarily nonlinguistic, nontextual expression in an interlingua of this character means that what is needed to compute true translation equivalents may already have been lost. The translations produced, while avoiding some of the obvious absurdities of more naïve approaches, might better be called paraphrases.

It is obvious that in the general case, translation may require access to real-world knowledge. However, requiring that a text be represented as an instantiation of an already present knowledge structure means that any knowledge in the text which is not predictable from that in the knowledge base can at best be treated in an *ad hoc* fashion. Rather, the class of possible textual representations must be characterized by some generative system, that is, one in which a finite knowledge source describes an infinite number of structures. Failure to acknowledge this is to deny any possibility of dealing with the essential creativity of language use.

2.1.3 Third-generation (transfer) systems

Apart from treatment of highly restricted texts, the interlingual approach to translation can be justified only by simplistic appeals to "psychological reality". The latter seems to refer to a fusion of SL text "understanding" and TL text generation capabilities in a single mind, rather than the psychological reality of expert translators performing their job. It has been demonstrated numerous times that it is significantly easier to approximate human-level performance in expert tasks involving conscious application of knowledge than in those we are genetically predisposed to do, and do unconsciously. Since human translation is at least partly conscious, it is worth studying in the interests of practical MT system design. The interlingual view that translation involves filling in the gaps in meaning in a universal language is an old one. That any linguistic task involves in some sense the filling in of "gaps" can hardly be disputed. Winograd puts it like this:

> The design of an utterance depends critically on the producer's expectations
> that the comprehender will make use of knowledge and intelligent reasoning to
> find interpretations and fill in the information that is not explicit. (Winograd
> 1983: pp. 14f)

The "meaning" of an utterance will vary according to the context in which it occurs. In the extreme, according to the semiotic view of language, "the meaning of a sign consists of all the effects that [it] may conceivably have" (Pierce 1934[1]); "the *meaning* of a linguistic form [is] the situation in which the speaker utters it and

---

1. Quoted by Newmark (1981: p. 5) [original footnote; actually, the quote as given by Newmark is as follows: ". . . effects that may conceivably have practical bearings on a particular interpretant . . .". — HLS]

the response which it calls forth in the hearer" (Bloomfield 1933: p. 139, emphasis original). This sort of 'meaning' is potentially infinite. The information that needs to be made explicit in any process of interpretation (mapping from one system of representation to another) is defined, i.e. made finite, by a set of goals specifying what needs to be computed. Though the computation is carried out in terms of the initial system of representation, the goals themselves are a function of the final system.

In translation, the aspects of meaning that may be relevant for defining equivalents in any language also tend towards the infinite. The determination of equivalents must be driven principally by the linguistic resources of the TL, which is the reason for the universal requirement that a translator be primarily a TL expert. Knowledge of what aspects of the meaning are to be made explicit in the TL text allows the expert to phrase a finite set of questions which must be asked of the SL text. That is, translation is goal-driven. Of course, the SL text must initially provide an indication of what questions are likely to be relevant, and it provides a framework in which they can be answered, but this is not the same as computing the answers to all possible questions.

This implies that an MT system should incorporate an initial monolingual analysis of the SL text, followed by a phase using bilingual knowledge. Such a system is said to be transfer based. The representational system which carries textual information between the two specifies what are variously called "normalized", "intermediate" or "interface" structures. This system is sometimes called an interlingua, perhaps to suggest that its form would be suitable for any SL. Nevertheless, the content of a "sentence" in it is SL specific, and is manipulated subsequently by a module employing bilingual knowledge, so the use of the term is misleading.[2]

Monolingual synthesis in current transfer MT systems is generally of little significance. If there exist multiple translation equivalents that cannot be decided between on the basis of bilingual knowledge then synthesis must usually make an arbitrary choice. This may change as a more sophisticated treatment of stylistic factors is incorporated into the system. In any case, synthesis is essentially deterministic, and not, in any interesting sense, the inverse of analysis, a claim which is often made by advocates of the "transfer as a poor substitute for interlingua" philosophy.

The analysis of a text using SL-specific knowledge into an interface representation (IR) of a text serves two primary functions. The first of these is to eliminate monolingual ambiguities (see Chapter 3) and the second is to convert the text into a form which makes the definition of translation equivalents as straightforward as possible (see Chapters 3 and 4).

An interesting variation of the transfer philosophy involves the use of "attached transfer procedures" (see METAL, Chapter 11). As each part of the IR is built, the

---

2. Most significant MT systems of recent design are of the transfer type (e.g. AVIATION, ARIANE-78, POLA, SALAT, EUROTRA), so it seems an unequivocal aspect of the state of the art in design. The above discussion of interlinguas has been provided in an attempt to counteract the notion (even among designers of transfer systems) that the transfer approach is merely a transitional stage, necessitated by insufficient knowledge of the problem, on the way to a "final solution" via interlingua. In fact, this notion detracts attention from the problems that do need to be solved in contrastive linguistics and in the knowledge representation appropriate for the task of translation.

information needed to compute a translation equivalent in the TL is attached to the structure. Transfer is merely a matter of traversing the IR and executing the attached procedures. This not only reduces the problems of discovering appropriate rules in transfer, but it also restricts the possibilities of large-scale structural reorganization of the IR, and is thus only appropriate for translation between closely related languages.

2.2 Text type considerations

It is generally stated that MT is suitable for a limited class of texts, variously called "nonliterary" or "informative". In practice, this has meant machine instruction manuals, technical articles, textbooks, minutes of meetings, etc. This section attempts to justify the suitability of such texts for machine treatment from the point of view of the present state of the art and the type of translation required.

Human translation is subject to conflicting aims. On the one hand, there is the need to capture as much of the "meaning" of the SL text as possible, including the connotations of individual words, with the different resources of the TL. On the other hand, there is the necessity of not straining these resources beyond certain limits of acceptable style.

The relative weight given to these aims depends to an extent on the purpose of translation, text type and other factors. Nevertheless, both aims are always important, and translators are obliged to define equivalents at various levels of the text, and, more importantly, between different levels in SL and TL texts.

Texts suitable for MT are so because they do not present this conflict of aims to such an extent. Translation, as has been claimed above, must involve computing only the information needed for defining equivalents. Thus in texts which make reference to a real-world fragment common to SL and TL cultures, the quantity of real-world knowledge that must be considered is minimized. In terms of word-level equivalents, such texts may use a good deal of terms for which there are internationally standardized translations; the MT environment is ideal for ensuring consistency of such terminology. At the other end of the scale, stylistic equivalents are clearly defined by cross-linguistic conventions applicable to the particular text type, resulting from the existence of international communities with common aims.

Of course, the problems of word-level and supra-sentence-level equivalents remain to an extent sufficient to make MT for these text types far from trivial. What MT does provide is an environment in which the well-studied phenomena of clause- and sentence-level equivalents define a framework for incorporating approaches to these other problems. The ease with which translation quality can be evaluated by appropriate experts makes MT highly suitable as a test-bed for alternative theoretical approaches.

Another aspect of informative texts that makes them particularly suitable for MT is the fundamental applicability of syntactic notions of well-formedness. It is desirable, from a purely monolingual viewpoint, that such texts are clearly written, which presupposes no significant departures from grammatical norms (well-formedness). If an MT system fails to provide an analysis for a sentence, it may be due to unclear writing rather than an incomplete grammar. If the MT system is embedded in an environment which provides interaction with the writer, it may be possible to elicit an alternative of greater clarity. In fact, in some environments, input to a system consists of texts drafted in a restricted language. Writers, and their employers, seem satisfied that this promotes genuine improvements in the quality of the SL texts.

In general, the use of restricted languages is not acceptable, and interaction with original writers is not possible. Thus the system must provide a capability of accepting "ill-formed" input. Although it must be handled, ill-formedness in informative texts need not be translated (cf. literary texts). There is thus no problem of defining translation equivalents between types of ungrammaticality, only the problem of incorporating analysis procedures which degrade gracefully in the face of ill-formed input.

In informative texts, intentional ambiguity does not play a significant part. Thus, again, MT in an interactive environment has the potential for improving the clarity of SL texts on a purely monolingual basis, by drawing the writer's attention to ambiguous constructions.

Certain MT systems are intended to deal with a very limited, highly formalized text type, such as the weather reports handled by MÉTÉO (Chapter 8). In cases such as these, the grammar-writing tools available to linguists may be unsuitable for more general text types.

In the case of more general-purpose systems, the linguistic knowledge incorporated in grammars may still be appropriate only for a restricted subject area (e.g. nuclear physics articles, telecommunications system manuals). These restrictions reduce the problems of dictionary compilation, ambiguity in word senses, etc. However, the range of syntactic phenomena which must be treated remains formidable, so a restricted system of this type must still incorporate grammar-writing tools of some generality.

Finally, in systems which aim to translate texts in a variety of subject areas, the amount of knowledge incorporated will be vast. In such systems, the generality, flexibility and perspicuity of the grammar-writing tools is a paramount design aim, since the process of grammar writing consumes far more human resources than does the initial design of the system.

2.3 The role of humans

The nature of the relationship between the human and the machine has been touched upon in the previous section. Here we present a brief summary of the types of MT available from the translator's point of view.

The sole function of the machine may be to act as a multilingual terminology bank. Such an arrangement is usually designated "Machine-Aided Translation" (MAT), and is not of relevance to the present discussion.

The machine may produce a complete translation, though based on a fairly superficial syntactic analysis of texts, and hence of quite limited quality. However, the system may provide a sophisticated text-editing environment and interactive dictionary creation routines, and hence contribute to significant improvements in translator productivity.

As a development of this type of system, the nature of the interaction with the translator may be extended, so that the user provides information during the translation process to resolve ambiguities. The ALPS system is of this type.

Both these types of system are essentially translators' aids, producing output which needs post-editing by someone familiar with both SL and TL. A possible direction which future system design could take would be as a translation aid for monolingual writers. The machine would be primarily a TL expert, with meta-knowledge about what it needed to know to produce high-quality output. This meta-knowledge would be used to drive an interactive interrogation of the writer, expressed in SL terms. Obviously, such a system would be very language-pair specific, and much of its knowledge would need to be replaced for it to be applicable to other language pairs. Nevertheless, for those pairs where bilingual human expertise is rarest, it could fill an important gap in the market.

Finally, there exist systems where no human intervention in the translation process is possible; these are run in batch mode and the raw output generally requires extensive post-editing. However, it is sometimes possible to replace post-editing by pre-editing in which the writer uses a controlled language which the machine is guaranteed to be able to handle. This is the approach adopted by Xerox in preparing texts for their SYSTRAN system.

Raw translations of unedited texts may also be of value for users, enabling them to gain a rough idea of the content, and hence to decide whether it is worth commissioning a polished translation (by post-editing or otherwise)

It is thus true that within the present state of the art, MT does not offer the possibility of replacing human skills entirely. Present MT systems can be considered as tools to improve the productivity and throughput of the translation process, and otherwise to meet needs that could not be met with human resources alone. Even so, the widespread use of MT is indicative of genuine cost effectiveness.

3
Linguistic problems in translation

In this chapter, a tentative distinction is made between problems for analysis, which can be classed as various types of ambiguity, and problems for transfer, which are more diverse (and include what may be called transfer ambiguities). In addition to the basic appropriateness of solving them using monolingual or bilingual knowledge, this distinction must also be based on the avoidance of unnecessary computation, which can occur in two, mutually antagonistic, ways. Analysis may compute information that is never used for determining equivalents in transfer (this is analogous to one of the problems of interlingual systems). Alternatively, a computation that is necessary may be performed more than once in different transfer stages (which in the limiting case would result in a number of direct systems). The principal advantage of a transfer organization is that it allows a practical resolution of the trade-off which is embodied in the above.

The relative importance of various linguistic problems, as well as the partitioning of their solutions across the analysis/transfer boundary, can only be definitively decided with regard to the languages involved in the system, the text type, nature of human–computer interaction, etc.

3.1 Ambiguity

Even with regard to a single language, "ambiguity" is a hazy notion. What is potentially ambiguous at one constituent level, e.g. word or sentence, may be resolved at a higher level, e.g. sentence, text. This resolution is usually performed unconsciously by humans, i.e. without ever being recognized. Nevertheless, the notion of ambiguity at the sentence level is indispensable within any current MT framework. The preferred reading of a sentence may depend on its context, and it is certainly infeasible to attempt to define translation equivalents between entire texts. In addition, even if a human finds a sentence unambiguous in isolation, MT based on rules which capture generalizations may still assign it different readings, and a different type of rule will be required to discriminate between them.

We enumerate below various sources of ambiguity that can occur in texts, illustrating each with an example which is ambiguous out of context, and glossing the alternative readings. A very similar example follows, in which the ambiguity does not arise. This is sometimes owing to the unacceptability of one reading on syntactic grounds. More often, one reading becomes overwhelmingly more likely on semantic grounds. Most of the treatment of ambiguity in practical MT systems is based upon defining these semantic criteria which assist in intra-sentential resolution. No concerted attempt to deal with residual ambiguity (requiring a larger context) has been made (but see Wilks's Preference Semantics (Chapter 10), which attacks the anaphor–antecedent problem).

3.1.1 Structural ambiguity

If a single word may be more than one part of speech (a "homograph"), two or more such words in a single sentence may give rise to structural ambiguity as in (1)

    (1) He saw her shaking hands.

        He saw her hands, which were shaking.

            poss.-adj.   adj.

        He saw her   shake hands (with someone).

          obj.-pron. verb

If the ambiguous constituent is subject rather than object, subject–verb agreement eliminates one or other reading as in (2).

    (2) a. Her shaking hands were obvious.

        b. Her shaking hands was obvious.

Substituting another word for *shaking* may also make one reading overwhelmingly more likely as in (3).

    (3) a. He saw her trembling hands.

        b. He saw her holding hands.

This sort of ambiguity is most common in "isolating" languages like English and Chinese. Other structural ambiguities arise from the possibility that an element has been deleted. This is exemplified in (4) and (5).

(4) *Wǒ kàn nǐmen hěn gaōxìng.*
   I SEE YOU VERY HAPPY
   $\simeq$ I see you, you very happy
   'I see that you are very happy.'
   $\simeq$ I see you, I very happy
   'I am very happy to see you.'
(5) *Wǒ kàn huà hěn gaōxìng.*
   I SEE FLOWERS VERY HAPPY
   $\simeq$ I see flowers I very happy
   'I am very happy to see flowers.'

In many languages, a relative clause can be considered as a sentence containing a "hole" which corresponds to the head noun. This can give rise to the ambiguity illustrated in the German noun phrases (6) and (7).

(6) *die Frau, die die Magd sah*
   THE WOMAN, THAT THE MAID SAW
   'the woman that the maid saw'
   'the woman that saw the maid'
(7) *die Frau, die die Blume sah*
   * 'the woman that the flower saw'
   'the woman that saw the flower'

In Japanese, a similar problem arises because complements can be freely omitted. This is shown in (8).

(8) *hon o okutta hito*
   BOOK SENT MAN
   'the man who sent the book'
   'the man to whom I/you/he etc. sent the book'

English embedded clauses with verbs having two different transitivity patterns may also give rise to ambiguity, as in (9).

(9) the man I want to leave
   i.e. 'I want the man to leave'
   or 'I want to leave the man'

Gross structural ambiguities also arise not from diffcrent readings of a constituent, but from different ways of combining the constituents. This is is demonstrated in (10–13),

(10) I saw the man in the park with a telescope.
   i.e. 'saw with a telescope'
   or 'man with a telescope'
   or 'park with a telescope'

but:

(11) I saw the man in the park with my own eyes.
   i.e. 'saw with my own eyes'
(12) I saw the man in the park with a blue shirt.
   i.e. 'man with a blue shirt'

(13) I saw the man in the park with a wall.
     i.e. 'park with a wall'
Conjoining constituents may result in ellipsis of identical material in the second conjunct. No general syntactic treatment of this phenomenon has been proposed, and it is a serious problem in MT. In many cases, such as that in (14) (contrasted with (15)), the extent ("scope") of this ellipsis gives rise to ambiguity.
     (14) old men and women
          (A (N and N))
          'old men and old women'
          ((A N) and N)
          'women (of all ages) and old men'
     (15) old men and children
          'children and old men'
          ? 'old men and old children'

3.1.2 Complex nominals

The relationship between the elements of a complex nominal may be ambiguous, as in (16),
     (16) border plants
          'plants for the border'
          'plants in the border'
while superficially similar complexes may demonstrate completely different relations between the elements, as in (17) and (18).
     (17) alligator shoes
          'shoes made from alligators'
     (18) horse shoes
          'shoes made for horses'
   Problems of scope also occur in complex nominals, e.g. (19).
     (19) adult toy manufacturers
          ((N N) N)
          'manufacturers of toys for adults'
          (N (N N))
          'adult manufacturers of toys'

3.1.3 Ambiguities in antecedents of anaphors

Anaphoric elements, e.g. pronouns, are those which refer back to some previously mentioned word, phrase or concept, the "antecedent". Often, there are several alternative antecedents, which need not occur in the same sentence. Syntactic devices (e.g. gender and number agreement, constraints on Rules of Construal in GB theory (Chomsky 1982)) will resolve some of these, though others (e.g. (20) and (21)) require semantic and even pragmatic resolution.

(20) She threw the vase at the window and it broke.
    the vase broke
    the window broke
(21) She threw the vase at the wall and it broke.
    the vase broke
    ? the wall broke

3.1.4 Word-sense ambiguity

Multiple senses for a single (orthographic) word (homonymy) are common in all
languages. An English example of this is *board* (22).

    (22) a. He asked about the board.
          'He asked about the committee.'
          'He asked about the blackboard.'
          'He asked about the lodgings.'
       b. He asked the board.
          'He asked the committee.'

In this case, the senses are distinct, but not all cases are so clear cut. Metaphorical
usage allows effectively unlimited extension of word sense (polysemy), and the
point at which two usages become sufficiently distinct to warrant being called
different senses (homonyms) cannot be definitively ascertained. In terms of dictionary
entries for MT analysis, it is important that only monolingual criteria of word-sense
differences are considered. Treatment of a word as ambiguous because it has several
potential translations in a given TL leads to all the problems described in Chapter
2 with regard to interlingual MT.

3.2 Translation equivalents

3.2.1 Lexical equivalences

As stated in the previous section, the dividing line between lexical ambiguities and
multiple lexical equivalents is far from clear-cut. Some examples (from English)
which can be unequivocally assigned to the latter group are as follows (23):

    (23) a. corner = Spanish *rincón* (inside) *esquina* (outside)
       b. put = German *stellen* (upright) *legen* (lying)
       c. river = French *fleuve* (main) *rivière* (tributary)

In any of these cases, the ability to compute the correct equivalent would not be
guaranteed. However, various *ad hoc* techniques can be used. One such technique
is shown in (24) and (25).

    (24) on the corner *en la esquina*

    (25) in the corner *en el rincón*

This type of useful, but *ad hoc*, treatment is ideally located in transfer.

3.2.2 Other linguistic phenomena

In a given language, only a fraction of the potential "meaning" of an utterance conditions its linguistic realization. The particular features which are relevant vary from language to language, particularly features of time (tense, aspect), modality and discourse features. It may be possible to compute from the context of an utterance the values of those features which are not marked linguistically. Nevertheless, it is essential that this computation is performed on a need-to-know basis, i.e. language-pair specifically, both in terms of saving unnecessary (and possibly very costly) computation, and in terms of defining the computation processes in a way which corresponds to expert bilingual knowledge. This also avoids the problem of regarding an utterance as ambiguous, merely because it is not possible to compute the value of some attribute which is not marked linguistically in the SL, and hence having to pass multiple representations from analysis to transfer.

Discourse phenomena such as definiteness and topic/focus structure are particularly troublesome for translation. The same phenomena may be realized in different languages (and even within the same language) using different grammatical resources. Conversely, values from one grammatical system (e.g. word order, articles, inflections) may realize different discourse phenomena in different languages. These systems are further complicated by their interaction with syntactic phenomena, such as the transitivity patterns of verbs, and voice of sentences. It is impossible to characterize discourse systems in a language-independent manner because much of the meaning depends on the linguistic facilities that are available but not used, that is, a value takes its meaning only from the other values in the system.

For instance, definiteness, realized in English by a system of articles, is partly a function of word order in Russian (26),

> (26) a. The woman came out of the house.
> *Ženščina vyšla iz domu.*
> b. A woman came out of the house.
> *Iz domu vyšla ženščina.*

while in Finnish, definiteness may be indicated by nominal inflections in some circumstances (in constructions with "impersonal verbs") (27),

> (27) a. *Kuuman veden tulisi olla heti valmiina.*
> 'The hot water ought to be ready soon.'
> b. *Kuumaa vetta tulisi olla heti valmiina.*
> 'Some hot water ought to be ready soon.'

and by word order in others (28).

> (28) a. *Hevonen on pihalla.*
> 'The horse is in the yard.'
> b. *Pihalla on hevonen.*
> 'There is a horse in the yard.'

In English, information about topic/focus is carried by a variety of syntactic devices, such as passivization, which serves other purposes, such as argument suppression. Definiteness is carried by an independent system of articles. In Japanese, on the contrary, the thematic system is based on particles, and there is no marking of definiteness as such.

Computation of equivalents for the values of such attributes as tense and modality is subject to the same sorts of complexity as discourse features. Modality information is carried by a variety of linguistic devices (verb inflections, modal verb systems, as part of the meaning of lexical verbs, etc.). In a given language, a particular value chosen from one linguistic system may represent various different modalities according to a much wider context.

Intuitively meaningful modality features such as permission, possibility, moral necessity, legal necessity and logical necessity define a multidimensional conceptual space. Points of this space are expressed as values of a linguistic system (such as auxiliary verbs) in such a way that the space is partitioned very differently in different languages. Determining on which side of a conceptual boundary a particular use of a linguistic value in the SL text falls presupposes the definition of the boundary. This is a function of the TL, and so must be handled in transfer.

4
Linguistic representation of texts

The nature of the class of text representations which carry information between analysis and transfer stages is a crucial question of system design.

In order to compare the linguistic content of various systems of representation we attempt to abstract from the details of their implementation and from the means whereby they are computed.

In its most general form, the representation of an utterance may be considered as a set of objects. An object is a set of attribute–value pairs, each associating some named attribute with some value of that attribute. Different systems of representation may be characterized by the nature of the attributes they permit, which are of two principal types, relational and intrinsic.

Relational attributes have as values other objects (e.g. "to the right of", "subject of", "constituent of"), and thus serve to impose a structure on the set of objects. Intrinsic attributes serve to characterize individual objects. They generally have values taken from some finite enumeration (e.g. "singular", "dual", "plural"; "definite", "indefinite", "unmarked").

The set of objects may be viewed as a directed graph with labelled vertices and labelled directed edges. The label on a vertex corresponds to the intrinsic attributes with their values, and the labels on the edges proceeding from that vertex to the relational attributes whose values are the vertices towards which the edges are directed.

4.1 Intrinsic attributes: dictionary and morphology

The initial text from which a representation is computed consists of character strings, i.e. words, separated by spaces. At this stage, each object can be considered to have the single intrinsic attribute "word", with values taken from the set of all character strings. Relational values are of the form "to the right of" or "to the left of". Morphological analysis and dictionary lookup associate with the object some further set of intrinsic attributes. It is probable that one such attribute will be a lexeme or lexical unit, which is the canonical or dictionary form corresponding to a character string. Conversion to canonical form involves the removal of inflections and the expression of the information carried by these as values of other attributes such as "gender", "number".

In certain cases, morphological analysis may map one "word" onto several lexemes (e.g. compound words in German) or several "words" onto one lexeme (some types of idiom).

The dictionary will also associate an attribute to each lexeme that will be used subsequently to express generalizations about its distribution in sentences, that is, its category. Typical values of such an attribute are conventional syntactic ones such as "noun", "verb", "preposition" etc. Some systems have a more semantic concept of category. For instance, Wilks's Preference Semantics system (see Chapter 10) treats verbal lexemes as members of semantic categories such as "cause", "move" and "do", and nominal lexemes under such category headings as "animate", "potent", "physical object". So-called semantic ATNs use highly domain-specific categories such as "ship", "port", "officer". In the normal case that categories are syntactic ones, further attributes may subcategorize these, either syntactically (e.g. transitivity of verbs) or semantically (e.g. animacy of nouns). In Q-system grammars, such as those used in MÉTÉO (see Chapter 8), syntactic categories, syntactic and semantic subcategories and computed morphological information are not distinguished formally. That is, each possible value of each attribute is considered as an attribute having a boolean value: present (indicated by the presence of the name of the attribute) or absent (indicated by its absence). Boolean-valued attributes are generally called features.

A contrast to this basically unstructured organization of grammatical information is illustrated by EUROTRA[1]. A hierarchical structure may be imposed upon grammatical information by allowing values of one attribute to act as many-valued attributes in their own right, and also to define further sets of attributes which become relevant. Such structuring is made explicit in declarations to the system, such as in (1).

> (1) a. CAT is (NOUN, ADJ, DET)
> b. DET is (ARTI, ARTD, POSSPRON)
> c. DET has (NUMBER, GENDER)
> d. NUMBER is (SING, PLUR)

---

1. The EUROTRA formalism referred to here is the first "user language", described in a report to the CEC (Maegaard & Maas 1985), but which was never described in the public domain, since it was soon superseded by the <C,A>,T formalism, with which some readers may be familiar. This in turn was later superseded. — HLS

Here, the `is` declarations specify the range of values that a particular attribute may take, whilst the `has` declarations specify the attributes that are relevant if some other attribute has the value given on the left-hand side. Note the blurring of the distinction between attributes and values.

4.2 Phrase structure

Many MT systems base their representation of the content of an utterance upon the notion of phrase structure, which represents a grouping of sentence items into higher level constituents. The legal structures which constituents may have are defined by a context-free grammar, a series of such rules as (2).

    (2) NP ← ART + ADJ + NOUN
        NP ← NOUN
        VP ← VERB
        VP ← VERB + NP
        S ← NP + VP

Symbols such as NP, VP, and S are nonterminal values of "category". The symbol "←" indicates the relational attribute "dominates" and the symbol "+" the relational attribute "precedes". The structure assigned to a sentence such as (3) would be (4), in which the "dominates", or "daughter", relation is shown explicitly, and that of "precedes", or "sister", corresponds to the order of the daughters on the page.

    (3) The small girl eats meat.

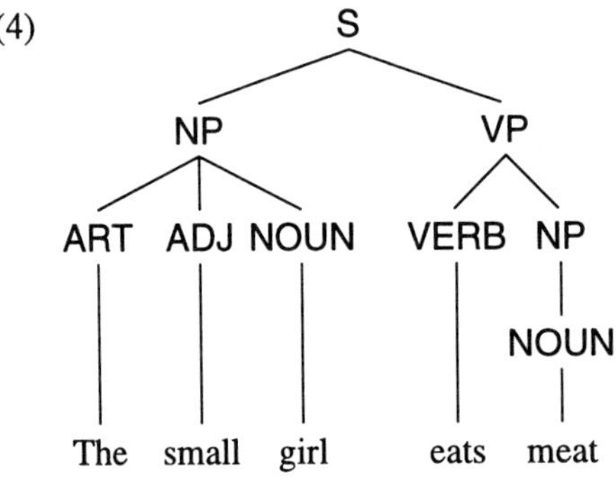

Context-free rules may be augmented to include conditions on the values of other attributes, for example (5),

    (5) S   ←   NP   +   VP
               [NUM = x]   [NUM = x]

which specifies that for this rule to apply, the values of NUM (i.e. number) on the NP and VP, which will have been "inherited" from one of their daughters, must be the same.

The most important aspect of this conception of sentence structure is its emphasis on well-formedness. A sentence is well-formed if the context-free rules assign to it a structure with a root having the distinguished nonterminal category (here S). If this is not the case, the sentence is ill-formed, and will be assigned no structure. The notion that "deviant" utterances should be assigned no structure (i.e. given no interpretation) has been much criticized; it has often been pointed out that this is exactly what humans do not do.

Nevertheless, the well-formedness approach is of value in an MT context for two reasons. First, as mentioned in Chapter 2, it is probably a necessary, though certainly not sufficient, prerequisite of textual clarity. Secondly, well-formedness rules provide a convenient means for eliminating those constituent readings that cannot be incorporated into a higher level structure. For instance, the context-free rule with augmentation for number agreement (5) given earlier can be used to assign appropriate structures to the pair of sentences given in Chapter 3 (assuming other appropriate rules). These structures are given in (6) and (7).

(6)

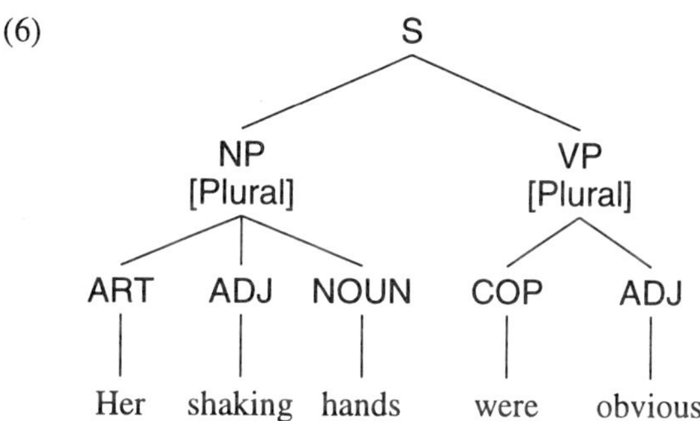

(7)

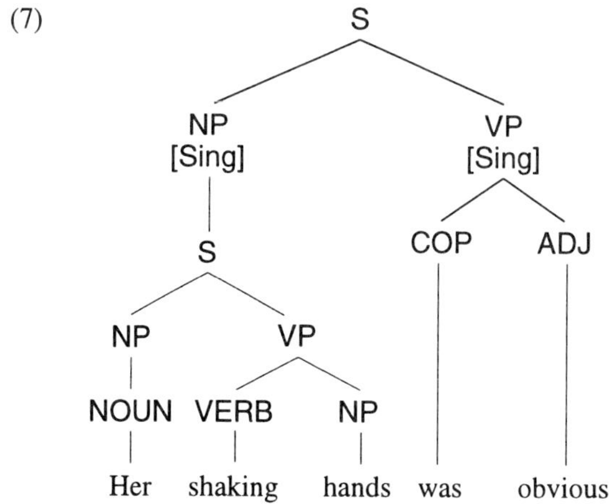

4.3 Dependency

An alternative means of representing linguistic structure is the dependency tree. The constituent structure is realized, not by the introduction of nonterminal categories, but by the definition of one item in a constituent, the head, as the most important, to which the other items are related by the attribute "dependent". Thus the dependency structure assigned to (3) would be (8).

(8)

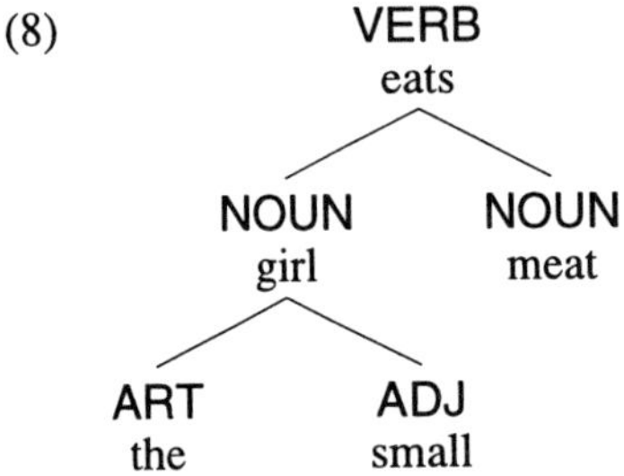

The dependency representation is of value because it indicates the possibility of interpreting the single relation "dependent" as a set of more functionally motivated relations. The various dependents of a constituent may be considered as the fillers of named slots defined by that constituent. For instance, a particular verb may specify the functional relations (i.e. slots) "subject", "object" or "indirect object", which will be filled by nouns. In turn, a noun may define slots for a "determiner", several "modifiers" and several "qualifiers", to be filled by an article, adjectives and relative clauses respectively.

Once purely structural relations such as "daughter" or "dependent" have been replaced with functional ones like "subject", sentences with different word orders but the same functional relations between constituents may be given a common representation. For instance, the three sentences (9a-c) may each be represented by (9d).

    (9) a. John gave the book to Mary.
       b. The book was given to Mary by John.
       c. Mary was given the book by John.
       d.

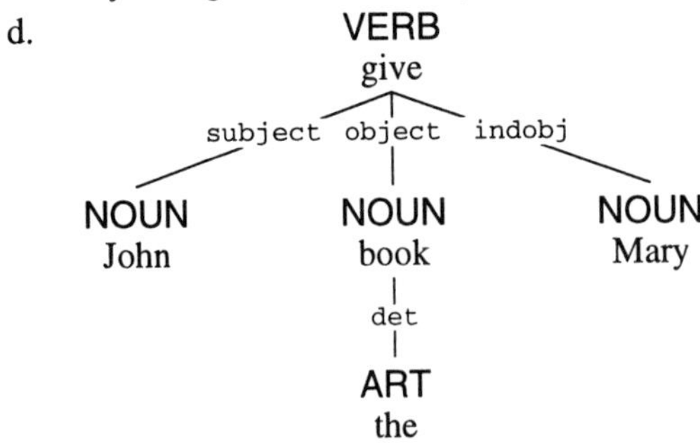

Information about the original surface word order may be represented as values ("active", "passive", "indirect object passive") of an attribute "voice" associated with the verb.

Of course, the three sentences above may also be given common representations as a canonical phrase structure tree (as in the earliest versions of transformational grammar (Chomsky 1957)). However, a direct representation of the relational attributes defined by a verb seems less arbitrary than expressing them as structural configurations, such as "leftmost NP dominated by S" (= subject).

Representations adequate for translation will need to express other relational attributes, such as that between anaphors and their antecedents, and the head nouns of relative clauses and their canonical position in the sentence from which the clause is derived. This is often achieved by coindexing, e.g. (10) (ignoring other structure), where i is the value of the attribute "antecedent of" for *vase*, and also the value of the attribute "anaphor of" for *it*.

(10) She threw the vase$_i$ at the window and it$_i$ broke.

Similarly in (11) where j is the value of the attribute "boss of" for the NP *the man*, and the value of the attribute "trace of" of the dummy object t.

(11) The man$_j$ I want to leave t_j.

This device thus serves to represent only one reading of these ambiguous sentences.

4.4 Case frames

A set of functional relations (slots) associated with an object is called a frame. The most widespread use of this notion in language processing is in the form of a case frame associated with verbs. Each slot in a case frame specifies a semantically motivated relation between the action expressed by the verb and one of the participants in that action. The relation is one of a small set (typically about 10) of cases intended to be appropriate for expressing the case frame of any verb.

A typical set of cases might be:

AGENT	The animate instigator of the action
PATIENT	The entity acted upon
INSTRUMENTAL	The entity by which the AGENT effects the action
EXPERIENCER	The animate entity experiencing the action
BENEFICIARY	The entity benefiting from the action
SOURCE	The entity or place from which the action originates or moves
GOAL	The place to which the action is directed, or the entity resulting from the action

The case frame associated with a verb sense will specify the central arguments, that is, case slots which must be filled in the sentence, and may also indicate other slots which will be optionally filled. What is important about case is not so much the particular list of cases chosen, but rather the way the case frame permits expectations about the linguistic environment of the verb to be organized. These expectations are of two principal kinds, syntactic and semantic.

4.4.1 Syntactic expectations

Syntactic expectations specify the way(s) in which a slot in the case frame of a particular verb may be realized in a sentence. These include its position relative to the verb and/or its surface case (e.g. surface subject/object, nominative, accusative, dative) and the type of constituent (e.g. noun or noun phrase, prepositional phrase plus characteristic preposition, infinitival clause, sentential clause). In fact, such expectations may not be specifically associated with a slot. They may be generated as needed from other sources, such as rules which state generalizations about the relationship between active and passive sentences for a large class of verbs.

4.4.2 Semantic expectations

In general, syntactic clues are not adequate to assign cases unambiguously. Thus the case frame must also specify expectations about the semantic attributes of the slot fillers. So, for instance, the verb *open* might have the following frame:

```
AGENT           animate
PATIENT         physical object (such as door, box, window)
INSTRUMENT      physical object (such as key, hairpin)
```

This frame, in conjunction with the appropriate syntactic expectations, permits the assignment of canonical structures to sentences (12–14), where *e* denotes an empty element.

(12) a. John opened the door with a key.

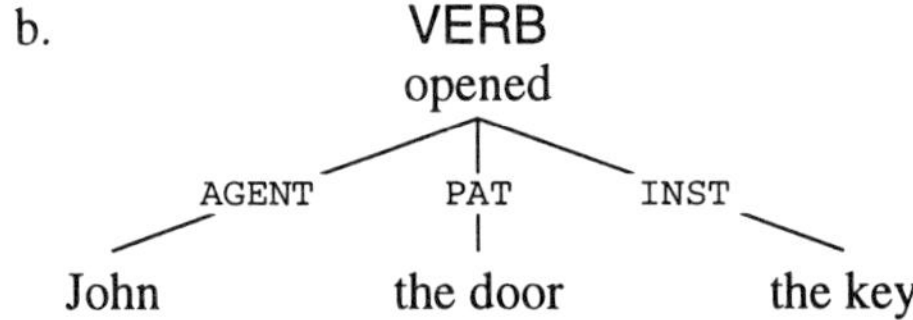

(13) a. The key opened the door.

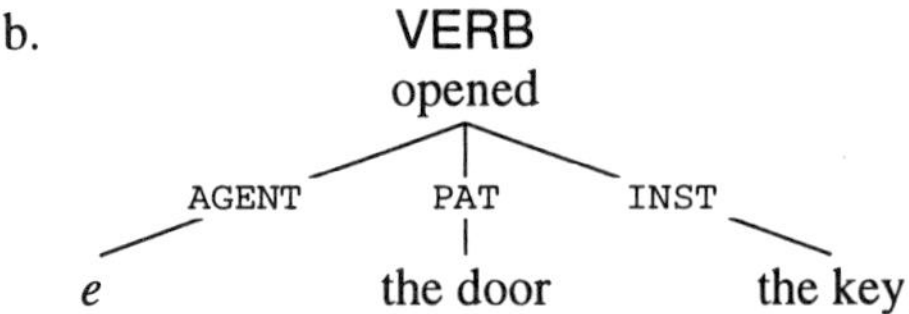

(14) a. The door opened.

b.

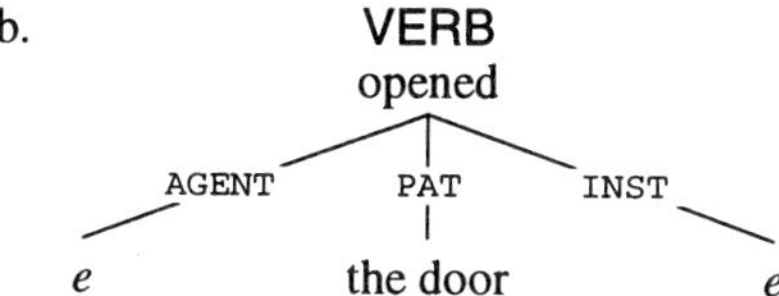

Semantic expectations provide a means for various types of disambiguation, for example:

- Multiple noun senses

    (15) He asked the board.

    ask will specify that what fills the EXPERIENCER role be animate, hence the 'committee' sense, rather than the 'blackboard' or 'lodgings' sense, of *board* will be chosen.

- Multiple verb senses

    (16) The teleprinter was running.

    run in the sense of 'locomotion' requires an animate AGENT, so the 'operate' sense will be chosen here, its expectation for a "machine-like" PATIENT being filled by *teleprinter*.

- Ambiguity of extraction site

    (17) a. *Die Frau, die die Blume sah.*
        b. *Die Frau sah die Blume.*
        c. * *Die Blume sah die Frau.*

    sehen expects an animate EXPERIENCER, so the sentence underlying the relative clause will be read as (17b) rather than (17c).

- Ambiguity of prepositional phrase attachment

    (18) He hit the boy with a blue shirt.

    Here, *with a blue shirt* could be read as the INSTRUMENT of *hit*, but *shirt* would not fulfil the expectation for some rigid physical object, so it is read as a modifier of *the boy*.

- Ambiguity in antecedents of anaphors

    (19) She threw the vase at the wall and it broke.

    Here, *it* might be read as *the wall* or *the vase*, but the latter will fulfil the expectation of *break* for a fragile PATIENT, and so will be chosen in preference to *the wall*.

All these examples of ambiguity resolution presuppose that the requisite semantic attributes, e.g. "animate", "machine-like", "nonrigid", "fragile" are associated with the appropriate nouns. Obviously, choosing and assigning a set of such attributes is a nontrivial task. In addition, if such specific attributes define absolute restrictions on role fillers, it may be impossible to assign readings to many sentences. It is thus important that expectations are treated only as preferences (see Chapter 10), with the reading of a sentence which satisfies the most preferences being chosen.

4.5 Generalized frames

A case frame is a particular organization of knowledge intrinsic to a verb. The instantiation of a case frame, i.e. the allocation of case roles to sentence constituents, is a means of representing the structure of an utterance. The case frame itself is said to represent a type of concept, in this case the concept of the class of events which may be expressed by means of the verb. Its instantiation is a token of the same concept, that is, it denotes a specific event of that class.

The notion of a frame can be generalized to permit the organization of real-world knowledge, i.e. knowledge which is not directly realized linguistically in an utterance, for a wide variety of concepts. In Yale's MT system (Lytinen & Schank 1982), for instance, "scripts" represent high-level frames organizing knowledge about typical chains of events.

Such frames allow information not expressed in the text to be inferred by means of default values for the slots; they may be organized hierarchically into classes, so that a concept may inherit features from the classes of which it is a member. Another important feature of generalized frames is that they permit procedures for determining slot fillers to be associated with slots. Broadly speaking, a knowledge base which is structured as generalized frames presupposes the following mode of processing: a word "pulls in" a frame and this drives the processing of the surrounding textual environment. As discussed in Chapter 2, translation really needs to be driven by the linguistic resources of the TL, not by nonlinguistic knowledge, and texts are best represented as linguistic objects, rather than as instantiations of rich extra-textual knowledge structures, so the generalized frame approach is not directly applicable to MT. A thesaurus-like structuring of dictionary entries provides some of the same facilities as frames, which can be exploited if necessary, but does not dictate the course of processing and hence the form in which text is represented.

4.6 Concluding remarks

The notion of levels is used to refer to systems of representation for which there is not a one-to-one correspondence between the relational attributes defined by the systems (nor, perhaps, between the objects themselves).

In general, transfer needs access to information about the source text of various levels, ranging from surface syntactic objects and relations to underlying conceptual ones. Which are actually computed by analysis and passed as part of the intermediate representation depends on the usual system parameters – languages involved, text types and human interaction. Two principal alternatives are to compute only to a shallow level, and to compute several levels, representing each in a multilevel intermediate representation, such as that of the GETA system, or EUROTRA[2].

In the first case, computation of "deeper" levels may be tailored to the particular requirements of the TL in a "pretransfer" phase, or may be performed in transfer on an *ad hoc* basis as necessary. This approach is efficient but leads to a large transfer phase, and hence is best suited to single language-pair systems. Computing multilevel representations in analysis reduces the size of transfer and is thus more appropriate to multilingual systems.

---

2. Again, this observation was true of the EUROTRA design at the time of writing. Subsequent changes led the EUROTRA researchers to prefer a more strictly stratified approach, suggesting the third alternative, namely a *sequence* of intermediate representations. — HLS

5

Knowledge representation and parsing

In this chapter, we discuss the question of how the linguistic knowledge which is used to construct representations of text is itself represented. In translation of all but the most limited text type, robustness of the system and quality of the output depend on the presence of large quantities of knowledge. Dictionaries and grammars are generally created and updated by several people over a long period. Their form should therefore be dictated by considerations such as the ease with which the appropriate knowledge can be specified in the formalism, and the ease with which errors in specification can be located and corrected.

In describing formalisms for representing linguistic knowledge, we address related questions such as determining the applicability of a particular piece of knowledge (fact) and choosing between several applicable facts. The facilities provided for the construction of various forms of text representation (see Chapter 4) are also introduced.

5.1 Basic concepts

Conceptually, the linguistic knowledge incorporated in an MT analysis has two components. The first of these defines the language which can be handled, that is, it characterizes an infinite set of legal sentences (text strings). If explicit, this knowledge can be applied by a recognizer which returns success or failure according to whether the sentence is legal (well-formed, grammatical) or not.

The second component of the knowledge consists of implicit or explicit structure-building actions, the application of which converts a recognizer into a parser that assigns some structure or structures to any legal sentence.

Languages fall into four classes, definable in two equivalent ways: by the form of rewrite rule needed to specify the legal strings, and by the type of automaton needed to recognize them. The classes of languages constitute the Chomsky hierarchy of power, such that a type n grammar is able to characterize languages of type m, for all $m \geq n$. Table 5.1 gives the equivalence of rewrite rule and automaton for each type.

Table 5.1 The Chomsky hierarchy and types of automaton.

Type	Name	Permissible form of rewrite rule	Automaton
0	general rewrite	$x \leftarrow y$	Turing machine
1	context-sensitive	$xNz \leftarrow xyz$	linear automaton
2	context-free	$N \leftarrow y$	pushdown automaton
3	regular	$N \leftarrow tM$ $N \leftarrow t$	finite state automaton

Key M,N any non-terminal symbol
t any terminal symbol
x,y,z any string of terminals and nonterminals

Context-free grammars have been mentioned in Chapter 4, and are important for several reasons. First, context-free power is the minimum necessary to characterize natural languages, because of the recursive nature of constructions such as (1).

(1) The cat the dog bit died.

Whether such power is sufficient is a major point of dispute in theoretical linguistics today.

Secondly, context-free languages may be parsed very efficiently, since much research has been devoted to algorithms for parsing programming languages of this power. Thirdly, the structure assigned to a sentence by a context-free parse will include a contribution, in the form of one node, from each of the rules that applied in its construction. Hence the rules may be recovered from the parse tree. The value of this is discussed in Section 5.5.

General rewrite grammars, the most powerful, are capable of handling any construction found in natural language. Descriptions of the relationship between structures in different systems of representation or at different linguistic levels seem to require such power, though this may not be true in fact. Parsing with such grammars can present certain problems (see Section 5.4). Despite this, most language analysers are of general rewrite power. Often this power is achieved by taking a context-free formalism and augmenting it with devices increasing its power to that of general rewrite.

5.2 Interpretation schemes

Whatever form it is expressed in, the linguistic knowledge must, in some sense, act as a program for a machine, either a real one (a von Neumann computer), or, more often, an abstract one. A von Neumann computer is made to behave like an abstract machine by running a program called an interpreter, e.g. a recognizer or parser, for which the linguistic knowledge is data.

The rewrite rule and automata theoretic approaches to knowledge representation, though formally equivalent, presuppose significantly different types of interpreter.

In order to illustrate this, let us view any computation as the progression of the system through a series of states. A state is a total configuration of the data (the text, and stages in its representation) and the interpreter. The linguistic knowledge that a system incorporates serves to define possible transitions between states.

In expressing knowledge for an automaton, the states which the interpreter may be in are made explicit. That is, facts are expressed in the form "if the system is in state S_i, and certain other conditions obtain, then the system moves into state S_j, and certain other actions are performed". The form of the other conditions and actions that are permitted define the power of the automaton (see Section 5.3).

Thus the interpreter embodies a locus of control, which moves from state to state. Facts are associated with states, and are considered applicable when control arrives at their state. The behaviour of the interpreter is intimately bound up with the knowledge that the system possesses. This permits the grammar writer to regulate finely the order in which facts are considered. However, this order must be specified even when it is irrelevant, the independence of facts (modularity) is lost, and a single fact may have to be specified several times if it is to be used several times. These properties are characteristic of procedural knowledge representation and control-driven computation schemes.

If knowledge is expressed in the form of rewrite rules, the states in which the system may be are not made explicit. Instead, they correspond to configurations of the data structure. The rewrite rule is a statement of equivalence between one configuration of the data structure (e.g. that specified by the left-hand side) and another configuration (e.g. that specified by the right-hand side). Thus the applicability of facts is determined solely by the existence of similarities in pattern between the data and the facts. The primary job of the interpreter is to perform this pattern-matching. The specification of knowledge does not include a specification for how it is used and in what order. Thus the knowledge is modular, a fact may be used in different ways at different points, and new facts may be more easily added. Such a knowledge representation scheme is said to be declarative, and it presupposes a pattern-directed computation scheme.

5.3 Augmented Transition Networks (ATNs)

Procedural approaches to knowledge representation are typified by the ATN (Woods 1970). The ATN formalism is based on the concept of the Recursive Transition Network (RTN), a representation for grammars of context-free power. An RTN is expressed as a set of subnetworks of states and transitions each corresponding to a nonterminal symbol of the grammar it realizes. For instance the context-free rule (2) would be expressed as a subnetwork of an RTN like (3) (where the Si are states and the arrows are transition) which would be linearized as input to the interpreter as in (4).

(2) S ← NP + VP

(3) S:

$$(S1) \xrightarrow{\text{NP}} (S2) \xrightarrow{\text{VP}} (S3) \xrightarrow{\text{POP}}$$

```
(4) S1   PUSH NP: GO TO S2.
    S2   PUSH VP: GO TO S3.
    S3   POP:.
```

Here, only a single transition is associated with each state, but in the general case, there may be an unlimited number. Each transition has a test part and an action part, separated by ":". If the test part succeeds, then the actions are carried out. In an RTN, tests are limited to the following forms:

PUSH <nonterminal category> This transfers control to the first state of the subnetwork corresponding to the named nonterminal category, and succeeds if this subnetwork succeeds.

CAT <terminal category> This succeeds if the current word in the input string is of the category stated.

WRD <word> This succeeds if the current word in the input string is the word stated.

JUMP This always succeeds.

POP This always succeeds.

The only permissible action is GO TO <state>.

If this is associated with a CAT or WRD test, then the focus of control is moved over one word in the input string. Transitions with POP tests are associated with the final state(s) of subnetworks, and have the implicit action of returning control to the higher level subnetwork from which it came.

Since the form of tests and actions is restricted in an RTN, the syntax of the example was unnecessarily complex. State S1, for instance, could be expressed as S1 NP:S2, with greater clarity. The more complex notation is necessary if we wish to permit a greater range of tests and actions, and thus augment the RTN to an ATN, with Turing machine power. This is effected by adding memory in the form of "registers" to the RTN model. Actions may then assign values to registers and tests may be made on these values. The POP test is given the side-effect of returning the value of a register called "*" to the calling subnetwork. Thus the value of * when the POP transition of the highest level subnetwork is taken is the result of the parse of the sentence.

Number agreement between NP and VP would be handled in an ATN as follows. An action which sets the value of a register to the number of the NP will be associated with the NP transition. The VP transition will have a test which accesses the register to compare it with the value of number for the VP. Note how a concise description of the phenomenon of number agreement has been lost, since it is now partitioned between different transitions.

By providing the appropriate register setting facilities, the ATN can be used to build linguistic structures of any level. Once again, the procedural nature of the ATN means that it is difficult to observe a succinct statement of the relationship between structures of different levels.

The ATN formalism commits the grammar writer to several choices of parsing strategy. Control is initially focused at the first state of the highest level subnetwork (which will usually be that for "sentence"), and at the leftmost end of the input string. During processing, control is transferred to the networks of lower level constituents, building a representation of the parse as it goes, and moving rightwards through the input string. These strategies are known respectively as "top down" (since the parse tree is built from the root downwards) and "left to right". One problem with such strategies is that an error in the input string will terminate the parse completely at that point, so that processing of the sentence beyond the error cannot be used for fail-safe purposes. More important than such specific drawbacks, which can be overcome, is that the knowledge represented is inseparable from aspects of the parsing strategy. We see below how declarative formalisms do not require such a commitment to particular strategies and thus both free the grammar writer from concern about them and allow the possibility of interpreting a grammar in different ways.

5.4 Production Systems (PSs)

Computation schemes appropriate for application of knowledge represented declaratively can often be characterized as Production Systems (PSs) (see Davis & King 1977). The basic components of a PS have already been introduced, that is:

- a database, which is the representation of the text at various stages in its processing;
- an unordered set of rewrite rules, which define equivalences between configurations of the database, that is, defining transitions between implicit states;
- an interpreter, which has the functions of determining applicable rules on the basis of pattern-matching between one side of a rule and the database, choosing which of several applicable rules to apply, and applying the chosen rule.

A PS can be used to realize the application of a context-free grammar in a straightforward manner, either top down or bottom up. In a top-down parse, the database will initially consist of the distinguished symbol (e.g. S). This will be matched against the left-hand side of a rule such as (5).

(5) S ← NP + VP

The entire rule can then be treated as a description of the new state of the data base, by interpreting the rewrite symbol as a 'dominates' relation as (6).

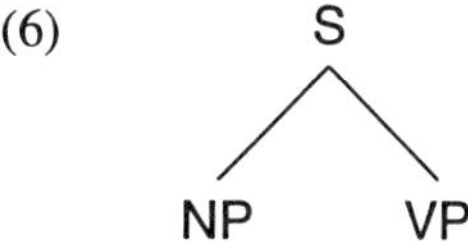

The leaves of this tree will then be matched against the left-hand sides of further rules, and further structure will be built. Finally the leaves of the tree will be matched against the words or word categories of the input string.

In a bottom-up parse, the database is initially constituted from the input string. Word categories are assigned to the words by matching against the right-hand sides of dictionary-type rules such as (7), the application of which causes the building of the structure (8).

(7) N ← dog

(8)   N
        |
        |
       dog

Strings of categories are successively matched against the right-hand sides of further rules, until all subtrees are finally subsumed under an S node by the application of a rule with the left-hand side S.

A PS can also be used to apply rules of general rewrite power, by interpreting the rewrite symbol as a substitution of, for example, the right-hand side (called the "action" or "image") for the left-hand side (the "pattern" or "schema"). Such rules are usually expressed as equivalences between structures rather than between strings, and their application can thus effect the building of structures at any level.

5.5 Variations on the PS model

Large monolithic grammars expressed in general rewrite form can give rise to certain problems, particularly unintended nonterminating cycles of rule application. This problem can be circumvented by the use of tactical labels. These are information planted in the database by certain rules designed to "trigger" or "block" pattern matching against certain other rules. However, this "proceduralization" of the PS detracts significantly from the clarity and perspicuity of the represented knowledge.

A preferable approach is to provide facilities which allow the grammar writer to specify any required ordering between rules and sets of rules without allowing this to obscure the underlying declarative representation. These facilities can take the form of a control language, defined by a context-free grammar with named rules as the terminal symbols (Georgeff 1982). The nonterminal symbols represent packets of rules. Such packets may also be provided with pattern-matching conditions on their applicability, by associating a structural expectation with each rule packet (as in EUROTRA[1]). In this way, a hierarchical structure is imposed on the grammar as a whole.

A context-free surface grammar can also be directly augmented to allow the construction of structures at other linguistic levels. This can be done merely by associating procedures with each rule, that may arbitrarily reorder the daughters at the time that the rule is applied. Thus the surface structure is recognized, but a different level of structure is actually built, as with ATNs.

Another possibility is to build explicitly the context-free surface structure, but provide a mechanism in the grammar that allows a "deeper" structure to be "read off" it. Since the surface structure includes a structural contribution from each rule which built it, the rules can be reinstantiated from the structure. In Lexical-Functional Grammar (Kaplan & Bresnan 1982) this is done as follows. Each nonterminal in the right-hand side of a context-free rule is associated with an equation, e.g. (9).

$$(9)\ \text{S} \quad \leftarrow \quad \text{NP} \quad + \quad \text{VP}$$
$$(\uparrow \text{subject}) = \downarrow \qquad \uparrow = \downarrow$$

The surface structure is built without taking account of the equations, with each node given a unique number (10).

$$(10) \qquad \text{S (1)}$$

$$\text{NP (2)} \quad \text{VP (3)}$$

The equations are then instantiated in any order, with $\uparrow$ being bound to the node on the left-hand side of the rule, and $\downarrow$ to the node above the equation, giving in this case (11).

$$(11)\ (1\ \text{subject}) = 2$$
$$3 = 2$$

The equations of all the rules used in the building of the structure are similarly instantiated. This complete set can then be solved for all variables, resulting in a functional structure independent of, but complementary to, the surface structure. This additive approach to computing various levels of representation is of obvious appeal in an MT context, given the conclusion of Chapter 4.

---

1. The device alluded to here was a feature of the first EUROTRA software design, described in Johnson et al. (1983, 1985), but later abandoned. — HLS

5.6 Conflict and ambiguity

The term "conflict" is used to denote the situation which may arise during the course of parsing in which the interpreter is faced with several applicable rules. In an ATN, several transitions whose tests succeed may leave a given state. In a PS, the pattern of several rules may match some configuration of the database. Three approaches to conflict are available.

The normal strategy adopted in an ATN is to treat transitions leaving a given state as ordered, and to take the first. If the parse is subsequently blocked, control backtracks to an earlier point of conflict and follows the next alternative. This is known as the depth-first strategy, since a single parse (hopefully the correct one) is produced. A successful parse can also be used to initiate backtracking, so that all legal parses are eventually discovered.

The depth-first strategy can also be used in a PS. Alternatively, all alternatives may be followed in parallel, in which case the parse is said to be breadth first. In order to keep track of all alternatives, a PS can use a chart as a database. The chart allows the application of rewrite rules to update the database by addition rather than by substitution. Thus a structure which corresponds to the pattern of an applied rule is not lost, and can be matched against other rules. Thus the PS is rendered commutative, i.e. insensitive to the order in which applicable rules are applied (see MÉTÉO, Chapter 8). The chart can also be used in conjunction with a depth-first strategy to store constituents that have been correctly parsed, even though this may have been during the course of an ultimately unsuccessful parse. In this usage, it is acting as a well-formed substring table.

A third possibility, requiring a significantly different framework for parsing that it is not appropriate to discuss here, is for all decisions to be postponed until the correct alternative can be chosen. This is called deterministic parsing (Marcus 1980).

The above are principally approaches to the problems of local syntactic ambiguity, and do not address directly the question of choosing between alternative successful parses. In some situations, it may be possible to determine the acceptability of intermediate results of parsing by passing these to a semantic processor as they are built. Such interleaved semantics is most appropriate within a depth-first framework, since it eliminates unacceptable paths as early as possible. However, there is little in the way of consensus or theory about what such a semantic processor suitable for MT might look like.

For MT purposes, it seems more appropriate to produce all structures which are well-formed, either depth first with forced backtracking or breadth first. The structures may then be ranked according to some metric, and the highest ranked chosen. This metric could be "number of case expectations satisfied", but it is not clear that a successful version of such a metric has ever been realised in a practical MT system. Representation of ambiguity, metrics of semantic and contextual likelihood of readings and strategies for applying them are probably the most fruitful areas for further MT research.

Part II
Descriptions of systems

6
SYSTRAN

6.1 Introduction

Development of SYSTRAN began in the late 1960s, when Peter Toma left the George-town University MT project to produce a system on a commercial basis. The first operational system, installed by the US Air Force for Russian–English translation and vice versa, was completed in 1973. In 1975, what was later known as the Commission of the European Communities (CEC) bought an English–French version, which it has since developed further and extended to cover French–English and English–Italian. Other language pairs available or under development include German–English, German–French, German–Spanish, English–Portuguese, English–Arabic and English–Persian[1].

6.2 Basic nature of the system

SYSTRAN can best be characterized under the following headings:

Modularity   The system's modular design is usually claimed as its main "second generation" characteristic. Modularity is displayed in the following features:

---

1. The list of languages has continued to grow ever since: see Hutchins & Somers (1992: p. 177) — HLS

40

- Programs are of two main types: system programs, written in assembler code, are independent of the particular languages being treated (e.g. control and utility programs, and those responsible for dictionary lookup); translation programs, written partly in a higher-level "macro-language", are dependent on the languages being treated and therefore subject to variation with each language pair.
- The translation process is broken down into a number of steps, with separate program modules being principally designed to cope with different linguistic phenomena (e.g. homograph resolution, clause-boundary definition, subject–predicate recognition; but see below). A module itself may consist of a number of distinct routines or submodules.
- Translation programs fall into three types: SL specific, language-pair specific and TL specific. The system therefore has the nature of a transfer system, with separation, in principle, between SL analysis and TL synthesis.

In important respects, however, the system's modularity is more apparent than real. In particular, the linguistic operations performed by different modules are rarely discrete; rather, the operations of one module are often taken up again in a later module which uses pertinent information computed in the interim. Neither is the distinction between analysis and transfer as well-defined as in other systems which can be called transfer based. These issues will be considered further at appropriate points in what follows.

Linguistic vs. computational components   SYSTRAN's most significant "first generation" feature is its failure to observe a strict separation between linguistic data and the algorithms that act upon those data. Apart from hampering the extensibility of the system to additional languages, this has contributed directly to the problems outlined below.

Linguistic strategy   The difficulty, resulting from the above, of updating the system to incorporate developments in linguistic theory, has meant that SYSTRAN's linguistic strategy remains relatively primitive in comparison to that of later systems. Little attempt has been made to found the strategy in any coherent, formal model of grammar. Rather, an essentially empirical approach has been taken – particular translation problems have tended to be dealt with as they arise by local additions or modifications to the program, without reference to a broader linguistic framework.

6.3 Data structure

SYSTRAN uses a linear data structure, the sentence analysis area, created in core memory by the routine **GETSENTN**, following initial dictionary lookup. The analysis area may hold a maximum of 105 words, and consists of 160 bytes of memory per word plus a variable-length area for homographs. GETSENTN loads into the analysis area each word of the sentence to be analyzed, together with the grammatical information and translation equivalent(s) associated with the word by dictionary lookup. In the case of high-frequency words, the word is simply accompanied by its offset address to the grammatical information table already held in core memory.

Each byte in the byte area associated with a word has a particular function. In general, the byte number specifies some grammatical attribute of the word, and the content of the byte is the value of that attribute drawn from a finite range. However, the attribute coded by one byte may be dependent upon the value of another byte, e.g. if byte 1 has the value "noun", the attribute associated with byte 3 is its surface case; if byte 1 has the value "verb", byte 3 represents the tense, mood and voice. Certain bytes are also used to represent a set of binary features, that is, they are interpreted as bit strings. All byte values are expressed in hexadecimal. Attributes are of two principal types. The first of these represents information pertaining to the word alone, either specified in the dictionary or computed according to its use in the sentence. Examples of such bytes are shown in Table ?.

Table 6.1 Contents of bytes (examples).

Byte no.	Content
1	Primary part of speech (POS) e.g. finite verb, noun,adjective, adverb, article.
2	Person and number (of verbs and personal pronouns).
3	Surface case (of nouns/pronouns); tense, mood, voice (of verbs).
4	Gender and number (of nouns).
5, 9, 10	Prepositional government.
6, 7	Transitivity and complementation patterns of verbs.
11	Semantic/syntactico-semantic features of nouns (e.g. human, animate, count/mass, abstract/concrete).

The second type of information is relational, i.e. representing sentence, clause and phrase structure. Bytes of this type thus contain pointers to the byte areas, such as a governed/governing word or a word in concordance with the current word. For example, bytes 18 and 28 are used to indicate object relations: byte 18 of the governing word points to the object word, while byte 28 of the object word points to the governing word. Such grammatical relations are established during analysis by the STRPASS and PREP1 routines (see Section 6.6.6).

6.4 Dictionaries

SYSTRAN's lexical data base (LDB) consists of two bilingual dictionaries: the stem dictionary of single-word entries, and the dictionary of multi-word expressions (LS/idioms). These master dictionaries are held on magnetic tape in a format designed to facilitate creation and updating of entries using the lexical data control system (LDCS). From them are automatically created a series of translation dictionaries, held in a more compact format on indexed disk for fast random access. It is the latter that are consulted during the actual translation process.

6.4.1 Types of entry

Distinctions are made between the following types of lexical entry:

Stems

These include abbreviations, punctuation marks and certain numerical strings as well as stem forms as such and/or full-form words. Where more than one stem form of an SL word exists, each form is listed as a separate entry, with cross-reference to a designated basic entry containing common grammatical information. When the SL is English, all English inflected forms (i.e. full-form words) are so entered, obviating the need for morphological analysis. For more highly inflected SLs, a morphological analysis procedure is included in dictionary lookup, to reduce the multiplicity of full-form entries.

Idioms

An idiom is defined for SYSTRAN purposes as an invariable (i.e. contiguous and noninflectable) expression (string of words) whose meaning differs from the sum of the meanings of its constituent words. Upon identification of an idiom in the SL text, the TL translation as given in the dictionary entry is attached to the first word of the idiom, and the expression is marked as translated. This does not, however, exclude it from subsequent analysis. Typical examples of English idioms are *by the way, at all costs, on the one hand.*

Idiom replaces

These are a special kind of idiom, used whenever it is possible to assign to the expression a single part of speech. In such cases, the expression is replaced by one with "." inserted between its constituent words (e.g. ON.ACCOUNT.OF), this replacement form being specified in the dictionary entry for the original form. The expression is subsequently treated as a single "pseudo-word" for translation purposes, and may feature as part of a larger dictionary-defined expression (idiom, limited semantics or conditional limited semantics). Typical examples of idiom replaces are: compound prepositions and conjunctions, e.g. *on account of, as far as*; compound verbs, e.g. *give rise to, carry out*; and nominal expressions consisting of a verb modifying a noun, e.g. *dwell chamber*, *disengage button* (see later for further explanation).

The distinction between idioms and idiom replaces is difficult to justify on theoretical grounds. The need for it here seems to be based on the fact that SYSTRAN does not incorporate a notion of nonterminal categories – hence the need for syntactic analysis of syntactically complex idioms. However, there seems no reason why the examples of idioms (as opposed to idiom replaces) cited should not be treated as idiom replaces and assigned the category "adverb".

Limited semantics (LS) expressions

Like an idiom, an LS expression constitutes a single meaning unit, unanalyzable in terms of its constituent word meanings; it differs from an idiom in allowing one or more words in the expression to be inflected, though the expression must be otherwise contiguous. Only the basic form of the expression is entered in the dictionary. All other inflected forms are automatically recoverable since LS lookup is based not on the variant word strings themselves but on invariant identification codes attached to the words during stem dictionary lookup. It follows that each constituent word of an LS expression must have an entry in the stem dictionary in order for LS lookup to be successful. Hence the requirement that the nominal expressions such as *dwell chamber* referred to earlier be treated as idiom replaces – the verbal component (*dwell*), which functions as a noun for analysis purposes, would not normally have a noun homograph entry in the stem dictionary.

LS entries are in fact reserved for nominal expressions only, variable verbal expressions being encoded as CLSs (see later). This apparently arbitrary stipulation seems to have been dictated by circumstances obtaining in the early stages of SYSTRAN's development, and exemplifies the tendency to give greater weight to the programming status quo than to linguistic motivation.

Typical examples of LSs (with their French equivalents) are: *blast furnace / haut fourneau, developing nation / pays en voie de développement, kitchen garden / potager*.

LS/idioms

These are nominal expressions which must be considered as integral units for syntactic reasons. They differ from the above entry types in that their constituent words retain their individual meanings, i.e. no special "idiomatic" meaning is attached to the expression in the dictionary. Essentially, the LS/idiom facility provides a means of defining a group of words as a noun phrase in order to resolve possible syntactic ambiguity, e.g.

- to indicate that an adjective has a strong affinity for a certain noun. Thus *hydraulic brake* would be encoded as an LS/idiom to ensure the correct translation of e.g. *hydraulic brake fluid* ('fluid for hydraulic brakes' rather than 'hydraulic fluid for brakes')

- to indicate that a present participle is functioning as the head noun in an NP, e.g. *equipment cooling* ('cooling of equipment' rather than 'equipment which is cooling')
- to indicate that a present participle is functioning as an adjective modifying a noun rather than as a verb taking that noun as its object, e.g. *attaching bolts* as in *tighten the engine attaching bolts*.

Conditional limited semantics (CLS) expressions

These are a type of LS expression supplemented by rules which impose conditions on instantiation. An important use of such rules is in dealing with noncontiguous expressions. Unlike LS expressions, CLS expressions are not limited to nominals.

The word by means of which a CLS expression is accessed is called the principal word (PW). A CLS expression may consist of any number of rules interspersed with any number of words, except that the PW must be to the left or right of all rules. If the PW is to the left, then each rule in the CLS expression applies to the word immediately to the left of the rule, and vice versa.

CLS rules may be divided into two principal types: those which impose conditions on relations between words (type 1) and those which impose conditions on the information associated with a single word (type 2). Both can occur in a single CLS expression.

In the following, WORD1 is assumed to be the PW unless otherwise specified:

Type 1 CLS rules   These can be further divided into four types, examples of which are given below.

Rule (1a) indicates that byte n of WORD1's byte area must point to WORD2 (conversely, if WORD2 is the PW). WORD1 and WORD2 are not required to be contiguous, as shown in (1b) which specifies that byte 26 of **PRACTICE** must point to **CURRENT**, i.e. *current* must be an adjectival modifier of *practice*. Similarly (1c) indicates that *provision* must be the object of *have* and must govern *for*.

    (1) a. WORD1 $C–Bn WORD2

        b. CURRENT $C–B26 PRACTICE

          (PW)

        c. HAVE $C–B18 PROVISION $C–B24 FOR

          (PW)

Rule (2a) succeeds if the word which is pointed at by byte n has the associated semantic feature represented by **SEMCAT**. For example, (2b) specifies that *remove* must have as its object (pointed at by byte 102), a word subcategorized by the semantic code **ATTACH** (e.g. *clamp, bolt, washer*).

    (2) a. WORD1 $C–Bn $C–SEMCAT

        b. REMOVE $C–B102 $C–ATTACH

          (PW)

In rule (3) M indicates that the meaning of WORD2 remains unchanged (normally CLSs, like LSs, cancel the meanings of their component words).

    (3) WORD1 $C-Bn,M WORD2

In (4a) WORD2 must be one word to the right of WORD1. Variations on this rule are shown in (4b) – WORD2 must be x words to the right of WORD1, and (4c) – WORD2 must be x words to the left of WORD1.

    (4) a. WORD1 $C-BO WORD2
        b. WORD1 $C-BO,+,x WORD2
        c. WORD1 $C-BO,-,x WORD2

Type 2 CLS rules   Rule (5) specifies that byte n of WORD1 must be equal to YY (hex). An example of the use of this rule is (5b) which specifies that *drop* must be a noun (i.e. byte 1 = 10). The equality condition may be replaced by an inequality, as in (5c).

    (5) a. WORD1 $C-Bn,E,YY
        b. PRESSURE DROP $C-B1,E,10
           (PW)
        c. WORD1 $C-Bn,NE,YY

The form of rule exemplified by (6) is used when the value of byte n is interpretable as a bit string (array of booleans). For the rule to succeed, all those bits which are set in YY must also be set in byte n. If XX represents the value of byte n, then the condition for success is YY & XX = YY.

    (6) WORD1 $C-Bn,O,YY

The corresponding rule which tests for certain bit positions being clear is (7). The condition for success is YY & XX = 0.

    (7) WORD1 $C-Bn,Z,YY

The rule which tests for the presence of any of a number of set bits is (8).

    (8) WORD1 $C-Bn,NZ,YY

The condition for success is YY & XX $\neq$ 0.

6.4.2 Master dictionaries

The master stem and ID/LS dictionaries of the LDB are maintained in variable-length record format, each entry consisting of six records. The following is a description of the main types of information contained in an entry; in keeping with SYSTRAN practice, records are labelled according to the lines of the coding sheets used in preparing entries.

"-" line

This contains the stem or expression itself, along with codes indicating capitalization requirements, the type of entry (stem, idiom, LS or CLS), and PW in the case of LSs and CLSs. It also contains various control codes, e.g. dictionary code number distinguishing between different entries for a homograph.

A-line

For stem entries, this contains codes used in the automatic generation of additional word forms – especially important for English where each inflected form of a word is given a separate entry. If an English noun or verb participates in a regular inflectional paradigm, this paradigm is indicated by an A-line code, which is then used to create all additional entries for the paradigm.

For idiom replaces, the form which replaces the original text string is given, e.g. *as soon as* will appear in the A-line as $R- AS.SOON.AS.

B-line

Contains codes indicating:
- primary part of speech (POS), e.g. infinitive, finite verb, auxiliary, noun, adjective, pronoun, adverb
- secondary part of speech (BPQ), e.g. common noun, proper noun, definite article, indefinite article, possessive pronoun, demonstrative pronoun, interrogative pronoun
- gender
- number (nouns, pronouns, adjectives)
- case (used in English for possessive/objective pronouns)
- capitalization
- high frequency word or expression homograph type (see Section 6.7.1)
- person and number (verbs)
- tense

A CLS priority code may also be included, to impose a priority ordering on conflicting CLS expressions, i.e. expressions which contain different rules and have different TL translations, but which may in certain instances apply to the same string.

C-line

Contains detailed syntactic or syntactico-semantic codes, including information as to the contextual properties (government, modification) of the entry. Any number of codes from a predefined set may be listed, separated from each other by commas. The following is a sample of the codes used for English verbs and nouns:

Prepositional government code (PREPR)   A word may be coded as governing one or more of 24 common prepositions, e.g. *arrive*: PREPR = AT, *talk*: PREPR = (TO, ABOUT).

Verb codes

TRAN	always transitive (e.g. *detest*)
UTRAN	usually transitive (e.g. *exchange*)
UINT	usually intransitive (e.g. *fly*)
AINT	always intransitive (e.g. *occur*)
IOBJ	can govern indirect object (e.g. *give*)

GI	can govern infinitive without intervening object (e.g. *want*)
GOI	can govern direct object + infinitive (e.g. *ask*)
GOO	can govern two direct objects (e.g. *elect*)
NCO	can take a noun clause as direct object (e.g. *know*)
INSUB	normally takes inanimate subject (e.g. *occur*) *
ANSUB	normally takes animate subject (e.g. *see*) *
HUSUB	normally takes human subject (e.g. *applaud*) *
MOTN	verb of motion or direction
NMR	present participle seldom functions as adj.mod. (e.g. *hit*)

* Similar codes exist for objects.

Noun codes

HU	human
AN	animate
AMB	animate/inanimate ambiguity
QUAN	quantity or measure
ABS	abstract
CON	concrete
CT	count
MS	mass
GI	can govern infinitive (e.g. *the attempt to*)
TP	time period
GRP	collective noun
NAP	can be followed by noun clause in apposition (e.g. *the proof that*)
GG	noun + prep. frequently governs gerund (e.g. *the method of working*)

D-line

Reserved for codes representing semantic markers of various kinds. Some 450 such codes have been defined for the system, originally designed to provide information about subject fields. In practice, only a fraction of these have been used in applications to date. They include:

- generalized markers, e.g.

PRGEN	generalized process
PRPHY	physical property
MATER	material
CONTNR	container
PROF	profession

- semi-specific markers, e.g.

CHCOM	chemical compound
CHELM	chemical element
FPROD	food product
FINAN	finance
GEOLOC	geographical location

- specific markers, e.g.

MONTH	month
CITY	city
COUNTR	country

Note that no attempt has been made to integrate these and other semantic features (e.g. **HU**man, **AN**imate, specified in the C-line) into any sort of hierarchy — the distinctions (if any) between general, specific and semi-specific markers have no functional value in the system.

The decision to incorporate particular markers is made empirically, depending on their usefulness in resolving specific problems of analysis or translation. In analysis, their main function lies in disambiguating enumerations (see Section 6.6.4). In transfer, semantic markers may be used to guide selection of the correct TL item. For example, *employ* would be translated into French as *employer* rather than *utiliser* whenever its object is designated as **PROF**. Also, certain markers may trigger more complex lexical routines during transfer. For example, **COUNTR** calls a routine ensuring appropriate translation and insertion of prepositions in e.g. *in Belgium and Luxemburg* — *en Belgique et en Luxembourg*.

E-line

This is the first bilingual section of the entry. It encodes the appropriate translation of any preposition(s) governed by or governing the item, where this translation differs from that given in the dictionary entry for the preposition itself. For example, *cover with* translates into French as *couvrir de*; hence the E-line for *cover* will include `WITH = (B = 12)` where B (before) denotes that the main item, *cover*, precedes the preposition, and 12 is the number of the preposition *de* as it appears in the TL preposition table. When the item is itself governed by a preceding preposition, as with *in French*, this is indicated by A (after) instead of B. Two or more prepositional codings for the item are separated by commas, thus: `WITH = (B = 6), TO = (A = 1)`.

F-line

Contains TL translation(s) together with morphological, syntactic and other specialized information required in TL synthesis.

The need to enter multiple translations for a given SL stem is reduced in SYSTRAN by:

- according separate dictionary entries to SL homographs;
- the use of separate idiom, LS or CLS entries to distinguish between different meanings of an SL word in different sentential contexts;
- the application, during transfer, of lexical routines which themselves provide the appropriate translation of any SL word for which they are called.

However, where polysemy is related to the more general extra-sentential context, it may be dealt with by entering multiple translations, distinguished by means of topical glossary (TG) codes. These codes are used to select the appropriate translation on the basis of text type/subject fields, explicitly prespecified when the text is input to the system. The CEC English–French system includes some 20 or so TG codes, e.g.

0   general
1   physics
2   electronics
3   computers, data processing

TG codes have in fact been little used in CEC versions, because of their inflexibility, e.g. at present the system has no way of recognizing changes in subject fields within a particular text.

Translation dictionaries

The lexical data represented in the LDB master dictionaries are reorganized into various disk files according to the needs of dictionary lookup at different stages of translation. These files, constituting the translation dictionaries, are:

`HFWD`	high-frequency word table
`HFIT`	high-frequency information table
`RID`	source idiom table
`EID`	target idiom table
`LDICT`	long-stem dictionary (>7 characters)
`MDICT`	medium-stem dictionary (4–7 characters)
`SDICT`	short-stem dictionary (1–3 characters)
`GDICT`	grammar dictionary
`LSDICT – LS/CLS`	dictionary
`XLSDICT – LS/CLS`	dictionary index

The `HFWD` contains high-frequency elements accounting for about 30 per cent of text "words" e.g. punctuation marks and function words. It also contains the first 15 characters of idioms, with offset address to the `RID`. Each word in the `HFWD` has attached to it an offset address to `HFIT`, containing grammar and translation information for that word. During analysis, the entire `HFIT` is kept in memory for rapid access via the offset addresses.

The `RID` contains the continuation of idioms (in excess of 15 characters), together with offset addresses to the `HFWD` and to the `EID` where TL translations for each idiom are stored.

Low-frequency stems are divided between `LDICT`, `MDICT` and `SDICT`, according to length of stem. Included in each entry are an offset address to `GDICT`, for corresponding grammar and translation information, and an offset address to `XLSDICT` if the stem can function as principal word of an LS expression.

6.5 Dictionary lookup and morphological analysis

6.5.1 LOADTEXT

For the first stage of dictionary lookup, the text is loaded into the high-speed core memory by the program **LOADTEXT**. Each word of the text is isolated into a separate text-processing record and given a text sequence number. At the same time **LOADTEXT** sets up in core memory the high-frequency word and idiom tables (HFWD, HFIT, RID, EID) and a table (LEXTBL) of words requiring special translation routines (see Section 6.7.3).

Each text word is then checked against:

- LEXTBL – a match causes an offset address to the corresponding routine to be attached to the word.
- HFWD (in a binary search) – a match causes an offset address to the corresponding grammar information in HFIT to be attached to the word.

If the string matched on HFWD is the first part of an idiom, the continuation of the idiom is looked up in RID using the offset address attached to the HFWD entry. If the idiom continuation is also matched, the TL meaning is accessed from EID and attached to the first text word of the idiom, subsequent words being marked as translated.

In the case of idiom replaces, the SL expression is replaced by the "dummy word" designated in the RID entry, so preventing the component words of the expression from undergoing individual lookup in the stem dictionary. For idioms as such (in the SYSTRAN sense), dictionary lookup and translation at this stage does not prevent subsequent lookup of component words in the stem dictionary, which may provide crucial grammatical information. The same is true of LS/idioms, which are "frozen" at this stage – in their case, subsequent stem lookup also provides the TL translation of component words.

In addition, **LOADTEXT** includes a special routine to deal with hyphenated words. These are broken down into their components which are individually looked up, to be ultimately reassembled in an equivalent TL form.

Finally, **LOADTEXT** invokes a routine (SORT 1) which sorts all low-frequency words into an appropriate alphabetical sequence, ready for the next stage of dictionary consultation.

6.5.2 MDL

The program **MDL** (main dictionary lookup) attempts to match the entries on the low frequency word list output by **LOADTEXT** against the low-frequency dictionaries (LDICT, MDICT, SDICT). These dictionaries are organized so that the longest match is obtained. Any unmatched portion of the text word is checked to ensure it is a valid affix for the paradigmatic type of the stem (see Section 6.5.3). These remarks do not apply in the case of English, where all paradigmatic forms are entered directly in the dictionary.

On finding a match, the corresponding grammar information is accessed from GDICT and copied into the processing record for the matched word. TL meanings are also copied, with MDL using the TG codes where applicable to select appropriate translations. When a homograph is encountered, all information relating to each usage is copied for later use by the homograph resolution routine at the beginning of syntactic analysis.

After all the words have been processed, the text is restored to its original word order by the routine SORT 2, using the sequence numbers assigned by LOADTEXT.

6.5.3 Morphological analysis

As noted earlier, SYSTRAN translation from English does not involve morphological analysis, dictionary entries being full-form words. For other SLs, e.g. French, morphological analysis is "included".

In French analysis, MDL calls two morphology programs, SYSNOUN and SYSVERB, which make it possible to recognize all inflected forms of nouns/adjectives (SYSNOUN) and verbs (SYSVERB) during dictionary lookup of basic stems. Both programs consist essentially of tables of inflectional endings accompanied by the grammatical information which each ending contributes, e.g. number and gender for nouns and adjectives, person and tense for verbs. On finding a potential stem match on the initial characters of a text word, the PST code located in the stem entry is used to access the list of possible endings for that stem; the remaining characters of the text word are checked against this list and, in the event of a match, grammatical information from the ending is attached to the text word along with information from the stem itself. Because of the search algorithm used by MDL, the first valid stem + ending combination encountered will be the one which gives a longest match on the stem (as compared with other valid combinations for the same word). It is not clear from the documentation whether or not the search continues for other valid combinations.

6.5.4 Not-found words

If dictionary lookup fails for any particular text word, the routine NFWRTN (not-found-word routine) is invoked. The word is first tested for the possibility of its being a number (numeric or alphanumeric, ordinal or cardinal); if it is, appropriate grammar and translation codes are attached. If not, the word is processed against a word-ending table in order to extract as much grammatical information as possible. A word for which no such information can be obtained is indicated by a POS value of EO.

6.5.5 LSLOOKUP

If a word is the PW of any LS, this information will be indicated in the appropriate byte of the byte area as a result of stem dictionary lookup. LSLOOKUP accesses the

LS dictionary for each word so marked, and determines whether any of the LSs are in fact present in the text, updating the information in the analysis area accordingly.

In some versions of SYSTRAN, this routine occurs after homograph resolution, though it would seem to be more appropriate at this point.

6.6 Analysis

After dictionary lookup has been completed, control is passed to the program INITCALL, which charges and executes the various translation modules, beginning with GETSENTN (see Section 6.3). Once a sentence has been loaded into the analysis area, it is analyzed by each of the following modules in turn.

6.6.1 HOMOR

This module attempts to resolve homograph ambiguity, using the information assigned during dictionary lookup. In SYSTRAN, a word is treated as a homograph if it can function as more than one part of speech (POS). For each SL, a set of homograph types is defined and encoded, each type representing a possible POS combination in which a given homograph may participate. For English, some 83 homograph types have been identified, e.g.

001   verb/infinitive (e.g. *go, have*)

006   verb/infinitive/past-participle/adjective (e.g. *read*)

027   auxiliary/noun (e.g. *might*)

039   noun/adjective/adverb/preposition (e.g. *outside, past*)

041   relative pronoun/interrogative pronoun/interrogative adjective (e.g. *which, what*)

061   adverb/preposition/subordinate conjunction (e.g. *since, before*)

All homographs are assigned the appropriate type-code when entered in the dictionary. The different parts of speech for each homograph are given separate entries, linked by offset addresses. On creation of the sentence analysis area by GETSENTN, only one (the most common) POS entry is loaded into the analysis area. In the byte area for this word, byte 137 indicates the homograph type and byte 55 contains a sequence number giving access to the other POS entries, which are stored in a special variable-length area following the analysis area. If the POS initially stored in the analysis area is determined by the homograph routine to be the incorrect one, the routine replaces it with the correct **POS** taken, along with its 160 bytes of information, from the variable-length homograph area.

HOMOR includes the following subprograms:

LEXFF – Exempts from consideration any homograph **POS**s marked in the dictionary as **FF** (semantically ambiguous). These will be processed at a later stage by special lexical routines (see Section 6.7.3).

HM PASS 1 – Identifies any homographs participating in an LS expression, and selects **POS** accordingly. The fact that no word in an LS expression can function as a verb reduces selection possibilities, and the homograph's position in the expression may give further clues as to its **POS**. This routine also searches for not-found words (**POS** = **EO**) and identifies them as nouns if preceded by an article, preposition or number.

HM PASS 2 – Treats remaining homographs by calling the resolution routine corresponding to the homograph code in each case. These routines may examine the surrounding environment as far to the left or right as necessary for successful resolution. As the pass is from left to right, resolution is based as far as possible on words to the left of the homograph, since any other homographs appearing there will have already been treated. In completely ambiguous cases, e.g. where resolutions of two or more homographs are mutually dependent, the **POS** originally entered in the analysis area is selected by default.

It is important to bear in mind that the routines have access to only basic grammatical information derived directly from the dictionaries. Other information, e.g. about clause boundaries and syntactic function, is established by subsequent analysis modules and is therefore unavailable to HOMOR. This necessarily limits the efficacy of the resolution routines, and means that their results are subject to later revision by other modules. This in turn not only is uneconomical, but also jeopardizes the claim to genuine modularity since, in effect, other modules with other professed aims are obliged to take on a function intended for HOMOR.

Certain more recent SYSTRAN versions are reported to have HOMOR following **LSLOOKUP** (see next section). This resequencing makes HOMOR's task somewhat easier by eliminating components of LS expressions from consideration (recall that LS expressions may contain only nouns). However, it does not substantially affect the criticisms just made.

6.6.2 STRPASSO

The purpose of this module is to:

- establish clause boundaries within the sentence, marking them with a subsentence unit (**SSU**) marker placed at the last word of each clause;
- set up pointers on either side of an embedded clause or parenthetical phrase so that these units may be skipped during subsequent analysis of the main clause;
- assign to byte 140 of each word a value indicating the type of clause to which it belongs.

Eleven types of subordinate clause are recognized for English: relative, noun, interrogative, restrictive, time, generalization, comparative, causal, purpose, conditional and concessive. Each potential clause opener (which may be an idiom replace) is encoded in the dictionary for the type of clause it may introduce, and it is this code that is assigned by the program to the other words of the clause.

STRPASS0 operates by examining each item of the sentence in turn, calling different subroutines depending on whether the item is a relative pronoun, subordinate conjunction, conjunctive adverb, semi-colon, colon, parenthesis, dash or comma. The subroutines scan the environment as far to the left or right as necessary, checking for the presence of other items (e.g. finite verb, punctuation) serving to define particular clause types.

6.6.3 STRPASS1

The main aim of this module is to establish the "primary syntactic relations", i.e. relations of government and modification, between words of the sentence. These relations are indicated by setting pointers between participating words, using the pairs of bytes reserved in the byte areas for this purpose. The sets of relations determined for English (numbers refer to the bytes used) are listed in Table **?**.

Table 6.2 Relations for English.

Bytes used	Types of words between which relationship exists
16-26	adjectival modifier + noun adverb + adjective or adverb
17-27	participle or adjective (following the noun) + noun infinitive (following the noun) + noun
18-28	verb + direct object preposition + object of preposition
19-29	verb + indirect object verb + adjectival complement (in verb + object + adj. complement sequence, e.g. *He painted the ball red.*) verb + second object complement (double object)
20-30	noun + noun modifier noun + possessive noun modifier
21-31	verb + infinitive verb + present participle noun + noun modifier noun + possessive noun modifier
22-32	antecedent + relative pronoun
23-33	adverb + verb
96-77	linking verb + predicate (noun or adjective)
118-119	noun + number in apposition

In each case, two pointers are set up, from the modifying or governing word to the modified or governed word and vice versa. Where more than one modifier is present, the second pointer points to the outermost modifier in the sequence (9).

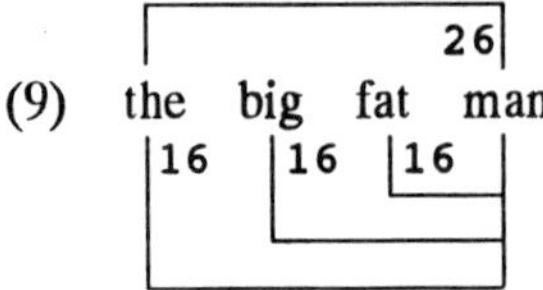

Note that relations are not established across coordinating conjunctions (e.g. *and*, *or*, comma) – this is left to a separate module, STRPASS2 (see Section 6.6.4).

STRPASS1 operates in a left-to-right pass, examining one word at a time and skipping over embedded clauses, which are scanned after the main clause. Syntactic relations are identified by specialized routines corresponding to particular POSs encountered during the scan. POSs already encountered are remembered by setting switches and saving word addresses, the appropriate switch being turned off whenever no more relations with a given word are applicable, or when an enumerative operator is encountered.

In addition, the module also performs the following:
- marking, by different bit combinations in byte 12, all words functioning as nouns, adjectival modifiers, finite verbs and pronouns. These are more general categories than the corresponding POSs, which they subsume. For example 'finite verb' here covers the POSs:

  04 finite verb (non-auxiliary)
  08 auxiliary verb (except those below)
  40 finite form of *be*
  54 finite form of *have*

- copying information on tense, person and number from nonmodal auxiliaries to the main verb, changing the code of the main verb to "finite";
- setting negative particles as "translated", and the appropriate word as negated;
- setting comparative and superlative adverbs as "translated", and marking the following adjective or adverb as comparative or superlative;
- changing the POS of a word, where necessary, on the basis of information contained in an LS expression.

6.6.4 STRPASS2

This module extends syntactic relations over enumerative sequences, i.e. sequences of subclausal items connected by enumerative operators. It establishes relations between the units themselves, and between them and other sentence elements, overruling where necessary relations established by STRPASS1.

The program makes a single left-to-right pass, searching for enumerative operators which have not already been identified by STRPASS0 as clause separators. On locating such an operator, the **POS** of the words immediately to its left and right are examined to determine invocation of the appropriate specialized subroutine: **NENO** (nouns), **ADJENO** (adjectives), **ADVENO** (adverbs), **PRENO** (prepositions), **VENO** (finite verbs), **INFENO** (infinitives) and **PTENO** (participles).

If the two words have the same **POS**, selection of the appropriate routine is straightforward. If they have different **POS**s, the program attempts to resolve the discrepancy before a routine can be invoked. In doing so, the **POS** of the word to the left of the operator is taken as a major guideline. For example, in (10) the fact that *camera* is a noun will cause the program to reject the adjective *other* as the potential second unit in the enumeration, and to select instead the noun which it modifies, *equipment*. The routine **NENO** can then be invoked.

> (10) the camera and other necessary equipment
>   NOUN   ADJ

The purpose of the routines is to make further checks to determine correctly the enumerative sequence, and to link the enumerated words by means of pointers, using bytes 47 and 48 to point forwards and backwards, respectively. The kind of checks necessary may be illustrated by the particularly problematic case of noun enumerations in English. A major problem here is presented by sequences of the type illustrated in (11).

> (11) NOUN1 and NOUN2 NOUN3

These are potentially ambiguous: **NOUN1** and **NOUN2** may be linked enumeratively as joint modifiers of **NOUN3**; or **NOUN2** may alone modify **NOUN3**, with **NOUN1** and **NOUN3** linked enumeratively as joint heads of the coordinate NP. The rules (or, more aptly, heuristics) applied to resolve the ambiguity include the following:

- If **NOUN1** is itself modified by an adjective or noun, it is assumed to stand in enumeration with **NOUN3**, as in (12).

  (12)   This study concerns physical fitness and body agility.

- Otherwise, it is linked with **NOUN2** as modifying **NOUN3**, as in (13).

  (13)   This study concerns alcohol and tobacco effects on the body.

- Where a finite verb occurs to the right of an enumerative sequence, its number may indicate the correct solution, as in (14).

  (14) a. Smog and pollution control are pressing issues.

  b. Smog and pollution control is under consideration.

- Where two of the nouns share the same semantic markers, they can be assumed to stand in enumeration with each other. For example, *production* and *sterilization* would have both been assigned the marker PRGEN (general process), leading to a correct solution in (15).

(15)   Production and sterilization plants were installed.
47 |________________| 48

- Similarly, the marker FPROD (food product) assigned to *fruit* and *vegetables* resolves the ambiguity in (16).

(16)   Fruit and vegetable markets did well last year.
47 |__________| 48

The strategy by which the above are applied is not clear.

After the 47,48 pointers have been set, the main program moves to its second task of finalizing syntactic relations between enumerated words and the rest of their environment. This is necessitated by the fact that STRPASS1 did not attempt to establish relations, enumerative or otherwise, across enumerative operators. In some cases, however, STRPASS1 will have correctly identified the relation between the first word in the enumeration and its preceding environment, requiring only a straightforward extension of that relation to succeeding words. In the following example (17), STRPASS1 has marked the 18,28 (verb-direct object) relation between *demands* and *speed*, and the 47,48 pointers have been set by NENO:

47 |‾‾‾‾‾‾‾‾‾| 48
(17)   This project demands speed and accuracy.
18 |______| 28

All that remains is to change byte 18 of *demands* to point to the outermost enumerated word, *accuracy*, and to set up the corresponding pointer in the reverse direction (18).

47 |‾‾‾‾‾‾‾‾‾| 48
(18)   This project demands speed and accuracy.
|18 |28 |28

In other cases, STRPASS2 will be required to rectify incorrect analyses resulting from STRPASS1. In the following example, STRPASS1 has correctly identified the 20,30 (noun–noun modifier) relation between *prices* and *fuel*, but on encountering *and* has ceased to search for further relations between *prices* and words to the left of *and*. It has therefore analyzed *food* as being the object of *about* (19):

47 |________| 48
(19)   The nation is concerned about food and fuel prices.
18 |___| 28   30 |___| 20

Having correctly established the 47,48 relation, STRPASS2 will now recognize *prices* as the head noun of the phrase and thus as the true object of *about*, and will reset the pointers accordingly (20):

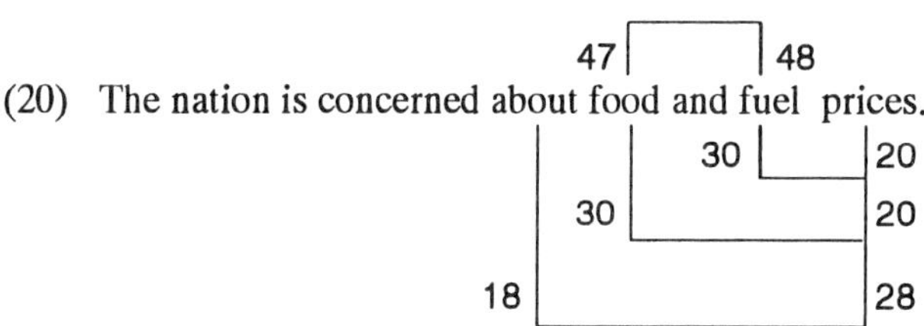

(20)   The nation is concerned about food and fuel prices.

Again, precise details of the algorithms involved are unavailable. However, such examples give further indication of how SYSTRAN's linear approach leads to "short-sighted" decisions being made in the earlier stages of analysis, which then have to be undone in later modules by highly specific corrective routines. A more coherent phrasal analysis, even if it required backtracking, would at least reduce the need for separate rules and routines having the sole purpose of rectifying earlier analysis errors, and so avoid much of the opacity of SYSTRAN's operation.

6.6.5 STRPASS3

This module identifies the subject and predicate of each clause and sets pointers to mark the relation. The task is relatively straightforward given the successful accomplishment of the previous passes. Verbs marked as finite by STRPASS1 are potential predicates, and nouns or pronouns not marked either as objects (of verbs/prepositions) or as modifiers are potential subjects.

The program begins by singling out each clause for treatment, setting pointers to the first word of the clause and to either the last word of the clause or the word before an embedded clause, using clause boundary information from STRPASS0. It then calls the subroutine PLOOP which scans the clause left to right for a predicate, i.e. (in English) a finite verb not immediately preceded by *as*. The location of this verb is registered in byte 108 of the first word of the clause, and a check is made to see if STRPASS2 has marked the verb as one of an enumerative sequence. If so, the verbs in enumeration arc linked by pointers in bytes 109 and 110 to indicate the presence of a multiple predicate.

The subject search routine SLOOP is then invoked. This begins by checking if the sentence ends with a question mark, indicating that a search to the right of the predicate is in order; if not, the subject is sought to the left of the predicate. Scanning left to right, the routine examines all words which have been marked by STRPASS1 as functioning as nouns. If such a word is found that has not also been marked either as an object of any kind or as a modifier of a second noun, that word is identified as the subject. Failing this, a search is made for other possible subject elements, i.e. a noun clause, infinitive, present participle or (in English) the word *there*. If no subject can be identified, the predicate is marked as imperative.

On identifying a subject, pointers are set up between it and the predicate, using bytes 108 and 111, and from the subject to the first word of the clause. Finally, byte 47 of the subject word is checked to see if it functions in an enumeration, in which case multiple-subject pointers are established.

It will be seen from this description that STRPASS3 appears to rely heavily on the results of the previous passes, especially of STRPASS1. It is not clear to what extent, if any, morphological agreement is used to verify independently subject–predicate relations.

6.6.6 PREP1/STRPASS4

PREP1 (English SL) is responsible for identifying the relation between a preposition and its governor, and for marking the relation by means of pointers in bytes 24 (governor to preposition) and 35 (preposition to governor). The program scans the sentence right to left for prepositions and, for each one encountered, searches to its left for a word whose prepositional government code (PREPR) specifies this preposition. If no such word is found before the current clause boundary is met, the program scans to the right for a main verb that may be the governor.

STRPASS4, as included in more recent versions of SYSTRAN (e.g. CEC French–English), subsumes the function of PREPPGM1 and in addition:
- identifies logical relationships between, for example, a predicate and its arguments;
- resolves any ambiguity as to gender and/or number of SL words.

6.7 Transfer

Certain of the more recent descriptions of SYSTRAN (e.g. van Slype & Pigott 1979) identify the modules described below as constituting a "transfer phase". They are indeed language-pair specific in that, in general, they involve selection of TL structures and/or lexical items on the basis of surface characteristics of the SL text. However, the same can be said of the "analysis" module LSLOOKUP, especially since it assigns TL equivalents to LS/idiom expressions, which are far less opaque in terms of the SL than "true" idioms. Hence the distinction between analysis and transfer is less clear-cut in SYSTRAN than in other systems that rely less heavily on dictionary translation of entire expressions.

6.7.1 CLSLOOKUP

This module operates in the same way as LSLOOKUP, sharing the same routines for identifying relevant expressions in the SL sentence (via the PW) and for assigning particular TL meanings to component words. In addition it includes specialized subroutines for interpreting and applying CLS dictionary rules. These rules are described in Section 6.4.1; as explained there, they impose conditions on the selection of particular TL meanings for certain SL words or expressions. The conditions involve reference to syntactic relations marked via byte-area pointers – hence the need to order CLSLOOKUP after the main analysis modules have established these relations. For example, the selection of *employer* rather than *utiliser* for the English *employ* is effected by a CLS entry embodying a condition on the presence of a direct object (active sentence) with the semantic marker PROF (profession). If included, the assignment of logical relations by STRPASS4 obviates the need for different active/passive versions of the rule.

It is possible for conflicts to arise between different CLS rules or between a CLS rule and an LS assignment, where these involve the same text item(s). In the former case, conflict is resolved by priority codes included where necessary in CLS dictionary entries. In the latter case, priority is given to translations already assigned by LSLOOKUP.

6.7.2 PREP2

This module selects the appropriate translation for each SL preposition that has not already been marked as translated by CLSLOOKUP.

Where applicable, the selection is determined by preposition-translation codes attached to the governor or object of the preposition from the E-line section of the dictionary entry for these words (see Section 6.4.2). For each nontranslated preposition encountered, its governor and/or object is located (via the pointers set by STRPASS1 and PREP1/STRPASS4) and checked for the presence of any such code applying to the preposition in question. If found, the specified TL preposition is retrieved from the TL preposition table and attached as the appropriate translation to the SL preposition.

Where no such code is present, the translation specified in the dictionary entry for the preposition itself is selected by default.

6.7.3 LEXICAL

A number of highly specialized lexical routines may be invoked at this stage to deal with words (and constructions containing them) which present particular problems for translation. Routines are written for individual words and for semantic or syntactic categories of words. Word-specific routines are accessed via offset addresses, attached to the text word by LOADTEXT from the file LEXTBL. Category-specific routines are listed in a separate file LEXLIST, consulted directly by the main LEXICAL program. The program operates in a left-to-right pass, examining the byte area of each word for either an offset address to a routine or a syntactic/semantic category code matching on LEXLIST. The corresponding routine is then applied.

There is virtually no limit, apart from programming constraints and the general nature of the SYSTRAN data structure, on the operations that may be performed by lexical routines. They may specify target translations for words and constructions; insert, delete, and reorder elements to conform with TL structure; change SL or TL grammar codes; and attach special markers to influence TL synthesis procedures. The following examples, from the English–French system version 1, give an indication of their use:

APPLYR This routine marks the verb as reflexive when necessary, e.g. in *this applies to all methods* but not in *apply heat to X*.

CITYRTN Assigns to all words encoded with the semantic category **CITY** a special marker preventing article insertion; when governed by *in* or *at*, selects the translation *à*.

EXPECTR Determines the appropriate translation of constructions involving *expect*, e.g.

> (22) a. He is expected to come.
> *On s'attend à ce qu'il vienne.*
> b. He expects to come.
> *Il s'attend à ce qu'il vienne.*

GOIVERBR Determines the appropriate translation of constructions involving certain verbs coded as **GOI** (may govern infinitive), (23) shows one such constriction.

> (23) They required him to vote.
> cf. They required the ballot to vote.

ITR Determines whether *it* is impersonal (to be translated as *il* or *ce*) or anaphoric. In the latter case, the routine finds the antecedent (it is not clear how) and translates *it* as *il* or *elle* accordingly.

WHICHR (for all relative pronouns) Determines number, gender, animate and concrete features of antecedent and copies this information into the relative pronoun.

Further details of the operation of individual routines are unavailable. However, given the relatively superficial nature of SYSTRAN's structural analysis, it is clear that many of the routines must themselves incorporate very *ad hoc* analytical procedures in order to achieve their results (**ITR** and a handful of other routines dealing with anaphoric reference are a case in point). It is presumably this criticism that has motivated the introduction and extension of CLS rules to cover much of what was originally the domain of lexical routines. (Unofficial reports suggest that this has recently been taken further, with the introduction of a new type of CLS rule capable of changing grammatical codes in the byte area; no details of these have so far been received.) However, although CLS rules as described in Section 6.4.1 are subject to more formal constraints than lexical routines, they are even less general since they can be invoked only by specific words rather than word categories.

6.8 Synthesis

The synthesis phase consists of two modules: **ESYN** and **REARR**.

6.8.1 ESYN

This program makes a left-to-right pass through the sentence, translating each item on the basis of:

- the appropriate TL item (or full form) selected by previous modules,
- synthesis routines specific to certain parts of speech.

The French module contains 16 synthesis routines, e.g. for verbs, nouns, pronouns, adjectives, adverbs, articles, comparative conjunctions. As an example, the verb routine **VERBR** includes:
- determination of person, number, gender, tense and mood
- insertion of negative particles
- choice of auxiliary (*être/avoir*)
- determination of participle agreement
- ending affixation, using a table of regular and irregular paradigms.

6.8.2 REARR

This imposes the correct TL word order where different from SL. The program makes a right-to-left pass, calling appropriate rearrangement routines for particular POSs and syntactic relations, e.g. noun–adjective, noun–noun modifier, verb–adverb etc.

The French module also includes two additional routines, called after all reordering has been completed. The first of these is invoked for all words marked **APOS**, indicating that their final vowel is to be elided before a word beginning with a vowel or mute *h*; the routine deletes the final vowel and inserts an apostrophe, where appropriate. The second routine anticipates the possibility that the subject of the following (as yet "unseen") sentence may be the pronoun *it*. The program scans the current sentence for a potential antecedent and saves its gender for later use in translating the pronoun should it occur. (No provision appears to be made for nonsubject *it* or for other pronouns with extra-sentential antecedents.) The criteria used in selecting the potential antecedent are not documented; however, since this routine follows the rearrangement routines rather than being included under **LEXICAL**, for example, it presumably depends on TL word order, and possibly does little more than select the last nominal to have a nonhuman reference. Note that this routine represents the only attempt in SYSTRAN to take analysis beyond the sentence level.

6.9 Hardware details and dictionary sizes

The original system was designed to run on IBM 360 and 370 series machines, with a core memory of 400 kbytes and slow memory of about 3 Mbytes. The CEC English–French version runs on an IBM 370/145 under OS/Vl, on an IBM 370/158 under OS/VSl, and on a Siemens 7740. Texts for translation are prepared on punch cards or magnetic tape, or keypunched directly.[2]

---

2. Since the time of writing, these hardware specifications have changed. In particular, most users have interfaced SYSTRAN with a word-processing or work-station environment, so that text input and post-editing is much more user friendly than previously. — HLS

The raw translation speed of the CEC system is 2000 words per CPU-minute on the 370/145 and 6000 on the 370/1-58. The total cost of finished translations per 100 words is estimated as in Table ?.

Table 6.3 Cost of translations.

Stage	Price (Belgian francs)
Data capture	100
Machine translation	35
Post-editing	300
Typing	40
Total	475

Source: van Slype & Pigott (1979: p. 158)

The post-editing cost is for a translator working in a large institution, and is significantly lower for freelance work. Since post-editors usually work on hard-copy output, which is subsequently retyped, there would appear to be large savings available were the system to be more integrated with the translation process, with documents produced originally in machine-readable form and each translator/post-editor working with a dedicated word-processor.[3]

The cost of creating new dictionary entries has been estimated at US$2.50. As of 1979, the versions of SYSTRAN listed in Table ? were being used or developed, with the dictionary sizes shown[4].

6.10 Documentation

Guazzo, J. 1980. *Short description of SYSTRAN*. Report no. CEC-TH24B3–A5, SYSTRAN Institute, Luxembourg.

Haller, H. & J. Guazzo-Jansen 1980. *Second quarterly report*. Report no. TH24A, CETIL/194/80, SYSTRAN Institute, Luxembourg.

Masterman, M. & R. J. Smith 1980. *The automatic annotation of SYSTRAN*. Contract TH-29, Final Report, Cambridge Language Research Unit.

Pahl, T. 1980. *Second quarterly report*. Report no. TH24B, CETIL/198/80, SYSTRAN Institute, Luxembourg.

---

3. See previous note. More recently, a fairly thorough MT feasibility survey for the Canadian government (Gobeil 1981: pp. 110ff) gave the following cost estimates per word (in Canadian dollars): text entry (using OCR) and correction 2.6¢, translation 8.4¢, revision 5.9¢: total 16.9¢. — HLS

4. Hutchins & Somers (1992: p. 177) list several additional language pairs including English–German, English–Japanese and vice versa, English–Russian, Spanish–English, German–Italian, plus about 15 pairs under development More recent figures also suggest, as one would expect, larger dictionary sizes: for example, German–English is now 153000 words, French–English 142000, English–Italian 131000, English–French 125000, and so on (Siebenaler 1986: p. 44). — HLS

Table 6.4 Versions of SYSTRAN and dictionary sizes (in 1979).

Language pair	Dictionary size	Subject area
Russian–English	1 500 000	20 scientific areas
English–French	72 000	Engineering, automobile technology
English–Spanish	6 000	Reprography
English–French (CEC)	70 000	Agriculture, economics etc.
English–Italian (CEC)	70 000	Agriculture, economics etc.
French–English (CEC)	40 000	Engineering etc.
German–English/ French/Spanish	15 000	Automobile technology
English–Arabic/ Portuguese	20 000	Technology (pilot system)

Source: 'Systran Report', EurOnet DIANE News *17, December 1979*

Pigott, I. M. 1980. How does SYSTRAN translate? A brief description of the workings of the European Commission's English–French machine translation system. Paper prepared for a meeting of the Natural Language Translation Specialist Group of the British Computer Society.

Toma, P. P., L. A. Kozlik & D.G. Perrin (n.d.) *SYSTRAN Machine Translation system.* LATSEC Inc., La Jolla, California.

Van Slype, G. (n.d.). *Le système SYSTRAN. Etat de la question sur les activités multilingues en matière d'information scientifique et technique.* Note de travail n° 6.1, Bureau Marcel van Dijk, Bruxelles.

Van Slype, G. & I. Pigott 1979. Description du système de traduction automatique SYSTRAN de la Commission des Communautés Européennes. *Documentaliste* **16**, 150–9.

World Translation Corporation (n.d.) Documentation of English–French system supplied to CEC, version 1.0.

World Translation Company of Canada (n.d.) An introduction to the SYSTRAN II computer dictionary. WTCC, Ottawa.

6.11 Further references

The following bibliography includes references in the footnotes, as well as important sources published since the first edition appeared.

Gachot, D. A. 1989. The SYSTRAN renaissance. *MT Summit II*, Final Programme, Exhibition, Papers. pp. 60–5. Munich.

Gobeil, F. 1981. *Machine Translation feasibility study: final report.* Planning, Management and Technology Branch, Translation Bureau, Secretary of State Department, Ottawa.

Hutchins, W. J. & H. L. Somers 1992. *An introduction to Machine Translation,* Chapter 10. London: Academic Press.

Siebenaler, L. 1986. SYSTRAN for ESPRIT and ECAT Bureau service. *Terminologie et Traduction* 1, 40–6.

Trabulsi, S. 1989. Le système SYSTRAN. In *Traduction assistée par ordinateur: perspectives technologiques, industrielles et economiques envisageables à l'horizon 1990,* A. Abbou (ed.), 15–34. Paris: Editions Daicadif.

Wheeler, P. 1987. SYSTRAN. In *Machine Translation today: the state of the art,* M. King (ed.), 192–208. Edinburgh: Edinburgh University Press.

7

TAUM-MÉTÉO

7.1 Introduction

The MÉTÉO system is an MT system used for the translation of weather reports from English to French. It was commissioned by the Canadian government from TAUM (*Traduction Automatique de l'Université de Montréal*) in 1974, and became operational in 1976[1]. The computational features of MÉTÉO, including the formalism for writing the grammars, are closely based on those of the Montreal MT prototype of 1971; the linguistic component of the system, that is, the content of the grammars, defines a language whose syntax and lexicon are heavily constrained according to the standard practice of meteorological bulletins.

7.2 Basic nature of the system

It is a difficult matter to locate MÉTÉO at a precise point on the spectrum of strategies for MT, i.e. direct—transfer—interlingual. On the one hand, the process of translation is highly language-pair specific, with target language lexical items being inserted prior to analysis, and no specific stage which could be termed "transfer". On

---

1. In October 1984 a new version of MÉTÉO, written in the special-purpose programming language GramR[TM], was installed at John Chandioux Consultants Inc., running on microcomputers. Translations of weather bulletins are now provided to the Secretary of State on a contract basis by Chandioux's company (cf. Chandioux 1989). — HLS

the other hand, the operations of analysis and synthesis are notionally separated; the structure which mediates between the two could be considered a syntactic interlingua, representing an abstraction of structural features from the limited syntax source and target languages, and using target language lexical items as a matter of convenience (i.e. a limited subset of French vocabulary is the lexicon of this interlingua).

7.3 Data structure

The data structure used in the MÉTÉO system comprises two components. The first of these is the tree, which is the representation of any well-formed constituent at any stage of the translation process. The nodes of the tree are labelled by character strings (*etiquettes*). A legal *etiquette* is any character, followed by any number (including none) of alphanumeric characters; an *etiquette* may correspond to a terminal, nonterminal, or feature of the grammar, though these functions are not distinguished formally. The root of a tree will normally be labelled with the nonterminal category of which the tree is a (well-formed) example. The forest of trees corresponding to a single tree with the root absent is termed a list. The members of a list (the daughters of the root) are separated by commas. Thus the tree in (1a) would be represented as the list (1b), where each of the strings (1c)–(1e) are lists.

(1) a.

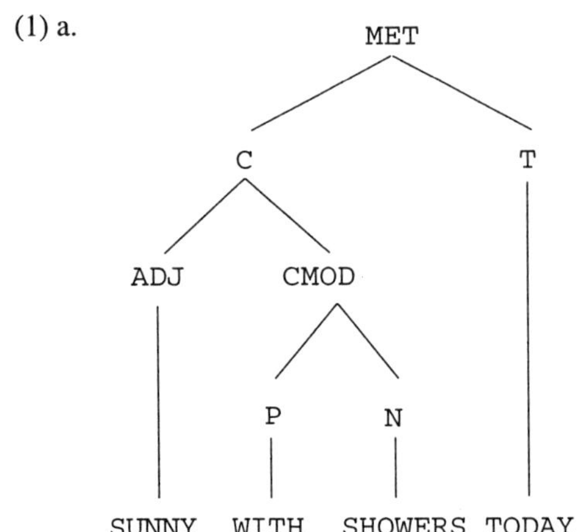


```
b. MET(C(ADJ(SUNNY),CMOD(P(WITH),N(SHOWERS))),
              T(TODAY))
c. P(WITH),N(SHOWERS)
d. ADJ(SUNNY),CMOD(...)
e. C(...),T(TODAY)
```

The other component of the data structure is a cycle-free directed graph, with unique entry and exit vertices, whose edges are labelled by trees as described above.

The two components together constitute a chart. The chart is a convenient device for representing the results of a bottom-up parsing algorithm which finds all possible analyses of a sentence.

The chart is initially constituted from the text as an unbranching graph, where each edge is labelled with a single lexical etiquette (i.e. a degenerate tree). Thus the text (2a) will give rise to the graph (2b). (The arrows point from right to left, since this is the direction in which the chart is actually traversed.)

    (2) a. Sunny with showers today.

       b.

In the text writing formalism, the entry vertex of a graph is designated by $-01-$, the exit vertex by $-02-$, and all other unbranching vertices by +. Thus the chart in (2b) would be written as (3).

    (3) -01- SUNNY + WITH + SHOWERS + TODAY + . -02-

A series of edges labelled with trees, such as the above is called a *chaîne* (path).

As parsing progresses, new edges (and new vertices) will be added to the chart. An edge spanning two vertices will indicate the existence of a well-formed constituent comprising those lexical items which label the original path between those two nodes. Two or more edges spanning the same pair of vertices indicate alternative parses; the structures assigned by these parses are given by the trees which label the edges. An edge spanning from entry to exit vertices indicates a parsing of the entire sentence.

Branching vertices, in intermediate representations of the text, are designated by integers, as in (4), indicating alternative readings for *talk*. These edges will each be part of one or more paths, but a single path may not include both.

    (4) -03- VERB(TALK) -04-
         -03- NOUN(TALK) -04-

7.4 Dictionary entries and grammatical rules

The dictionary entries and grammatical rules of MÉTÉO are expressed in a formalism known as a Q-system. A Q-system is a generalized path transducer, that is, each rule specifies the transduction of one path, or concatenation of tree structures, into another. Since a path cannot include alternative branches, all vertices indicated in a rule have the form +. A Q-system rule has the following components:

- an LHS, or pattern, specifying a path to be found in the chart
- an RHS, or action, specifying a path to be added to the chart
- an optional condition, which must evaluate "true" for the rule to be applied, i.e. for the RHS to be added.

That is:

```
<Q-system rule> ::= <pattern> == <action> /
   <condition> .
```

In principle rules are invertible: if a grammar (i.e. a collection of rules) is preceded by the reserved word -INV-, the RHS of each rule acts as the pattern and the LHS as the action. In what follows, the uninverted correspondences are assumed.

Example (5) is a Q-system rule:

```
(5) AN + ADDITIONAL == CIRC(INV(ADDITIONALLY),/,*DEG).
```

When applied to a graph containing the path specified by the LHS, this rule will create a new edge spanning the same vertices as this path, and will label the edge with the tree specified on the RHS.

The etiquette slash (/) (not to be confused with the slash introducing a condition) indicates that the right sisters of the node thus labelled may be construed as features on its left sister node, though, as stated above, the rule interpreter does not discriminate between these different types of etiquette.

An example of a rule in which the RHS is a path comprising more than one edge (and hence will cause the addition of a new vertex to the graph) is (6), which effects the morphological decomposition of an irregular word form.

```
(6) WORSE == ADJ(BAD,/) + *(ER).
```


7.4.1 Variables

It is obvious that in order for such a grammar to capture significant generalizations about language, there must be a facility for partially specifying structures (i.e. for specifying classes of structures). To achieve this, a Q-system rule may include what the documentation calls *paramètres*, but which are best termed variables. A variable of a given type appearing in the LHS of a rule will match any structure of the same type appearing in the database. A variable appearing in the RHS must also appear in the LHS, and will cause the building of the structure against which it was matched. Thus for a rule to be invertible, no variable must appear on one side only.

A variable is a letter followed by * and an optional digit. Variables may be of type etiquette, tree or list; the type is indicated by the first letter of the variable name, thus:

```
'A'..'F'       etiquette
'I'..'N'          tree
'U'..'Z'          list
```

The use of variables may be illustrated by rule (7), which will recognize the concatenation of any adjective with the morpheme *-er*, and generate a tree including a feature indicating comparison of that adjective.

```
(7) ADJ(A*,/,U*) + *(ER) == ADJ(A*,/,U*,INV(MORE)).
```

This rule will apply to the structure which was used to rewrite *worse* in (6) (i.e. A* = BAD, and U* = -NUL-, the empty list) as well as any other structure of the appropriate form, e.g. originating from an adjective with a regular morphology.

7.4.2 Conditions

A variable may match against an infinite number of patterns. In order to constrain the number of patterns to the members of a finite set, a rule may include a condition. This is a boolean function defined on the variables of the LHS, and must evaluate "true" for the rule to be applicable.

A condition is constructed using relational operators. There are four of these. Two, = and =/, are operators on lists, with the obvious semantics. The other two, -DANS- and -HORS-, are operators on sets of trees (which are syntactically identical to lists) and correspond to inclusion and exclusion. The documentation defines them as follows:

```
let a and b be any etiquettes
let i and j be any trees
let u and v be any lists
then:
-NUL- -DANS- u = "true"
u -DANS- -NUL- = u = -NUL-
i,u -DANS- v = i -DANS- v et u -DANS- v
i -DANS- j,v = i -DANS- j ou i -DANS- v
a(u) -DANS- b(v) = a = b et u -DANS- v
-NUL- -HORS- u = "false"
u -HORS- -NUL- = "false"
i,u -HORS- v = i -HORS- v et (u -HORS- v ou u = -NUL-)
i -HORS- j,v = i -HORS- j et (i -HORS- v ou j = -NUL-)
a(u) -HORS- b(v) = a =/ b ou u -HORS- v
```

The boolean terms (primaries) obtained by means of these relational operators may be built up into more complex conditions using the logical operators -ET-, -OU- and -NON-. To exemplify the use of conditions, consider rule (8) which might be found in a grammar for treating the English possessive form -'s:

```
(8) NP(U*) + 'S + A*(V*) == NP(U*) + 'S + ART(DEF) + A*(V*)
    / A* -DANS- ADJ,N,QUANT -ET- I,YOU,HE,SHE,IT,THEY
    -HORS- U*.
```

If two rules have a component (LHS, RHS, or condition) in common, they may be written adjacently, with the common component of the second replaced by -- . This is used to economize on storage, and, in the case of identical LHSs, to improve the efficiency of pattern-matching against paths in the data structure.

7.4.3 String handling

In order to process individual characters of an etiquette (as in a morphological analysis or synthesis), the latter must first be converted from a string to a list. This is achieved by means of the disintegration operator $$. For instance, rule (9a) applied to an edge labelled SHOWERS would produce a new arc labelled with the tree (9b).

```
(9) a. A* == MOT($$A*).
    b. MOT(S,H,O,W,E,R,S)
```

This kind of structure could then figure in a rule such as (10).

    (10) MOT(U*,S) == MOT(U*) + S.

The $$ operator is reversible, so if it appears on the LHS of a rule it will effect the reverse transduction from list to etiquette.

7.5 Rule compilation

The Q-system rules are checked for correct syntax and compiled into an internal representation by a program written in FORTRAN. The original compiler was written in ALGOL-60, but this was found to be too inefficient.

A node of the tree is a triple of the following form (where ↑ means 'pointer to'):

↑ left daughter

↑ left sister in LHS path or ↑ right sister in RHS path or list

etiquette

Rules are accessed by means of debreg, an array of pointers. debreg is indexed by means of a hash function on the value of the root of the rightmost tree of the LHS of the rule, when that root is an etiquette. Rules which hash to the same index of debreg form a linked list (through the next rule field in the rule header, see below). All those rules which have as the rightmost constituent of their LHS a variable, or a tree whose root is a variable, form another linked list. For each rule, there is a header of six elements with the following functions:

↑ next rule

↑ LHS

↑ rule with identical LHS

↑ condition

↑ RHS

rule number

This header is accessed from debreg or from the previous rule in a list. It is also accessible from the left sister field of the leftmost tree of the LHS, so that when a pattern match (which ends at the left of a path) is found during parsing, the RHS and condition parts of the rule may be accessed.

7.6 The chart traversal algorithm

The rule interpreter, also written in FORTRAN, accepts the compiler output and a text formatted as described earlier (Section 7.2). The chart is constructed from the text as triples of the same form as the grammar rules, chart edges being analogous to tree nodes. However, the chart must include a facility for representing alternative paths (in addition to the left sister and left daughter properties). Thus the root nodes of trees labelling chart edges are actually quadruples. The fourth field contains a pointer to the next edge in the edge set of the right-hand vertex. Of course, in the degenerate chart initially constituted from the input text, this `nextedge` field will always contain the special value `nil`. A more complex chart will be created during parsing, and this may form the input to subsequent Q-systems.

Thus a chart of the form (11a) may be represented with the structure (11b).

(11) a.

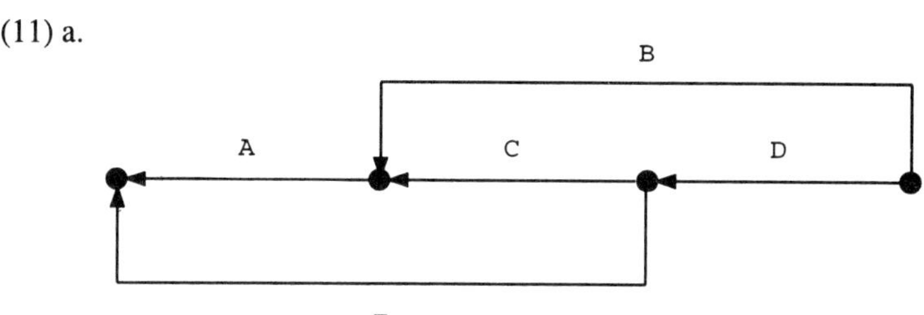

b.

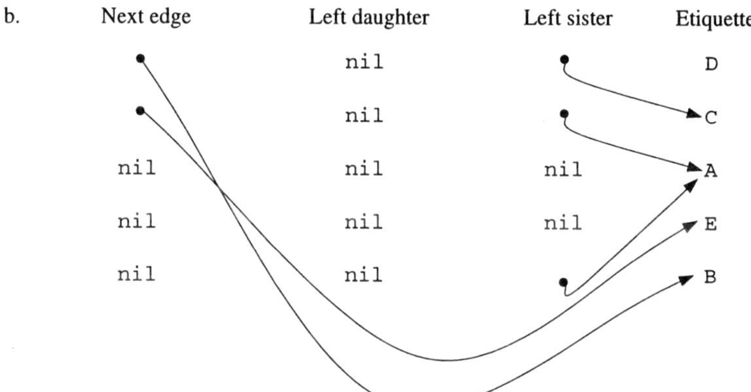

The task of the interpreter is to traverse the chart in such a way that each and every path through it is matched once against the rule base, even though new paths may be added during the course of traversal. Because vertexes are not represented explicitly, it should be understood that when the algorithm is referred to as being focused at a particular vertex, it means that what is being considered is the rightmost edge of a particular path proceeding from that vertex. The remaining edges from that vertex are accessible by following the pointer in the `nextedge` field of that edge's quadruple.

The rule application algorithm has two principal components. The first (TRAVERSE) is a procedure which enumerates the rightmost edge of each path, and the second (PATTERN-MATCH) uses the root of this edge's label to access the linked list of rules via `debreg`, attempting to match the LHS of these rules against all paths proceeding leftwards from each such edge.

TRAVERSE has the following form (in informal ALGOL-like notation):

```
procedure TRAVERSE (x:↑edge)
   var  c:↑edge;
begin if x <> nil then
   if  UNMARKED(x)  then
      begin c  := x;
            repeat TRAVERSE(c.leftsister);
                   MARK(c);
                   PATTERN-MATCH(c,possible-rules);
                   c:= c.nextedge
            until  c = nil
      end
end;
```

TRAVERSE is called initially with the first edge of the rightmost vertex. The leftsister pointers are followed recursively until the leftmost vertex is reached. As the recursion unwinds, PATTERN-MATCH is called for the set of paths starting with the current edge, and this edge is marked as visited. New paths which are created are added to the edge set of the current vertex. TRAVERSE then iterates through this edge set, each time recursing along a path until a marked edge is encountered. This algorithm is very similar to that of Kay (see Kaplan 1973). The Q-system traversal algorithm adds paths while moving its focus from left to right, though the pattern-matcher examines paths of increasing length starting from their rightmost edge. The algorithm is totally combinatorial, in that the result of applying a grammar which is guaranteed to terminate is independent of the order in which the rules of the grammar are applied. However, it is easy to write grammars which will never terminate, and the system makes no checks for this.

When applied to the example chart (11), TRAVERSE will enumerate rightmost edges of paths in the following sequence:

A   C   E   D   B

PATTERN-MATCH will thus attempt to match each possible applicable rule against paths in the following order:

A   C   AC   E   D   CD   ACD   ED   B   AB

New paths resulting from successful rule application have not been included in this list. They are added as follows. PATTERN-MATCH maintains a stack of edges, such that at any time, the edges on the stack correspond to a path (leftmost on top, rightmost on bottom). When a path corresponding to a rule LHS is found, the RHS path is built. The leftsister pointer of the leftmost edge specified in the RHS is set equal to the leftsister pointer of the topmost stack element. The other edges are then built from the rule RHS. Finally the nextedge pointer of the rightmost edge of the new path is set to the value of the nextedge pointer of the edge at the bottom of the stack, and the latter is set to point to the rightmost edge of the new path. In this way, the new path is inserted into the edge set of the current vertex ahead of the parser focus.

As an example, suppose a grammar which is being applied to the chart given above contains the rule (12).

(12) C + D == X + Y.

When PATTERN-MATCH has recognized the LHS of this rule its stack will be in a configuration with (a pointer to the quadruple for) C on top and D beneath (on the bottom). It then builds a quadruple for X, and sets its leftsister pointer equal to that of C, i.e. pointing to A. The quadruple for Y is then built, with its leftsister pointing to X, as specified in the rule action. Finally, this quadruple is inserted as the nextedge of D (the current focus of TRAVERSE, at the base of the stack), with B as its nextedge..

This algorithm is bottom up: all well-formed constituents are discovered, regardless of whether they form a part of any top-level (e.g. sentence) constituent. It is also breadth first: no top-level constituent is discovered until the paths from the rightmost vertex are considered towards the end of the parse, at which point all such constituents are discovered almost at the same time. Both these strategies are appropriate in an MT context.

When the pattern-matcher builds a new path through the chart corresponding to the RHS of a rule, each edge of the LHS path (i.e. each edge on the stack) is flagged. When all applicable rules in one Q-system grammar have been applied, flagged edges are removed from the chart. Following this, all edges which are no longer in paths spanning from entry to exit vertices are also removed. This guarantees that the essential properties of the data structure are maintained.

The Q-system formalism permits the specification of unrestricted rewrite rules, and the parsing algorithm, through its use of chart position rather than constituent length as its "parsing variable", realizes a system of Turing machine power. The parsing variable of a bottom-up algorithm is a variable whose value at any given time defines a finite set of possible candidate strings for pattern-matching. Its value must change in such a way that all sets of strings are examined in a sequence which prevents the output of one set acting as a member of another, previously examined, set. For a grammatical formalism of context-free power, the number of terminal symbols incorporated in the pattern to be matched is a suitable parsing variable, and increasing this value is a suitable parsing strategy, since the RHS which is built will always incorporate at least as many terminal symbols as any of the LHS constituents. For rules of general rewrite form, this does not hold, and a different parsing variable must be used. In the Q-system, chart position is used. That is, the set of strings to the left of and including the current parser focus is the candidate set for pattern-matching. Only the current set may be extended by a successful rule.

7.7 Evaluation of Q-systems

In a Q-system rule, every action that the discovery of an applicable rule must effect has to be explicitly specified within the RHS of the rule. For instance, there is no shorthand way to specify that certain features on nodes should be automatically copied to higher nodes when higher-level constituents are built. Although this effect can usually be achieved using the etiquette / (see Section 7.3) and a list variable, the fact that features and hierarchical dependencies are not formally distinguished could force the grammar writer to express a particular grammatical theory in a not obvious manner.

Another drawback of the Q-system formalism is the lack of both a path variable (for specifying an arbitrary sequence of top-level constituents) and a "generalized dependent" variable (for specifying a vertical dependency relation of arbitrary depth). These omissions may complicate the precise characterization of complex structures.

The fact that there is no way of specifying directly that some component of a tree is at an arbitrary vertical distance from some other component causes particular problems with regard to lexical transfer. In the TAUM prototype, special grammars were written which effected the linearization of the tree resulting from analysis before lexical transfer and its recomposition after. The result of linearization was a linear graph including edges labelled by single lexical units and others labelled with the etiquettes [and] providing the information about the structure of the original tree. Leaving aside questions about the inefficiency of this approach, it is unsatisfactory as it severely restricts the possibility of lexical disambiguation from the surrounding structure.

The only method of passing control between Q-system grammars is to chain them in a linear fashion. There is no means whereby a conditional invocation of a grammar can be realized. This can cause problems when the function of a particular grammar is to treat some optional phenomenon which may or may not actually occur in the data structure. The grammar must be invoked in any case, and care must be taken to ensure that rules do not apply where they are not intended to. This often involves the use of "tactical" etiquettes, that is, those which have no linguistic significance, being solely designed to block or initiate the application of subsequent rules.

A final criticism of the Q-system formalism may be levelled at the machinery with which the grammar writer must effect morphological analysis. The necessity of decomposing words into characters explicitly using the $\$\$$ operator prior to morphological analysis, and subsequently recomposing them, is not only inefficient in terms of processing resources, but is also clumsier to use than alternative methods for achieving the same end that could be envisaged.

7.8 Organization of rules into grammars

The success of MÉTÉO is largely because the nature of the material to be translated enables the inadequacies of the Q-system formalism discussed above to be circumvented.

For example, there is neither a morphological analysis grammar, nor, as described in Section 7.1, a transfer phase. The absence of the former is made possible by the relative lack of inflected forms in English, particularly in the telegraphic English of meteorological bulletins, so that all inflected forms can be included in the dictionary. Even this could result in a dictionary of unacceptable size were it not for the highly limited vocabulary of meteorology. The problems of accessing leaves of the tree at arbitrary depths are obviated by the insertion of target language lexical items prior to analysis.

The difficulties of characterizing complex structures using the Q-system formalism are obviated in MÉTÉO, since the source texts contain no pronominal references, questions, relative or subordinate clauses or passives.

There are a total of 18 stages in the treatment of texts, which may be grouped as follows:

1–3. Preprocessing (three grammars): elimination of text units containing errors of transmission, treatment of header information, expansion of abbreviations.

4. The idiom dictionary: rewrites idioms (e.g. *blowing snow* → *poudrerie*) and normalizes other constructions (e.g. *kilometres per hour* → *KMH*).

5. The place-name dictionary: rewrites those English place names which differ from the corresponding French ones, or which require subsequent linguistic treatment.

6. The general dictionary: rewrites an English lexical unit as a tree with a root etiquette indicating syntactic category, and daughters including the corresponding French lexical unit and a list of morphological, syntactic and semantic features. In many cases a single lexical unit will be rewritten in more than one way, i.e. as a number of parallel edges (a bundle) carrying different French lexical units and different sets of features.

7–11. Syntactic analysis 1 (five grammars): recognition of phrases giving dates, times, temperatures and places. In general, these phrases may be adverbial, nominal or prepositional in form. Lexical units which have not been assigned a grammatical category by this point are assumed to be proper place names.

12. Syntactic analysis 2: recognition of the remaining nominal groups, which are expressions of meteorological conditions. Matching of features on adjectives and nouns will usually result in the selection of the appropriate edge from a bundle added by the dictionary phase. The edges of the bundle not incorporated in higher level constituents will be eliminated by the garbage collection procedure (see Section 7.6) at the end of this phase.

13. Syntactic analysis 3: construction of top level phrases from their constituents. A top-level phrase is one of five types (see Section 7.8) and failure to match the data with one of these types will result in a complete rejection of the partial analysis.

14. Elimination of text units for which analysis has failed.

15. Syntactic generation: decomposition of the tree into a linear form, including possible reordering of the phrases created in phases 6 and 7–11, positioning of adjectives, determination of adjective and article agreement, and insertion of appropriate prepositions before place names.

16. Morphological generation: generation of the final forms of words from their associated morphosyntactic features. This phase also deals with contraction (*de + le → du*), insertion (*ce + été → cet été*), and elision (*le + été → l'été*).
17. Application of stylistic rules.

7.9 Linguistic content of grammars

The linguistic content of the grammars is heavily application specific and hence of limited general interest. However, examples of the types of linguistic information used are provided here as they are one of the major reasons for MÉTÉO's success, and provide a good indication of the syntactic and semantic complexity which must be considered even in a very limited domain of discourse. Some of the complexity is attributed by MÉTÉO's designers to the telegraphic style of meteorological bulletins, with its lack of grammatical function words, e.g. prepositions and articles, which complicates the task of analysis. In addition, the output of the system is not intended to be to be post-edited, which imposes further complexities to guarantee the accuracy of translation. Even so, these factors are more than offset by the highly constrained nature of the input text.

7.9.1 Syntactic categories

Traditional syntactic categories constitute the basic subdivision of words into classes. The categories used are adjective, adverb, determinant, subordinating and coordinating conjunction, preposition, numeral, proper and common noun, and verb. The etiquettes corresponding to these are the roots of the trees which label the chart edges after the dictionary phases.

Nouns, adjectives, adverbs, and verbs are subcategorized with morphosyntactic features. Gender and number are indicated for nouns. As there is no morphological analysis, the dictionary phases rewrite English plural nouns as their equivalent French plurals directly, except in those cases where a singular French form is the correct translation (e.g. *skies → ciel*). Proper nouns also carry an indication of whether they require to be preceded by an article. Adjectives are subcategorized with features indicating their preferred position with regard to the noun they modify, and the method of formation of their feminine and plural forms, e.g.

FO Feminine formed with no change
F1 Feminine formed by addition of *-e*
F2 Feminine formed by change of *-eau* to *-elle* (e.g. *beau → belle*)
PO Plural formed with no change
P1 Plural formed by addition of *-s*
P2 Plural formed by change of *-al* to *-aux* (e.g. *local → locaux*)

Adverbs are subcategorized according to whether they may modify an adjective, verb or preposition, and verbs are marked for transitivity or otherwise.

7.9.2 Semantic subcategorization

Nouns, adjectives, adverbs and prepositions are sub-categorised with semantic features as shown in Tables 7.1 – 7.4.

Table 7.1 Semantic features for nouns.

Noun features		Examples
Acronym for time zone		*HAE*
Month		*juillet*
Day of the week		*mercredi*
Non-countable (mass noun)		*air, bruine, eau*
Measure		*degré*
Place		*secteur, comté*
Direction		*est*
Time	duration	*matinée*
	punctual	*matin, fin*
Possibility		*risque*
Meteorological phenomenon	stationary	*humidité, brume, chaleur*
	falling	*neige, pluie, grêle*
	blowing	*rafale, vent*

Table 7.2 Semantic features for adjectives.

Adjective features		Examples
Degree		*bas, mince*
Place		*avoisinant*
Direction		*du nord*
Possibility		*bon, faible, possible*
Measure		*médiocre, supérieur*
Time		*annuel*
Meteorological condition		*chaud, venteux*
Meteorological phenomenon	stationary	*dense*
	falling	*abondant*
	blowing	*fort*

Note that the last three examples in Table 7.2 are all possible translations of the English adjective *heavy*. The dictionary phase will add edges corresponding to each to the chart, and the phase which identifies nominal groups will eliminate the two incorrect translations.

Table 7.3 Semantic features of adverbs.

Adverb features		Examples
Time	durative	*pour peu de temps* ('briefly')
	punctual	*par la suite* ('afterwards')
Place		*partout*
Possibility		*peut-être*
Measure		*à peu près*

Table 7.4 Semantic features of prepositions.

Preposition features		Examples
Time	durative	*au cours de*
	punctual	*avant*
Place		*au-dessus de*
Measure		*environs*
Direction		*de* ('from')

In some cases, subcategorization features are merged with the root categories for compactness, e.g. `N((TEMPS),APRES-MIDI)` is replaced by `NT(APRES-MIDI)`.

7.9.3 Syntagms

The phrases which the analysis grammars are capable of parsing fall into five classes, distinguished by the root etiquette assigned to the tree built by stage 7 mentioned in Section 7.8, as follows:

1. `MET0` A list of place names.

2. `MET1` A meteorological condition for the day, including:

    `C` the condition itself, including:

    > `GN/ADJ`
    >
    > `CMOD` an optional complement

    `T` expression of time (optional)

    `LOC` expression of place (optional)

    e.g. `MET1(C(ADJ(SUNNY,...), CMOD(P(WITH,...),`
    `GN(N(SHOWERS,...))))), T(ADJ(TODAY)))`
    where `...` indicates that a list of features has been omitted.

3. `MET2` A phrase specifying temperature maxima and minima, including:

    `GN` – specifying highs or lows

    `GN` – temperature

    `T` – expression of time (optional)

    `LOC` – expression of place (optional)

    e.g. `MET2(GN(N(HIGHS,...)),GN(...15 TO 18...),`
    `T(ADV(TODAY)))`

4. `MET3` A phrase giving a future outlook, similar to `MET1`, except `C` is preceded by a `GN` dominating the words *outlook for* `X`.

5. `ORG` A stereotyped bulletin header of the form:
    `FORECAST FOR <area> ISSUED BY ENVIRONMENT CANADA`
    `AT <time><time zone><month><date><year> FOR <day or`
    `days>`

7.10 Software and hardware environment

The MÉTÉO translation programs are executed on the CDC Cyber 76 at the Canadian Meteorological Centre at Dorval[2], which is part of the communication network linking the various sources of meteorological data, regional centres where bulletins are drafted, and the central data bank in Toronto. The Cyber 76 is front-ended with a Cyber 71, which manages the collection of bulletins from the network and their submission for translation, and provides the software environment for translators working at VDUs to retrieve and check translated bulletins.

Bulletins collected by the Cyber 71 are automatically submitted for translation every 10 minutes as a batch job. A FORTRAN program, PREEDIT, extracts the material to be translated and formats the individual units of translation as Q-system input text strings. After translation, another FORTRAN program, POSTEDIT, reconstructs the bulletin in its original format, with successfully translated units replacing the source text, and the original English text reinserted in place of those units which the system was unable to deal with. The bulletins are returned to the Cyber 71, where they may be processed by human translators using the interactive editor-manager program GERANT. Those text units which have been translated may be considered accurate with a certainty of 99 per cent plus, so the translator is expected only to provide translations for text units in English. In other words, there is no human post-editing of the material translated by machine. When the bulletin is completely translated, it is reinserted into the communications network, to be used by shipping and the information media.

7.11 Documentation

Chevalier, M., J. Dansereau & G. Poulin 1978. *TAUM-MÉTÉO: description du système*, TAUM, Université de Montréal.

Colmerauer, A. 1971. *Les systèmes Q ou un formalisme pour analyser et synthétiser des phrases sur ordinateur* Publication interne no. 43, TAUM, Université de Montréal.

TAUM 1972. *TAUM 71: rapport de janvier 1971*. TAUM, Université de Montréal.

7.12 References

This bibliography includes references in the footnotes and some important sources published since the first edition of this work.

---

2. As footnote 1 indicates, this information is now out of date. — HLS

Chandioux, J. 1989. Météo: 100 million words later. In *American Translators Association Conference 1989: Coming of age*, D. L. Hammond (ed.), 449–53. Medford, NJ: Learned Information.

Hutchins, W. J. & H. L. Somers 1992. *An introduction to Machine Translation*, Chapter 12. London: Academic Press.

Kaplan, R. 1973. A general syntactic processor. In *Natural language processing*, R. Rustin (ed.), 193–241. New York: Algorithmic Press.

8

TAUM AVIATION

8.1 Introduction

The AVIATION system is an MT system designed to translate aircraft maintenance manuals from English to French. The system was commissioned by the Canadian government from the TAUM group following the latter's successful completion of the MÉTÉO contract. The texts for which AVIATION was specifically intended, and which acted as a corpus during its development, were the hydraulics sections of the maintenance manuals of the Defense Department's CP–140 aircraft. Although a version of the system has been delivered to the Bureau of Translation, it has yet to be installed or tested in a realistic operating environment[1], and the TAUM group itself is no longer in existence.

The theory underlying AVIATION represents a radical departure from the MÉTÉO philosophy. The latter system was constructed entirely as a sequence of Q-system grammars. With regard to AVIATION, the greater linguistic complexity of the texts to be translated and the shortcomings of the Q-system formalism encouraged the development of a variety of software tools intended to fill the specific requirements of different stages of the translation process.

---

1. Not long after this was written, the AVIATION project was ended. The failure of AVIATION was attributed not to poor translation quality – Isabelle & Bourbeau (1985: p.24) report the evaluation of Gervais (1980) in which "Raw machine output was deemed to have a degree of intelligibility, fidelity, and style that reaches 80% of unrevised human translations" – but to the high cost of revision: twice as high as for human translation. — HLS

8.2 Basic nature of the system

The AVIATION system is transfer-based, i.e. the translation process consists of a monolingual source language analysis, a monolingual target language generation and between the two, a bilingual transfer phase which replaces source language lexical items with their equivalents in the target language, using grammatical context to disambiguate between different translations of a word. Some structural rearrangement of the text representation is also carried out during transfer. Sentences in the text representation have a canonical predicate-argument structure.

The system also demonstrates a separation of the linguistic data from the algorithms which apply that data to the database (text representation), at least for all components other than those concerned with morphology.

8.3 Data structure

The data structure which is employed in AVIATION to represent a text at the various stages in the translation process is a development of that used for MÉTÉO, the chart. A chart is a directed graph with unique entry and exit vertices, whose edges are labelled with trees. The trees used in MÉTÉO employed a single data type, the character string (etiquette), to represent terminal and nonterminal symbols and features on these. However, in AVIATION, features on nodes are no longer represented as daughter nodes (leaves) in exactly the same way as the daughters which represent the hierarchical organization of grammatical structure. Instead, the features pertaining to a node are associated directly with that node as data of type "set of booleans", and are written in square brackets immediately following the etiquette to which they refer. They may be manipulated using set operators; it is not possible to define an ordering or superimpose a hierarchical structure on the members of such a set.

8.4 Morphological analysis

The phase which is called morphological analysis is concerned solely with inflectional suffixes, and has two principal functions. It segments input strings (words) to produce possible root-suffix pairs, which will be represented as a canonical root for dictionary lookup with a set of associated morphological features, and it builds the chart on which subsequent stages will operate, adding alternative segmentations of a particular word as labels on parallel edges spanning the same vertices. This phase is completed prior to dictionary lookup, so dictionary information cannot be used to eliminate impossible segmentations.

As an example, consider the input string *disturbs*, which will give rise to the two edges (1).

(1)

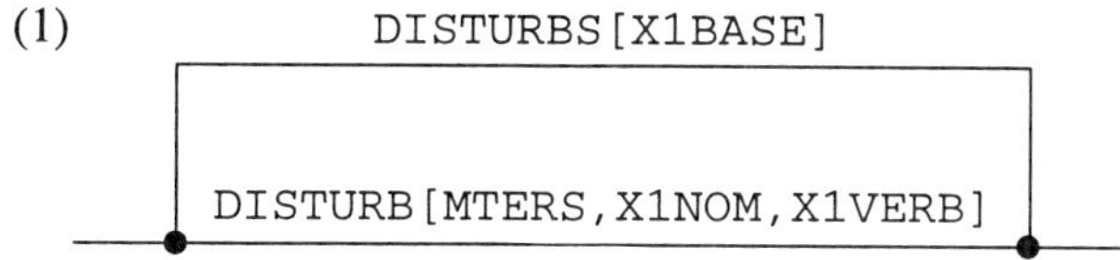

An edge with the feature X1BASE will always be generated, as the word may not be an inflected form (e.g. *bias*). In the example given, the other alternative indicates that the word may be a verb (feature X1VERB) or a noun (X1NOM) as it has the morphological ending *-s* (feature MTERS). The complete set of suffixes examined is {*-s, -ing, -ed, -', -'s*}.

The possible morphosyntactic features which will be assigned according to the suffix found are:

MPOSS	possessive (noun)
MROOT	root (infinitive) (verb)
MPAST	past (preterite) (verb)
MPASTP	past participle (verb)
MPRESP	present participle (verb)
MTERS	termination in *-s* (verb or noun)
X1NOM	nominal suffix found
X1VERB	verbal suffix found

The possessive terminations are checked first, as the remaining stem must still be checked for the termination *-s*, although the presence of this will not, in this case, cause addition of the feature X1VERB.

An edge will be added to the chart for each proposed root form, (i.e. for each possible segmentation of the word) with the morphosyntactic features compatible with the segmentation forming a single set. The morphological analyzer takes into account the various possible roots that could give rise to a particular inflected form. For instance, if the string remaining after removal of the suffix *-ed* ends in *-i*, the actual root form could end in *-y* or *-ie*, and an edge, with the appropriate feature set, will be added for both of these. The complete list of cases in which the ending of the remaining string causes special action is as follows:

After removal of *s*	stem ends in *u, ss, sse, che, zze, ee, ck, se, oe, ie, xe*
After removal of *ing*	stem ends in *ss, zz, ee, ck, ye, y*, any double consonant
After removal of *ed*	stem ends in *ss, zz, e, ck, y, i*, any double consonant

The algorithm which strips productive suffixes, adjusts the remaining root forms and assigns morphological features is coded directly as a Pascal program. However, it does make use of some external linguistic data in the form of a table of special (irregular) morphological forms (TFMS). This table is accessed for each word after segmentation of the suffixes *-'* and *-'s*, and contains all possible combinations of root plus features for an irregular word form, e.g. (2),

(2) BASES ⇒ BASES / BASIS[MPLUR] / BASE[MPLUR] /
     BASE[M3PRES]

thus eliminating the need for further segmentation.

The text file which carries TFMS is compiled by another Pascal program, SETMF-STAB, into a form suitable for use by the morphological analyzer, ENGLIMORPH.

The morphological analysis phase is thus independent of and prior to dictionary lookup, deals with a very limited set of inflectional suffixes, and has its linguistic data coded directly as part of the analysis algorithm. For a task of limited linguistic complexity, these characteristics are justifiable, particularly in terms of computational efficiency. However, for a language with a richer inflectional system than that of English, the separation of linguistic data from the program which manipulates it would be preferable from the point of view of clarity and manageability. For a language with a totally open-ended and highly productive system of word-compounding, such as German, a morphological phase of the AVIATION type would be totally unacceptable.

8.5 Analysis dictionary

The analysis dictionary of AVIATION comprises a set of rewrite rules of three different types. Although rule application is strictly ordered according to these types, the dictionary is conceived as a single entity to ensure integrity of organization and ease of update. The type of rule is indicated by the rewrite symbol used, thus:

Equivalence rules	=E=
Potential idiom rules	=P=
Fixed idiom rules	=F=

8.5.1 Equivalence rules

These have the effect of replacing a string of one or more etiquettes by a different string of etiquettes. They serve to establish exact lexical equivalences (e.g. between different spellings) in order to avoid duplication of rules of the other types with more complex right-hand sides (RHSs). For instance, the pair of rules (3a), are exactly equivalent to the pair (3b)

(3) a. e′ =E= e   e =F= a
    b. e′ =F= a   e =F= a

where e and e′ are any lexical etiquettes, and a is a tree giving the syntactic category of e, a set of features, and any other information necessary for syntactic analysis.

8.5.2 Potential idiom rules

These rules rewrite a path of one or more edges labelled with lexical etiquettes as a single spanning edge labelled with a tree. The root etiquette of this tree indicates a syntactic category and is associated with a set of features. The original lexical units, which do not appear in the RHS of the rule, are actually subsumed under the root, when the tree is constructed, as the leftmost daughter or daughters. Other daughters may be present if the word or idiom is verbal or adjectival: these indicate the arguments that are to be expected in conjunction with the predicate; if the word is a noun, daughters indicating restrictions on the formation of compound noun groups may be present.

8.5.3 Fixed idiom rules

These rules are of exactly the same form as potential idiom rules, and have exactly the same effect, except for the following proviso: if a particular lexical item occurs in the left-hand side (LHS) of more than one applicable rule, it will be rewritten only once, as part of the RHS of the rule with the longest LHS (i.e. with the largest number of lexical items). This avoids the addition of spurious edges to the graph in those cases where a particular sequence of words is always idiomatic, at least in the corpus being considered. Single words are also rewritten using fixed idiom rules. Thus the chart in (4) will be rewritten by the rules in (5) as (6).

(4)

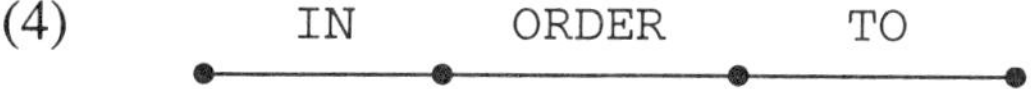

(5) IN =F= PREP ORDER =F= N TO =F= PREP IN ORDER TO =P= SCONJ

(6)

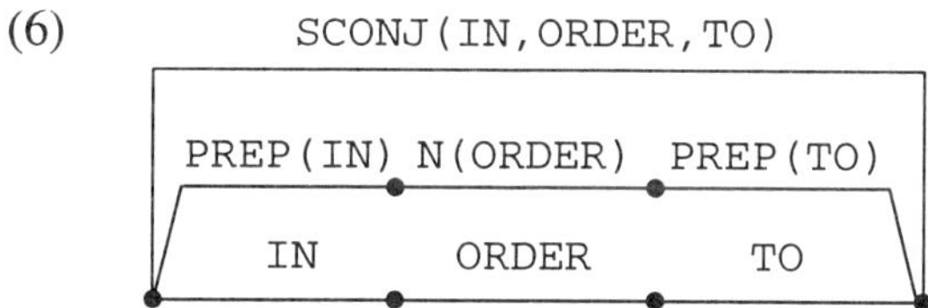

In this case, when the edges which have been rewritten (i.e. those which appear on the LHS of a rule which has been applied) are deleted from the data structure at the end of the phase, there will be two parallel paths in the chart representing a lexical ambiguity with which the structural analysis must deal. However, if the last rule were of the form IN ORDER TO =F= SCONJ, this would block the application of the other rules, so after deletion of used arcs, the result would be a single edge labelled with SCONJ(IN,ORDER,TO).

8.5.4 Example rules

As stated above, the dictionary rules rewrite lexical units as a syntactic category and an optional associated set of features, e.g. (7).

(7) a. ANY =F= [DLQ, DPRECOMPAR] ;
    b. CHECK VALUE =F= N [DC, DHPART, DP, DSG] ;

Predicates

In the case of verbs and adjectives, the root category will be assigned a list of daughter trees representing the expected arguments, with argument numbers as the roots of these. There may also be a daughter indicating the particles which may occur in conjunction with the verb, e.g. (8).

```
(8) a. FILTER =F= V [ DERG, DPP] (PART (OUT,OFF),
                            1(GN [DHUM,DP]),
                            2(GN [DDEFECT, DFL] ),
                            3(P(THROUGH)));
```

```
    b. PRESENT =F= ADJ (1(GN [ DDEFECT, DFL, DMAT, DVAR ],
                        2(P(IN)));
```

Application of the former rule will cause the building of an edge labelled with the tree structure (9).

(9)

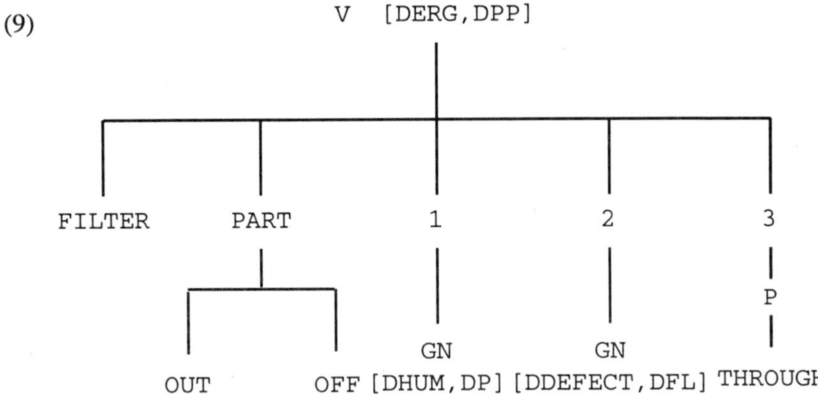

The feature DERG on the verb indicates that it is ergative, that is, the first argument may be absent, in which case the second argument will occupy subject position. DPP indicates that the past participle of the verb may be used adjectivally. The features on the nominal groups are fairly self-explanatory: DHUM human, DFL fluid, DP piece of equipment, DDEFECT unwanted substance, e.g. *dirt, debris*. This representation does not appear to be suitable for specifying different frames for the same verb, e.g. *filter y*, *filter x from y*, other than by means of binary features such as DERG.

Nouns

Like those for predicates, the dictionary entries for nouns provide semantic information to ensure the compatibility of elements in higher level constituents, in this case complex noun groups. This information is probably even more crucial than that associated with predicates, as there are few syntactic or morphological clues which can be used to ascertain the internal structure of a noun group. Compare, for instance, (10a) and (10b).

(10) a. booster poppet valve N (N N)

    b. pressure regulator failure (N N) N

Complex noun groups of this type are extremely common within the AVIATION corpus, and determination of their internal structure is essential for correct translation. To this end, the dictionary entries for nouns may specify co-occurrence restrictions, e.g. (11).

(11) SUCTION =F= N

```
           RESTRICT   OBJ[DFL]
                      FUNCTION[DCANALISATION]
```

This entry indicates that the noun *suction* may be the head of a noun group containing a noun bearing the feature DFL (e.g. *fuel suction*), and that the relationship between the two is that the latter is the object of the nominalization *suction*. Alternatively, *suction* may appear in a noun group with a noun having the feature DCANALISATION (e.g. *suction line*), in which case the relationship will be that this second noun has the function of *suction*. Although the AVIATION documentation claims that *suction* will be the head noun (*gouverneur*) in both cases, this is quite clearly not the case.

The complete list of semantic relationships which may exist between two elements Y and Z in a noun group is as follows:

FUNCTION	a Z for Y-ing something
HAS	Y has Z
SUJ	Y is the subject of the nominalization Z
OBJ	Y is the object of the nominalization Z
MAT	Z is made of Y
LOC	Y is the location of Z

The use of these relations in the structure built by the structural analysis phase is exemplified in Section 9.7.

8.5.5 Dictionary software

The high-level language in which dictionary entries are written is known as SYDICAN (*'SYstème de DICtionnaire d'ANalyse'*). The software which realizes the dictionary phase of translation is written in Pascal, and comprises two programs. The first of these is a compiler, which accepts as input a text file of rules of the form described above, producing an internal representation. The second is an interpreter which matches the LHSs of the compiled rules against the database and builds the structures indicated by the RHSs.

In addition to the updated data structure, the SYDICAN interpreter also produces as output a list of words occurring in the text for which no entry was found in the dictionary. The user may use this file to create a supplementary dictionary (*dictionnaire d'appoint*) by providing the necessary entries. This is then compiled and applied to the data structure using the SYDICAN software. Following this stage, those words to which no dictionary entry has applied are assumed to be proper nouns and are rewritten as such.

8.6 Structural analysis

Following dictionary lookup, structural analysis uses the syntactic and semantic information added to the graph by the dictionary, and a collection of grammatical rules, to assign a structure to the sentence (or noun group in the case of section headings). The grammatical rules are expressed in a formalism known as REZO.

The REZO formalism is very closely based on the Augmented Transition Network (ATN) of Woods (1970, 1973), a procedural formalism for top-down left-to-right parsing of natural language texts. It is possible to use the chart data structure in conjunction with an ATN grammar, acting as a well-formed substring facility, and thereby circumventing one disadvantage of top-down parsers: that they may reanalyze the same low-level phrase several times, once for each higher-level construction that uses it. It is not clear whether the chart is used in this way in AVIATION.

The use of the chart means that all alternative edges from a given vertex must be considered each time the parser is focused at that vertex. The default parsing strategy associated with an ATN, as with REZO, is depth-first, i.e. a single parse is discovered first, hopefully the correct one. However, the REZO grammar writer has the option to switch the parser to breadth-first mode, when, for instance, two alternatives are equally likely, and to follow both. In addition, as described above, the depth-first description applies only to those parses associated with a given path through the graph. Conceptually, a parse will be performed in parallel on each distinct path. It is not clear how choices are made at the end of structural analysis between alternative parses resulting from these two sources of parallelism.

8.6.1 The ATN and REZO formalisms

A finite-state transition network is a representation of a regular grammar, in which the transitions that relate the states are labelled by terminal symbols. An ATN is such a network that has been generalized to context-free power by allowing the transitions to be labelled with nonterminal symbols (construed as calls to the appropriate subnetworks) and further generalized to Turing machine power by associating arbitrary tests and structure-building actions (written in some high-level programming language) with the transitions.

An ATN or REZO grammar is a series of subnetworks, each of which corresponds to a nonterminal of the grammar. In REZO, each subnetwork has the form:

```
<sub-network>  ::=
    ssreseau <sub-network name>
    <declarations>
    <list of named states>
```

The order in which the list of named states is written is unimportant except for the first, which is the state to which control is transferred when the subnetwork is called. Each state is associated with an ordered list of transitions, i.e. test–action pairs, separated by *;*:

```
<state>::=
    <state name>
    <list of test-action pairs>
```

The parser steps through this list evaluating each test in turn and performs the actions associated with the first test which succeeds. As mentioned above, the writer of a REZO grammar may suspend the ordering of test-action pairs associated with a given state by preceding the state name with `ndeter`. In this case, the actions of all the tests which succeed are performed. Thus the REZO traversal algorithm, taking into account the form of the data (i.e. a chart) is as follows (in informal ALGOL-like notation):

```
procedure TRAVERSE (state; edge; right:boolean);
var transition
begin
repeat
  transition := FIRST-TRANSITION (state)
  repeat
    while EXISTS (transition) and
          not (TEST(transition))
      do transition := NEXT (transition);
    if EXISTS (transition) then
      DO-ACTIONS (transition);
    transition := NEXT (transition)
  until DETERMINISTIC (state) or
        not EXISTS (transition);
  edge := NEXT (edge)
until not (right and EXISTS (edge))
end;
```

The first call of this procedure is:

```
TRAVERSE ( first-state, FIRST-EDGE (first-vertex),
    true)
```

It may also be called recursively by DO-ACTIONS. For instance, the action `avancer <statename>` will result in the call:

```
TRAVERSE (statename, FIRST-EDGE VERTEX-AT-END-
    OF(edge)), true)
```

The action `avancer` thus carries out two operations: it shifts the focus of the grammar to the named state, and consumes the item labelling the current edge (i.e. it shifts the focus to a new vertex of the graph). On completion of this recursive call to TRAVERSE, edge will return to its original value, thus implementing the backtracking necessary for consideration of each path through the graph.

Another action, `nouvetat <statename>`, causes the following call to TRAVERSE:

```
TRAVERSE (statename, edge, false)
```

This shifts the focus of the grammar without consuming a data item (i.e. without changing the chart focus). `nouvetat` will normally occur as one of the actions following successful parsing of a lower level constituent (i.e. the test part of the transition will be a `push`), and the subnetwork will itself have advanced the chart focus. Alternatively, it may occur following some test which has indicated that an optional constituent is not present, or that some deep-structure constituent of the sentence has been moved and thus is not present in the surface structure.

In Woods' original formulation of the ATN, these different types of transition, and others, were distinguished by name (e.g. PUSH, VIR, JUMP). This is only a syntactic shorthand, and the REZO approach in which more primitive operations are available to the grammar writer gives slightly more control at the expense of having to do slightly more work.

Other facilities provided in REZO include the following:

Registers of different types   These may be declared at the head of any subnetwork and manipulated by the tests and actions using a variety of operators appropriate to the type. All registers in Woods' ATN were of type tree, but REZO provides the types shown in Table 8.1.

Table 8.1 Register types in REZO.

Register	Type	Purpose
`arbre`	tree	
`boolean`	boolean	
`nombre`	integer	Weighting or preference calculations
`etiquette`	character string	
`ensemble`	set	A subset of the complete feature set `traits` declared at the head of a REZO program, for manipulating the syntactic and semantic features associated with *etiquettes* by the dictionary entries
`liste`	list	Ordered list of trees

Privileged memory areas   Both ATNs and REZO predefine a register `*`. This is of type tree and is used to hold the current input item (i.e. the label on the current chart edge) or, on return from a subnetwork, the tree built by that subnetwork.

Other privileged memory areas in REZO are:

- `+1` – A list of the trees which may become the next input item (i.e. `EDGESET(VERTEX-AT-END-OF(current-edge))`)
- `pile` – This is of type tree, being the top element of a LIFO (last in first out) stack whose manipulation is under user control.
- `$` – A random access array, also under user control, the members of which are referenced by subscription with integers, e.g. `$1`, `$2`.

Predefined functions   REZO provides a wide variety of functions by means of which the grammar writer can operate on registers of various types, as in Table 8.2.

Table 8.2 Predefined functions in REZO.

Function	Parameters	Result
etiq	(a)	The root etiquette of the tree a
traits	(a)	The set of traits associated with the root of a
fils	(a)	The left daughter tree of the root of a
frere	(a)	The right sister tree of a
lfils	(a)	A list of all daughters of the root of a
elem	(l)	The first tree in the list l
reste	(l)	The list remaining after removal of elem(l)
nombre	(e)	The number represented by the string of numeric characters which constitute the etiquette e
etiquet	(n)	The etiquette obtained by considering the digits of n as characters
def	(r)	"True" if the register r is defined, else "false"
sommet	(a,e,t)	"True" if the root of the tree a is the etiquette e with a set of traits including the set t, else "false"
sommet	(l,e,t)	"True" if the list l contains a tree a for which sommet(a,e,t) is true, else "false"
liste	(a1,a2,...,an)	The list formed from the trees a1,a2,...,an
conclis	(l1,l2,...,ln)	The list formed by concatenating the lists l1, l2,...,ln
feuille	(a,a1,a2,...,an)	"True" if lfils(a) is empty and etiq(a) is equal to one of e1, e2,...,en, else "false"
feuille	(l,e1,e2,...,en)	"True" if the list l contains a tree a for which feuille(a,e1,e2,...,en) is true, else "false"

Pattern-matching   The REZO grammar writer may define a model, that is, a specification of a class of trees. The model is written as a tree, with the various components replaced by boolean expressions, including parameters (etiq and traits) which will be bound to the appropriate values from the tree against which the model is being matched.   Etiquettes may be tested for equality or inequality against expressions of type etiquette, and feature sets may be compared with expressions of type set using the standard set predicates. A model may include embedded models to allow specification of a class of subtrees, for example (12).

This will match successfully against any tree whose root is NP, with at least the associated features A,B,C, with a left daughter tree whose root is not XXXX, and at least one other non-null daughter (indicated by the final , before the)).

(12) `etiq = 'NP' traits ≥ [A,B,C] (etiq =/ 'XXXX' ,)`

8.6.2 Tests and actions

The facilities described above may be used to create tests and actions of arbitrary complexity. Expressions featuring in the action part may be conditional.

Tests

The test part of an arc is an expression of type boolean. As well as arbitrary tests on whatever registers, there are various expressions of boolean type whose side-effects are extremely important. These are:

push <sub-network>   This test causes a transfer of control to the named sub-network. It evaluates "true" only if the subnetwork succeeds in analysing a portion of the graph. Initialization of various registers in the subnetwork prior to transfer of control may be achieved by appending an `avec` clause, which consists of assignments of the form <register> `:=` <expression>.

pop <expression>   This test returns control to a higher subnetwork, indicating that a constituent of the type corresponding to the subnetwork in which the `pop` is found has been successfully parsed. It evaluates "true" only if the stack is in the same state as it was when the corresponding `push` was made. The associated expression is of type tree and after evaluation this will become the value of the register *, for use in the action part of the corresponding `push` arc. No actions may be associated with a `pop` arc.

depiler <model>   This test assigns `pile`, that is, the tree on top of the stack, to the register *. It evaluates "true" only if `pile` conforms to the specified model.

Each of the above tests may be preceded by a boolean expression. Another sort of test is the expression of conformity, which has the form

`<simple expression>` **conforme** `<model>`

where the simple expression defines the tree which is to be matched against the model. This test succeeds if a pattern match is found. The expression of conformity may be followed by an optional `pop` test as described previously.

The test part of an arc may also be empty. Obviously, such an arc will be the last associated with a given state, except if the latter is a nondeterministic state.

Actions

As with the tests, actions can be considered as general or special. General actions are those which assign to a register, thus:

`<register> <assignment operator> <value>`

The normal assignment operator (`:=`) replaces the register specified on its LHS with the value on its RHS. There exist two other assignment operators (`<=` and `>=`)

which expect a register of type list on the LHS and a value of type tree on the RHS, and have the effect of concatenating the tree to the left or right of the list, respectively. The value on the RHS of any operator may be an expression, or a register in another subnetwork, specified by preceding the register name with one of the reserved words `dernier, plus pres, premier`.

Two of the special actions, `avancer` and `nouvetat`, were discussed above. The others are as follows:

tuer <register>   This causes the named register to become undefined.

empiler <expression>   This causes the tree resulting from evaluation of the expression to be added to the stack.

ecrire <expression>   This writes the tree resulting from the evaluation of the expression to an output file. However, this action has an effect only when the final action of an execution is `succes` (see below).

succes | echec   These two actions have largely the same effect, to terminate a particular parse, and initiate the backtracking required to follow suspended alternatives. The only difference between them is that `succes` renders effective the `ecrire` actions that have been encountered up to that point.

Actions may be structured using `if...then...else` and `case`-like conditional constructs. It is not clear that this facility allows the grammar writer to do anything that could not be done in the test part of an arc, though it can be used to achieve a "factoring out" of actions common to more than one transition.

8.6.3 Example subnetwork

The following example illustrates the REZO formalism using the subnetwork SEN-TENCE and is taken from Kay (1977). It is not intended to be a definitive syntax for an English sentence. Other relevant declarations necessary to understand this subnetwork are the declaration of `traits` at the head of the REZO program:

```
traits active, passive, sing, plur, transitif,intrans,
     present, past, past perf;
```

and the declarations of the subnetwork PRINCIPAL, from which SENTENCE is called:

```
ensemble numfeat, tensefeat;
ssreseau SENTENCE
ensemble tense, voice;
arbre sujet, obj, verb;
 S1 (* search for subject *)
      DEF(sujet) : nouvetat S2;
      push NP     : sujet := *, nouvetat S2.
```

```
S2 (* identification of verb *)
   non (numfeat <= TRAITS(*) + TRAITS(sujet))
                 (* subject-verb agreement *)
             : tense := TRAITS(*) inter tensefeat,
               voice := [active]
               si ETIQ(*) = 'VERB' alors
               debut
                     verb := * ,
                     avancer S3
               fin
               sinon
               si ETIQ(*) = 'BE' alors avancer S6
                    sinon echec .
S3 (* intransitive verb may not have object *)
                 : si [intrans] <= TRAITS(verb)
                 alors nouvetat S5
                 sinon nouvetat s4.
ndeter
S4 non DEF(obj) : nouvetat S5
   [transitif] <= TRAITS(verb) : nouvetat S41.
S41    DEF(obj) : nouvétat S5;
         (* don't look for object if it is already found *)
   push NP : obj := *, nouvetat S5.
S5 (* end of sentence *)
   pop 'S' / voice
            ( sujet,
              'VP' ( 'AUX' / tense,
                   ( si DEF(verb) alors 'V'(verb)
                                  sinon nil),
                   ( si  DEF(obj) alors obj sinon nil))):.
S6 ETIQ(*) = 'PASTP' : verb := *, nouvétat S61.
S61 (* discovery of passive without backtracking *)
    [transitif] <= TRAITS(verb)
                 : obj := sujet,
                   sujet := 'DUMMY' (nil),
                   voice := [passive],
                   avancer S7.
ndeter (* no deep subject, or one introduced by 'BY' *)
S7                 : nouvetat S5;
   ETIQ(*)='BY'    : avancer S8.
S8 push NP         : sujet := * , nouvetat S5
```

8.6.4 Evaluation of REZO

The decision to use a top-down depth-first analyzer of the ATN type was based upon an extensive examination of the syntactic structures in the corpus. REZO represents a radical departure from TAUM's previous philosophy as embodied in the bottom-up combinatorial nature of Q-system grammars. The change is attributable to at least two factors. First, the large number of verb–noun homographs that exist in the AVIATION corpus would give rise to a vast number of different, mostly incorrect readings of complex noun phrases were a purely combinatorial approach to be followed. Secondly, the ATN approach, with its explicit ordering of arcs leaving a state, allows the statistical information about frequencies of particular structures to be utilized directly in the grammar (that is, the depth-first strategy is actually "most likely first").

The consensus of opinion among those researchers who work with ATN-like formalisms about the perspicuity of representation that they permit may have been another factor in the choice. It is claimed, for instance, that the simplicity of the underlying context-free model is retained despite the complex augmentations superimposed upon it. This may be true in terms of the efficiency with which such grammars may be interpreted; however, the perspicuity applies only to the context-free surface grammar. The REZO grammars also include an implicit inverse transformational component. As this is realized using a variety of different features of the formalism (tests, arbitrary structure building actions, privileged memory areas), the relationship between the grammar parsed and the structure built is far from obvious. In an ideal formalism, all the obligatory consequences following from the choice of a particular option would be deducible from the point at which that option is chosen. This situation is certainly not true of ATNs, and REZO, with its many facilities, is possibly even more opaque than simpler ATN-based formalisms. In any case, a large measure of the perspicuity of an ATN grammar in graphical form is lost as soon as it is linearized.

Another advantage claimed for the ATN is its ability to make intermediate results available for semantic processing (using some different software tool), though this is not exploited in the AVIATION system.

The fact that the structure-building actions on the arcs of an ATN are explicit provides a facility for experimenting with different structural representations; to this extent, at least, REZO grammars have a measure of flexibility.

The processing of conjoined sentence fragments in an ATN grammar is claimed to be tractable because of the explicit stack. That is, the parsing of the sentence may be restarted following the conjunction from some configuration available on the stack, and continued until it merges with the parsing of the suspended computation. However, without a special-purpose modification to the ATN interpreter to realize this (e.g. SYSCONJ (Woods 1973)), the treatment of conjunctions within the grammar imposes a heavy burden on the grammar writer. This is because the ATN is a predictive formalism, and it is very difficult to predict the occurrence of co-ordinating conjunctions, which may occur at almost any point in the sentence. REZO provides no special mechanism for dealing with conjunctions, and it is apparent that the latter cause significant problems in the analysis of sentences from the AVIATION corpus. The problem is, of course, a double one; it is necessary, first, to determine the scopes of a conjunction which are syntactically valid, and then, if necessary, to disambiguate using "semantic" features. A refinement of the existing semantic categories could probably cope with most problems of the latter type. However, the former problem rests with the difficulties of capturing generalizations in the formalism.

At present, the AVIATION analysis grammar fails to elucidate various readings of the scope of conjunctions. For example, (13a) results in the single (incorrect) translation (13b).

> (13) a. Connect nitrogen or dry air charging connection to the valve.
>
> b. *Relier l'azote ou le raccord de gonflage d'air sec.*

Here it appears that a semantic disambiguation between the possible readings, which would seem to be trivial, has not even been recognized as necessary.

Finally, the fact that properties must be expressed as sets of boolean features would seem to impose severe restrictions on the grammar writer. However, such a representation is not inherent in the ATN formalism, and could be improved without much difficulty.

8.7 Normalized structure

The AVIATION corpus contains a wide variety of sentences which can be considered as transformationally derived from "matrix" or "canonical" sentences. The transformations involved include the following: passive, dative movement, relative reduction, *there*-insertion, particle movement, extraposition, and those transformations applicable to ergative verbs.

The aim of the grammars is to produce from sentences displaying any combination of the above a normalized structural representation of the sentence. This involves recognition of the main verb, determination of the strongly (valency) bound arguments by comparison of the latter's features with those indicated as expectations on the former, and recognition of the other components of the sentence as legal, though optional, circumstantials. The normalized structure is then built by placing these different components in the canonical order: predicate (GOV), arguments, circumstantials. In general, both arguments and circumstantials are considered as prepositional groups (GPs); those which are actually nominal appear in the normalized structure with the dummy lexical item, BOF, as their preposition.

The normalized structure resulting from the example sentence (14a) would be of the form (14b).

> (14) a. When the air system is defective, the check valves retain pressure
>   in the reservoir.
>
> b. (see next page)

Missing from this tree are several feature sets, including those on the GNs, which are identical to those on the GPs which dominate them, and those on the nodes dominating BOF, which are always [XX].

(14) b.

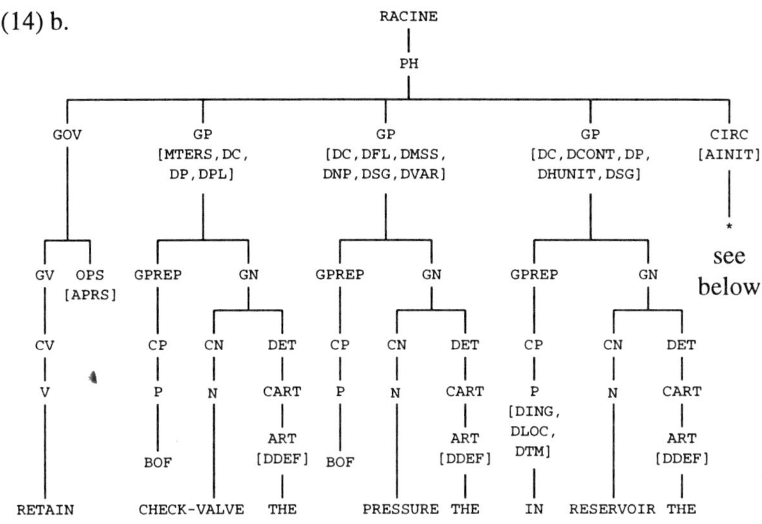

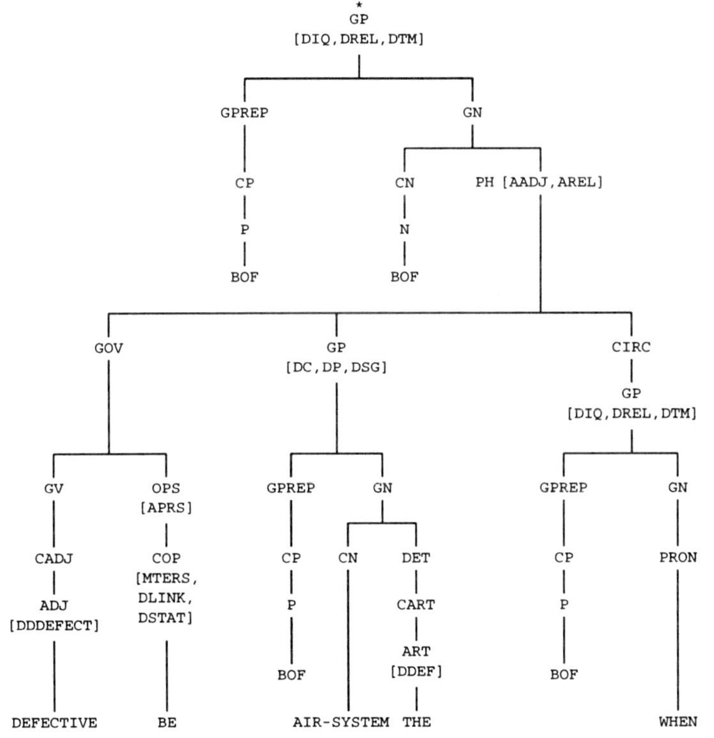

Within complex noun groups, the internal structure is indicated in the normalized tree by means of the semantic relation markers described in Section 8.5.4. For instance, the internal structure of the group in (15a) will be (15b).

(15) a. left engine fuel pump suction line

b.

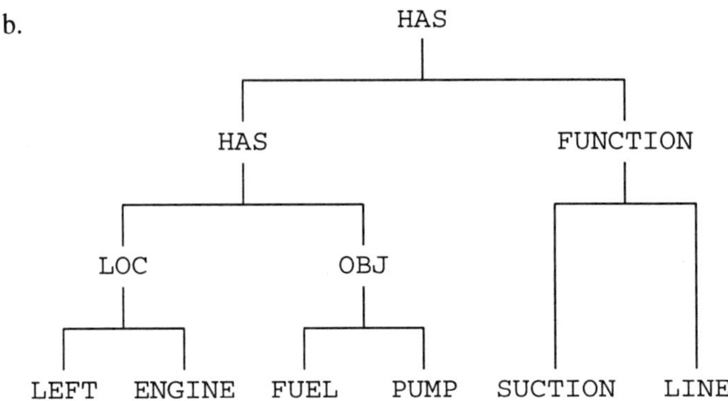

8.8 Lexical transfer

The normalized structure produced by the analysis grammars constitutes the input to the lexical transfer stage, during which the leaves of the tree (English lexical items) are replaced by their French equivalents.

It is often necessary to examine the structural environment of a given word in order to determine the correct translation. Similarly, when the correct translation has been chosen, this may make it necessary to effect certain changes on the data structure. The formalism in which the entries of the bilingual transfer dictionary are expressed allows the lexicographer to write procedural descriptions to carry out both of these tasks.

The LHS of a dictionary rule is a character string corresponding to an English lexical item. Further conditions on the context of the lexical item are included in the RHS. This is a specification of a traversal of the data structure starting from the leaf corresponding to the LHS, tests to be performed on the nodes thus visited, and their associated feature sets, and assignments to be made according to the results of those tests.

8.8.1 Traversal of the data structure

At the start of a transfer dictionary entry, control is considered to be focused at the node which directly dominates the lexical unit being considered (i.e. the LHS of the entry). This node is known as FC. Its label, which will be a syntactic category, may be interrogated using the function `nature`, e.g. `nature(FC) est N` is a boolean function which returns "true" if the label on FC is N and "false" otherwise.

The boolean function `parcours` takes as an argument a specification of a traversal of the tree starting from FC. This traversal is expressed as a series of node labels and tree relations between them. These relations are:

↑	is dominated by
/	is directly dominated by
\	directly dominates
_	has as sister

The function `parcours` returns the value "true" if the traversal can be made, otherwise "false". For instance (16a) will evaluate to "true" if the subtree in (16b) is found.

(16) a. `parcours /CV/GV\GPREP\CP\P`

b.
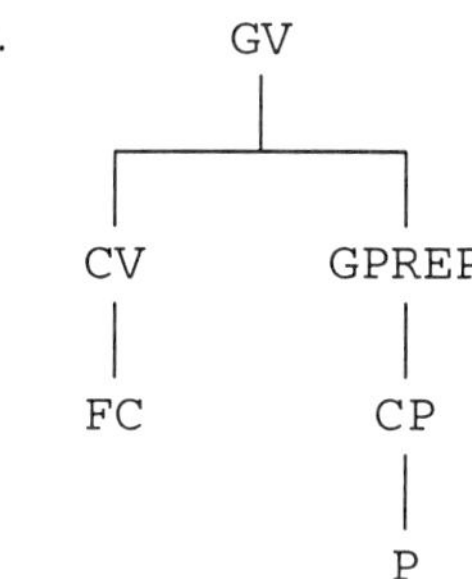

At any point in the traversal, the current node is the value of the identifier `ICI`, and additional conditions may be specified on this as part of the evaluation of `parcours`. These conditions will normally be composed of set and relational operations on the feature set of `ICI` and other (literal) feature sets, e.g. (17).

(17) `parcours /C ADJ/GV/GOV/PH telque traits(ICI) >=`
`[AREL] /GN`
`parcours /CQ/GQ_CQ\Q telque traits(ICI) inter`
`[ENUM] = [ ]`

It is also possible to specify that the value of `ICI` at some point be assigned to another named variable, which may then be referenced later in the entry. This is achieved by insertion of `$<string>` into the traversal. Subsequently, the identifier `<string>` will be bound to the value of `ICI` at the position immediately prior to the `$`, e.g. after evaluation of (18)

(18) `parcours /CADJ $ECADJ /GV $EGV/GOV $EGOV`

the variables ECADJ, EGV, and EGOV will be bound to the nodes bearing the labels CADJ, GV, and GOV respectively which were traversed during that evaluation.

In addition to the actual labels on nodes, traversals may also be specified in terms of the relational categories of nodes. For instance, the strongly bound arguments dominated by a PH node will all be labelled by GP. A particular GP may be chosen by specifying one of the predeclared relations SUJ, OBJD, OBJI. Similarly, all circumstantials will be dominated by a node labelled by CIRC. Particular ones may be specified by subscripting the CIRC label, e.g. `CIRC[1]`, `CIRC[2]`.

8.8.2 Assignments and tree manipulations

Variables of type ut, i.e. character string with associated set of morphological features, and type arbrelibre, i.e. tree, may be declared at the top of a dictionary entry, and subsequently assigned in the entry, e.g.

```
var A1:ut; A2:arbrelibre fin
debut
   .

   .

   .
A1 := 'Y' 'AVOIR'[B1]
A2 := CV ( V ut traduite A1)
   .

   .

   .
fin
```

The result of the assignment to A2 is to build the tree (19) which will subsequently replace any occurrence of the identifier A2.

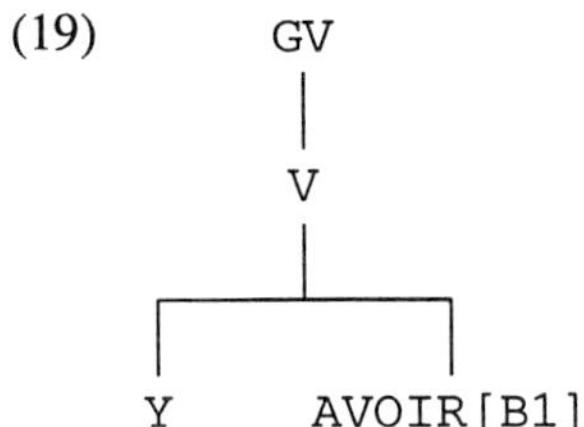

Notice that the assignment includes the infix operator traduite. There are several such operators, and to each there is a corresponding predefined procedure. In the case of traduite, this is traduire. Thus (20) will replace the lexical unit dominated by FC with the ut-valued literal 'PR2ESENT'[F1,P1]:

(20) traduire FC par 'PR2ESENT'[F1,P1]

As well as using a literal, the identity replacement may be specified as in (21), which will be used in those cases where execution of the dictionary entry has failed to pinpoint an acceptable translation.

(21) traduire FC par ut(FC)

Other procedures include inserer, copier and deplacer. Each of these has the form:

<procedure name> <tree> **en** <position> **sous** <node>

The tree may be a literal, a variable, or a named node or position. In the last case, the tree is that dominated by the named node. The semantics of these three procedures is not made clear in the documentation, though some idea of their action may be gleaned from their names.

To illustrate the use of these procedures, consider the fragment of a dictionary entry for the adjective *present*. This fragment performs the restructuring of arguments when a phrase such as *x is present* is converted to the form *il y avoir x*. (EPH is the PH node dominating the named subject position ESUJ):

```
SI parcours ESUJ_OBJD() $EOBJD alors
  debut
  inserer circ(EN GP DEPLACE (EOBJD)) en circ[1] sous
          EPH;
  copier ESUJ en OBJD sous EPH;
  deplacer GP(GPREP(CP(P ut traduite 'BOF')),en SUBS
          GN(PRON ut traduite 'IL')) en SUJ sous EPH
  fin
```

The procedure `effacer` takes a single named node as an argument and erases the tree dominated by that node.

Assignments may be made to the set of features on a named node, e.g. (22).

```
(22) traits en EGN := traits(EGN) + [TSTOPDET]
     traits en FC := TRAITS(FC) + [TNOREF]
```

8.9 The LEXTRA software

It is obvious that the language in which transfer dictionary entries are expressed, LEXTRA, is, like REZO, highly procedural. As with REZO, the linguist is provided with a software tool which allows very fine control over the operations to be performed, with very similar merits. The complexity of writing transfer dictionary entries for AVIATION is often cited as a reason for its lack of success.

One important consequence of the procedural nature of dictionary entries is that the linguist must take care to maintain the integrity of the data structure. To ensure that this is so, the LEXTRA compiler performs certain verifications on the entries, as well as compiling them into a suitable form for use by the LEXTRA interpreter.

The compiler takes as data a formal description of the normalized structure, and during the course of rule compilation ensures that the manipulations expressed in the rules, providing they are applied to a well-formed structure, will not result in a structure which deviates from that description.

The well-formedness of the structures passed by the analysis stage to the interpreter is verified by the latter, which also takes the formal description of the normalized structure, in addition to the compiled procedures for each lexical unit output by the compiler.

The interpreter traverses the data structure according to a predefined algorithm, which ensures that each leaf becomes in turn the value of FC.

8.10 Structural transfer and syntactic generation

Both structural transfer and syntactic generation are effected by means of Q-systems, which have been discussed extensively in Chapter 7. Certain limited changes must have been made to the Q-system interpreter to deal with the feature set data type.

The distinction between the two stages is not stressed in the documentation, but remains of some theoretical significance. The structural transfer stage has the task of realizing those aspects of the "deep structure" of French texts which are not conditioned by the presence of particular lexical items. This includes such transformations as the substitution of an impersonal subject and an active sentence structure in French for a passive in English, and the conversion of an English gerundive subject into a French subordinate clause. Structural transfer also deals with such phenomena as the sequence of tenses and choice of articles.

Syntactic generation serves primarily to flatten the tree output by structural transfer, giving a linear sequence of lexical items. It also effects the insertion of lexical items such as relative pronouns which are totally predictable from the information in the deep structure, and ensures that each word is associated with the correct set of morphological features dictated by rules of agreement.

The transformational model which underlies these phenomena, and their deterministic nature, renders them well-suited for treatment by means of Q-system grammars.

8.11 Morphological generation

The morphological generation phase, which is coded directly as a Pascal program, takes as input the output of the syntactic generation phase and a separately compiled table of morphological forms. The form of the output from syntactic generation is an ordered forest of very simple trees. Each tree is of the form of a syntactic category label with a set of features describing the required inflections (e.g. PLURAL, PASTPART, FEM) dominating the lexical item to be inflected, with a feature set giving that item's morphological class (e.g. P1, B6, F4) as added by lexical transfer. Invariable word forms have the root node INV, obviously without features. For example (23):

> (23) a. *Deux robinets sont situés dans le logement de roue.*
>   b. (see next page)

Morphological generation accesses the table of morphological forms using both sets of features. For instance, it will look up the conjugation of a verb of class B6 for a masculine, plural, past participle, which will result in the form *situés*.

This stage also takes care of phenomena such as elision (LE AVION → *l'avion*) and contraction (DE LE → *du*).

(23) b.

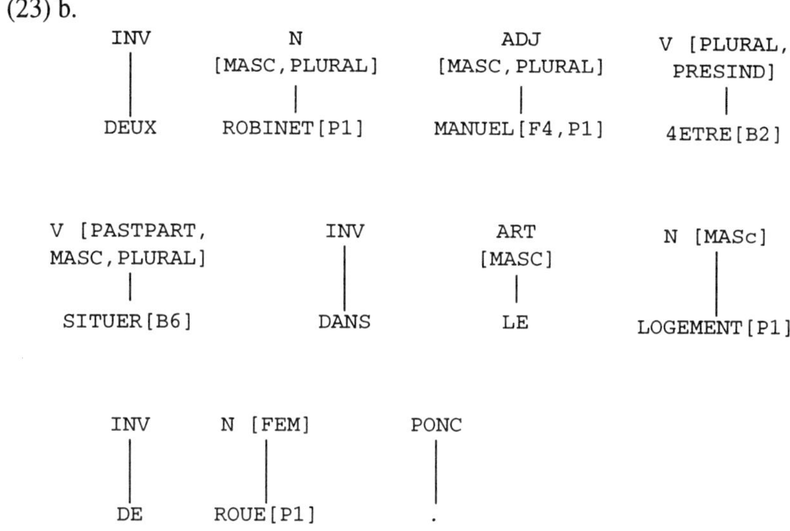

8.12 Software and hardware details of the system

The AVIATION system was developed on the University of Montreal's Control Data Cyber 173 with a NOSBE 1.4, level 508 operating system. Texts are automatically pre- and post-edited by application of rules written in a formalism known as SISIF (*Système d'Identification, de Substitution et d'Insertion de Formes*). Like those of the SYDICAN, REZO, and LEXTRA formalisms, the SISIF compiler and interpreter are written in Pascal.

In addition to the main components of the translation chain, AVIATION provides a software system for questioning and update of entries in both analysis and transfer dictionaries, called GEDIBADO (*GEstion de DIctionnaire en BAnque de DOnnées*). It is estimated that a linguist requires about three months of specialized training in order to write transfer dictionary entries.

As of March 1981[2], the analysis dictionary contained 4054 entries, as shown in Table 8.3.

The transfer dictionary contained 3280 entries, this lower figure being a result of the fact that a single transfer entry will deal with all homographs of whatever syntactic category.

The central memory required to execute each stage of the system is as in Table 8.4, and the size of the files (in kwords of 60 bits) is as in Table 8.5.

The cost of producing a revised translation of texts submitted to AVIATION was estimated to be C$0.183 per word, of which C$0.083 was the cost of unedited translation. This should be compared with the cost of a human translation of the same texts, C$0.145 per word. The total cost of producing an edited translation breaks down as shown in Table 8.6.

---

2. See Macklovitch & Bourbeau (1981); this is the source of all the data in Tables 8.3–8.8.

Table 8.3 Contents of analysis dictionary.

Entry	Number
Nouns	1674
Adjectives	871
Verbs	833
Adverbs	187
Prepositions	149
Equivalence rules	136
Quantifiers	79
Ordinals, pronouns, articles and conjunctions	124

Table 8.4 Central memory required.

Stage	kwords
Preprocessing	14
Morphological analysis	16
Analysis dictionary	16
Structural analysis	40
Transfer dictionary	16
Structural transfer/syntactic generation	23
Morphological generation	20
Postprocessing	14

Table 8.5 Size of files.

Stage	Source			Compiled		
	C	I	G/D	C	I	G/D
Preprocessing	5.9	3.7	1.3	4.3	1.5	6.0
Morphological analysis	1.2	7.4	2.3		4.8	7.7
Analysis dictionary		39.4	137.5		7.2	195.8
Analysis	15.8	11.1	15.9	15.5	5.6	20.5
Transfer dictionary	25.9	14.6	376.9	13.0	10.7	191.2
Structural transfer/generation	2.8	4.6	9.8	2.6	6.3	11.3
Morphological generation	0.8	6.9	5.8		6.4	9.9
Postprocessing	5.9	3.7	0.8	4.3	1.5	4.3

Key: C compiler; I interpreter; G/D grammar or dictionary.

Table 8.6 Breakdown of translation cost.

Task	% of cost
Preparation/input	8
Translation	43
Human revision	37
Transcription/proofreading	12

Of the C$0.083 per word cost of translation alone, the breakdown according to hardware resources is shown in Table 8.7, and according to translation stages in Table 8.8.

Table 8.7 Cost of translation according to hardware resources.

Resource	Cost (C$)
Central Processing Unit	0.0468
Input/output	0.0032
Central memory	0.0331

Table 8.8 Breakdown of translation cost by stages.

Stage	% of cost
Preprocessing	2.1
Morphological analysis	3.1
Analysis dictionary	19.1
Structural analysis	34.2
Transfer dictionary	13.0
Structural transfer/generation	20.3
Morphological generation	1.1
Postprocessing	7.1

The time required for translation was estimated at 0.63 seconds, of which 0.42 is CPU time, and 0.21 is input/output time. This is about half the time required for human translation. However, it is also stated that revision requires more qualified personnel than translation.

TAUM claim that optimization of software could significantly reduce the hardware resources consumed and hence the cost, and further savings could be achieved by improvement of the human interface. Furthermore, improvement in the grammars and dictionaries would result in a greater percentage of sentences being translated than the current 67 per cent, which would in turn reduce post-editing time and costs. It would appear, therefore, that translation by means of AVIATION is, in theory, an economically viable proposition. This view is obviously not shared by the Canadian Bureau of Translation.

8.13 Documentation

Bourbeau, L. 1981. *Linguistic documentation of the computerized translation chain of the TAUM-AVIATION system*. TAUM, Université de Montréal.

Bourbeau, L. & G. Poulin 1977. Analyseur morphologique du système TAUM-AVIATION. In TAUM (1977).

Chevalier, H. & J. Dansereau 1977. Catalogue des structures syntaxiques du corpus AVIATION. In TAUM (1977).

Dansereau, J. 1977. État des travaux. In TAUM (1977).

Isabelle, P. 1977. Traitement des idioms dans le système TAUM-AVIATION. In TAUM (1977).

Isabelle, P. 1981. A linguistic description of the TAUM-AVIATION computerized translation system. In Bourbeau (1981).

Isabelle, P., L. Bourbeau, M. Chevalier & S. Lepage 1978. TAUM-AVIATION: description d'un système de traduction automatisée des manuels d'entretien en aéronautique. Paper submitted to 7th International Conference on Computational Linguistics (COLING), Bergen, Norway.

Lehrberger, J. J. 1977. Complémentation des verbes. In TAUM (1977).

Lehrberger, J. J. 1981. The linguistic model: general aspects. In Bourbeau (1981).

Poulin, G. 1977. Le dictionnaire TAUM-AVIATION. In TAUM (1977).

Stewart, G. 1971. Opérations préliminaires à la formation du catalogue des structures syntaxiques. In TAUM (1971).

Stewart, G. 1978. Spécialisation et compilation des 'Augmented Transition Networks': REZO. Paper submitted to 7th International Conference on Computational Linguistics (COLING), Bergen, Norway.

Stewart, G. 1981. The role of computer science in the TAUM machine translation system: computational aspects of machine translation. In Bourbeau (1981).

TAUM 1977. *Projet AVIATION: Rapport d'Étape*. TAUM, Université de Montréal.

TAUM 1979. *Démonstration du 27 mars 1979*. TAUM, Université de Montréal.

8.14 References

This bibliography includes references in the new footnotes, and some important sources which appeared since the first edition.

Gervais, A. 1980. Evaluation of the TAUM-AVIATION Machine Translation pilot system. Translation Bureau, Secretary of State, Ottawa.

Isabelle, P. & L. Bourbeau 1985. TAUM-AVIATION: its technical features and some experimental results. *Computational Linguistics* **11**. 18–27.

Kay, M. 1977. Morphological and syntactic analysis. In *Linguistic structures processing*, A. Zampolli (ed.), 131–234. Amsterdam: North-Holland.

Lehrberger, J. & L. Bourbeau 1988. *Machine Translation: linguistic characteristics of MT systems and general methodology of evaluation*. Amsterdam: John Benjamins.

Macklovitch, E. & L. Bourbeau 1981. The principal characteristics of the TAUM-AVIATION system. In Bourbeau (1981).

Woods, W. 1970. Transition network grammars for natural language analysis. *Communications of the ACM* **13**, 591–606.

Woods, W. 1973. An experimental parsing system for transition network grammars. In *Natural language processing*, R. Rustin (ed.), 111–54. New York: Algorithmic Press.

9

GETA ARIANE-78

9.1 Introduction

GETA's ARIANE-78 system is a suite of software tools for the description and application of linguistic data, particularly for the purpose of translation. GETA (*Groupe d'Etude pour la Traduction Automatique*), based at the University of Grenoble, is one of the oldest MT research groups in the world, having been formed in 1961 (as CETA). The CETA system was developed over the 10 years to 1971, and was based on the interlingua philosophy. This system, which was designed for Russian–French translation of scientific texts, was not extremely successful, failing to translate well over half the sentences it treated. One of the principal reasons for this was the loss of potentially useful surface syntactic information during the production of the text in interlingual form.

9.2 Basic nature of the system

From 1971 onwards, GETA's approach to MT has been firmly based on the transfer concept, that is, a bilingual transfer stage is interposed between monolingual source language analysis and target language synthesis, eliminating the need for some abstract, unambiguous, language-independent, static text representation (interlingua). The ARIANE system is the latest development of this approach, but is strongly based on research carried out between 1971 and 1978. Although Russian–French translation still appears to be the main focus of linguistic work using the system, other languages (including English, Japanese, German and Portuguese) have also been studied. The system itself is claimed to be suitable for translation between any language pair, and it is in fact the algorithmic features which are of the greatest interest. The translation chain consists of six principal phases, namely:

- morphological and preliminary syntactic analysis
- syntactic (or multilevel) analysis
- lexical transfer
- structural transfer
- syntactic generation
- morphological generation

The ARIANE system offers to the user–linguist a set of metalanguages for expressing the linguistic data (dictionaries and grammars) appropriate to each phase. A formal separation between the linguistic data and the algorithms of application is observed, although certain data effect a direct influence on the algorithms. An important feature claimed for the system is that the simpler stages of translation, i.e. morphological analysis, lexical transfer and morphological generation, are realized by algorithmic models of correspondingly less generality (ATEF, TRANSF and SYGMOR respectively), with the more sophisticated ROBRA model being used for the remaining, more complex stages, namely syntactic analysis, structural transfer and syntactic generation.

9.3 Data structure

The data structure which represents a text between the stages of morphological analysis and morphological synthesis is a complex labelled tree. Each node of the tree is a complex label, i.e. a property list incorporating (the values of) any number of variables of various types. The use of this term is somewhat idiosyncratic, designating what are normally called attributes. It is retained here, but it should be remembered that it does not have its normal meaning, referring to a class of grammatical structures within a linguistic rule.

9.3.1 Variables

Variables are declared to the system in files of variables. Each variable is characterized by a name, a type (scalar or set) and a list of values. Declarations of scalar variables are preceded by the reserved word -EXC- (exclusive). Such variables may have at any one time only a single value, taken from the value list plus the special value "nil" (or undefined). Numerical variables are a particular subclass of the exclusives, and are declared by stating their maximum value, as a positive integer, in brackets after the name. Thus $ARIT(n)$ defines a numerical variable called ARIT whose values range over the integers from $-(n + 1)$ to n. UL (*unité lexicale*) is an exclusive variable predefined by the system whose values range over the lexical units included in the dictionaries. Set variables have their declarations preceded by -NEX- (non-exclusive) and have values taken from the set of all subsets of their associated list plus nil. The permissible operations on scalars are tests for equality and inequality on sets, these plus intersection, union and membership; and on numericals, the commonly found arithmetic operations. There is no means whereby the presence of one variable may be made conditional upon the value of another, in other words, no "variant record" capability, and thus no way of imposing a hierarchical structure within labels.

Given the declaration of variables in (1a), the structure of the subject NP *The linear systems...* after analysis might be of the form shown in (1b).

(1) a. **-EXC-**

    CAT := (ART, NOM, VB, ADJ).   syntactic category

    K := (NP, PP, VP).   syntagmatic class

    NB := (S, P).   number

    FS := (DES, EPIT, GOV, SUBJ, OBJ) syntactic function

b.

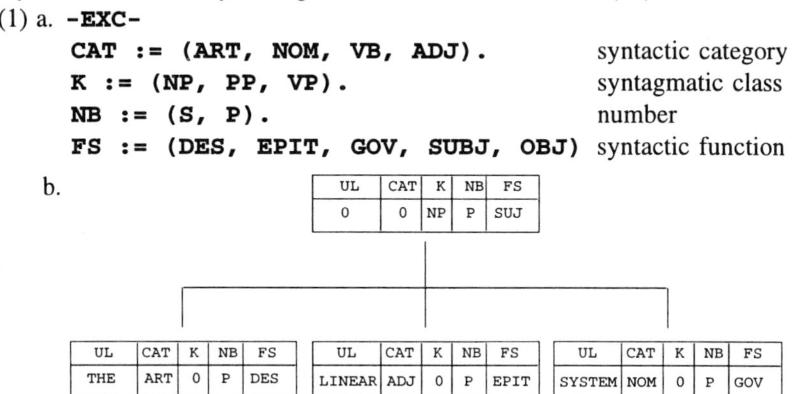

Labels are implemented as masks of variables, fixed-length records of 32 bytes, one each for exclusive and non-exclusive variables. Each variable will be mapped by the compiler into a field of such a record. This imposes a limit on the total number of values declared under each type. For exclusive variables this is 2^{240}, and for non-exclusive ones 240.

The nil value for a variable is represented by the identifier <variable name>0. Variables are initialized with their nil values by the system.

9.3.2 Formats

To simplify the writing of dictionaries and grammars, recurring combinations of variables with particular values may be defined. These are known as "formats". Each format is referred to by a name, and is declared in a file of formats.

Formats are declared as follows:

```
<format name> <card number> == <comment> .**
     <expressions> .
```

The expressions part may be empty, may assign values to variables (simple formats), or may call other formats (general formats). For instance, the assignments in (2a) (i.e. third person singular masculine pronoun) may be effected by calling a format declared as in (2b).

> (2) a. **CAT := (PRN)**
> **PER := (3)**
> **NB := (SING)**
> **GEN := (MASC)**
>
> b. **FOSIL 01 ==.** **CAT-E-PRN, NB-E-SING, PER-E-3,**
>   **GEN-E-MASC.**

9.3.3 Linguistic content of labels

From the linguistic viewpoint, the variables that constitute a label fall into four classes according to the type of information they express. The latter may be related to:

- the lexical item, including UL itself and all syntactic and semantic features derived from the source dictionary or computed during analysis (e.g. gender, animacy, count/mass);
- the actualization of the sentence (e.g. tense, aspect, number, degree);
- tactical variables, i.e. variables of no particular linguistic significance, but allowing the dictionary/grammar writer to prespecify in the linguistic data certain aspects of algorithmic operations, such as a particular sequencing of rules, or prevention of a such a sequencing;
- the level of interpretation (see next section).

9.3.4 Levels of interpretation

The system does not impose any *a priori* limitations on the "depth" to which a text is analyzed. This level is determined by the linguist when writing the analysis and transfer rules, and may in principle lie anywhere on the scale from the level of surface structure to an abstract interlingual level. In practice, however, the linguistic teams working with ARIANE have agreed upon transfer between source and target intermediate structures: structural descriptors containing both deep- and surface-level information.

A major advantage of GETA's data structure is that it allows different levels of interpretation to be represented simultaneously on a single labelled tree, rather than using separate graphical representations for each level. This gives the possibility of interaction between levels, and is particularly important as a fail-safe provision: i.e. in case of failure to compute deep-level information for some part of the translation unit, more superficial information is accessible to represent that unit while still allowing deep-level representation elsewhere (since, being on the same tree structure, all levels of representation are formally compatible). The levels of interpretation employed to date correspond to:

1. terminal and non-terminal syntactic classes (CAT), e.g. NP, VP, PREP, ADJ
2. syntactic functions (FS), e.g. SUJ (subject), OBJ(ject), COMP(lement)

3. logico-semantic relations (RL), e.g. arguments of a predicate (ARG1, ARG2, ...), argument qualifiers and determiners (QUAL1, DET)

Tree geometry has to be consistent with each of these levels. This is achieved by bracketing according to the set of nonterminal classes (level 1); thus the structure of the tree does not imply any linguistic dependency relation between connected nodes. This is dictated by the use of multilevel representation, since the ARIANE system itself is quite general in the type of structure it supports, e.g. immediate constituency or dependency. In a tree structured according to immediate constituents, levels 2 and 3 involve relationships between sister nodes, e.g. between verb and noun, noun and adjective. These relations are expressed in the label by employing the value GOV(ernor) of the variable FS, in addition to the FS/RL values which describe the relationship. For example, if node i bears the relationship R (e.g. subject of, first argument of) to node j, then node i will be labelled for the value R (i.e. its FS/RL variables will be assigned these values) and node j (which must be a leaf) will be labelled for the value GOV (i.e. its FS variable will be assigned the value GOV, its RL variable necessarily taking the value nil). Thus for every set of sister nodes, one will have the role of GOV, and all other (optional) nodes of the set will be dependent on the GOV node via their respective FS and RL values.

For example, the multilevel intermediate structure of the sentence (3a) would have the form (3b).

> (3) a. *Cette musique plaît aux jeunes gens.*
> 'The young people like this music.'

b.

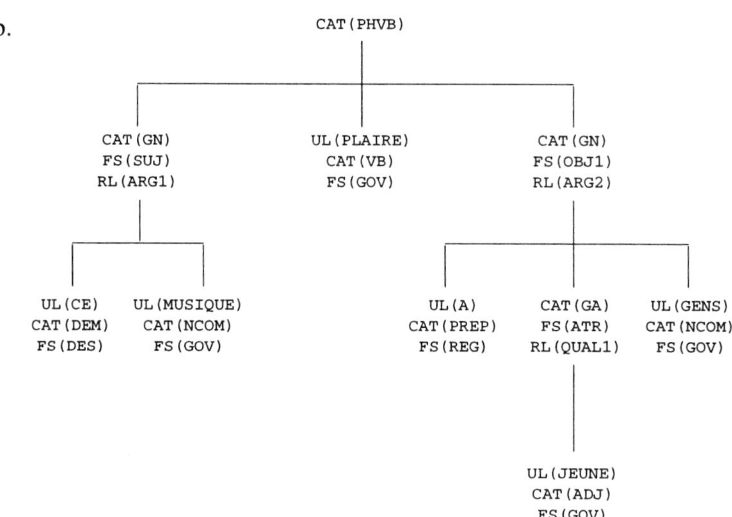

9.3.5 Declarations of data

The external linguistic data available to the various phases of the translation chain may be of the following kinds:

- variables (all components)
- formats (all components)
- dictionaries (ATEF, TRANSF, SYGMOR)
- grammars (ATEF, ROBRA, SYGMOR)

Variables and formats are declared for each phase separately, though variables which have already been declared for one phase may in certain cases be carried over in simplified form to the declarations of subsequent phases. Dictionaries and grammars are specific to each component which uses them. All four kinds of data are expressed in particular metalanguages, whose syntax and coherence is checked by the corresponding compiler. The compilers generate compact intermediate code which is interpreted at run time.

9.4 Morphological analysis

The component ATEF (*Analyse de Textes en Etats Finis*) is responsible for morphological analysis and the preliminary stage of syntactic analysis. Its function is to convert text strings into labelled trees, as input to the subsequent stage of multilevel analysis realized by ROBRA. The ATEF formalism is based on a nondeterministic finite-state transducer model; non-determinism is essential, since in general multilevel analysis must receive all possible interpretations of a form, as disambiguation between these may not be possible until this later phase.

The linguistic data available to ATEF comprise:

- declaration of variables and formats
- source dictionaries
- a grammar, each rule of which includes a list of calling formats, a set of conditions and a set of actions

The input text is considered as a string of forms. A form is a string of characters bracketed by two blanks, and usually corresponds to a word of the text. The text is analysed left to right, form by form. The direction (left–right or right–left) of analysis of each form is set by the linguist at compilation time.

The functions of the morphological analysis phase are twofold. First, to assign to each form a mask of variables representing the sum total of linguistic information characteristic of the form: this is achieved by segmenting each form into its component morphemes and integrating the information contributed by these. Secondly, to assign a basic tree structure to the text: the terminal nodes of this tree will consist of the masks of variables representing forms.

Nonterminal nodes, which are generated by the automaton, may have the following values of the variable UL (and otherwise empty labels):

ULTXT for the node corresponding to the text

ULFRA for the node corresponding to the sentence

ULOCC for the node corresponding to an occurrence of a word

ULMCP for the node corresponding to a compound word

For example, if the text consists of a single sentence (4a) the output may have the form (4b).

    (4) a. *Un physicien montre un semiconducteur.*

        'A physicist demonstrates a semiconductor.'

    b.

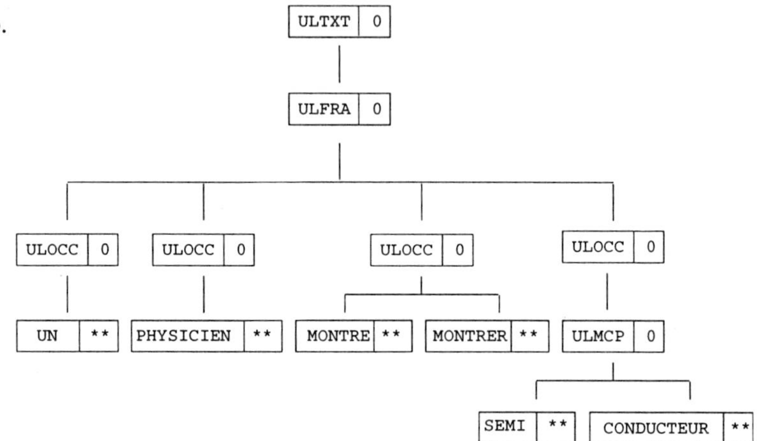

    ** and 0 stand for the values of the variables other than UL which make up the mask associated with each form. 0 indicates that all values are nil.

Note that unresolved ambiguities are represented as the multiple daughters of a ULOCC node for resolution in multilevel analysis (although this particular example of verb/noun homography would probably be resolved during the application of a realistic ATEF grammar).

9.4.1 Dictionaries

The ATEF system permits the user to define a maximum of six dictionaries plus a dictionary of idioms. There is at least one dictionary of stems and one of affixes; otherwise the number and arrangement of dictionaries is user defined.

The form of an ATEF dictionary entry is:

```
<dictionary entry> ::= <character string> ==
   <morphological format> ( <syntactic format> ,
   <lexical unit> ) .
```

The elements , <lexical unit> appear only in stem and idiom dictionaries. Morphological and syntactic formats are declared in separate files. Morphological formats incorporate only morphological variables (declared separately from syntactic variables); syntactic formats may not incorporate exclusive morphological variables. However, both morphological and syntactic variables may relate to information at any linguistic level (morphosyntactic, semantic, logico-semantic); the distinction between morphological and syntactic formats is therefore essentially strategic rather than linguistic, morphological formats being used to access particular ATEF rules.

For each application of the ATEF grammar, the set of dictionaries to be used must be initialized, and the type of control adopted must be specified. This is achieved via the obligatory rule RDICT, which comprises two main right-hand side (RHS) elements: a list of source dictionaries, and a control code, e.g. (5).

(5) RDICT: (1,2,3 / D).

The control code D indicates that the three dictionaries (which will normally be those for suffixes, stems and prefixes) are accessed in an order defined by the system. Alternatively, the control code N permits the user to control the current set of dictionaries and the order in which they are accessed by means of assignments to the non-exclusive tactical variable DICT in the grammar.

9.4.2 The ATEF algorithm

The basic (unconstrained) algorithm examines all possible segmentations of a form (which will number 2^n-1 for a string of n characters) by attempting to match character substrings exhaustively with entries in the available dictionaries. For example, the German word *Automaten* may have the potential segmentations shown in (6), assuming a likely set of dictionary entries:

(6) a. AUTOMAT + EN

   b. AUTOMAT + E + N

   c. AUTO + MATE + N

Of these "solutions", only (6a) will be retained as valid after application of the ATEF grammars. In general, valid segmentations are those for which:

- each segment is compatible with its co-segments (morphological coherence);
- the form itself, so analyzed, is compatible with the analysis of neighbouring forms, to a maximum of the four preceding forms and the immediately following form (syntactic coherence).

Morphological and syntactic coherence are determined by the ATEF grammar – specifically, by the conditions contained in individual grammar rules. These conditions relate to certain key masks of variables, designated by the following codes of origin: A, C, P1, P2, P3, P4, S.

P1...P4 represent the masks associated with the four forms preceding the form being currently analyzed, in order of increasing distance from that form. S represents the mask associated with the immediately succeeding form. These five masks are employed in determining syntactic coherence. Morphological coherence is determined on the basis of the two masks A and C. C represents the "current state" of the analysis of a particular form: the C mask embodies the sum total of information contributed to the interpretation of the form by the segments (morphemes) so far analyzed.

A step of the analysis begins by "cutting out" a prospective segment from the as yet unanalyzed part of the form. The dictionaries are scanned to find a corresponding entry. If one is not found, the scan is repeated with a shorter segment. A dictionary entry for a segment provides the mask A (argument state), i.e. A represents the information (morphological and syntactic formats and a possible UL value) characterizing the "new" segment. The morphological format associated with the segment is the calling format of one or more grammatical rules. The condition parts of each such rule are evaluated, and if "true", the specified actions are carried out. Thus a rule serves to determine whether mask A is compatible with mask C, and will update C accordingly.

After the applicable rules for a particular segment have been applied, the segmentation continues with a new segment until a blank, indicating the end of a form, is reached. Thus the left-to-right segmentation of a form *WXYZ* will examine all possible segmentations (unless interrupted by a standard function) in the order:

1. *WXYZ*
2. *WXY* — *Z*
3. *WX* — *YZ*
4. *WX* — *Y* — *Z*
5. *W* — *XYZ*
6. *W* — *XY* — *Z*
7. *W* — *X* — *YZ*
8. *W* — *X* — *Y* — *Z*

Failure to locate a dictionary entry for a particular segment will eliminate one or more of these segmentations. For example, if there is no entry for *WX*, 3 and 4 will be eliminated, and none for *X* will eliminate 7 and 8. Other segmentations will be eliminated by a failure to verify rule conditions. The search for solutions for a form may be characterized by a tree, which branches as a result of:

- several different segmentations of the form;
- the same segment being found in several dictionaries;
- several rules being called from the same dictionary entry.

In terms of the automaton which realizes the analysis, morphological formats specified in the argument label A and in the left-hand side (LHS) of grammar rules constitute the set of input elements to a transition, and the label C constitutes the output. A final state is reached at the end of a successful segmentation and is represented by the resulting C label for a particular form. The systematic traversal of the solution tree associated with a form (which is the realization of the nondeterministic nature of the algorithm) is effected by stacking and unstacking copies of the partially completed label C at appropriate times. However, by means of the standard functions described below, the user can intervene in this combinatorial enumeration and thus heuristically constrain the search for possible solutions.

9.4.3 The ATEF grammar: rules and operations

The ATEF grammar contains an unordered list of rules, of the form:

```
<rule> ::= <name of rule> :  <LHS> == <RHS> .
```

in which the LHS consists of a list of calling formats by which the rule is accessed (separated by –), while the RHS specifies the conditions on the application of the rule and the actions to be effected if the conditions are satisfied, thus:

```
<RHS> ::= <assignments and standard functions> /
    <conditions on current and previous forms> /
    <modifications of entry> / <conditions on the
    succeeding form> / <subrules>
```

The need to divide the set of conditions into two parts arises from the fact that, when analyzing a particular form, the variables associated with the succeeding form are not yet available. Hence `<conditions on the succeeding form>` come into effect retroactively, when that form is analyzed. In consequence, this part of the condition cannot make reference to P4 which, by the time the condition is evaluated, has disappeared from the field of the automaton.

Assignments

Values may be assigned to the variables of the masks C or S. These values may be literals, e.g. (7a), or may have been calculated during the course of analysis of earlier forms, in which case they are "situated" by subscripting them with the appropriate code of origin, e.g. (7b).

> (7) a. GEN(C) := MASC
>   b. GEN(C) := GEN(P1)

In the case of a non-exclusive variable, assignment may refer to a set of values, obtained by means of the set operators: -U- (union), -I- (intersection), -N- (complementation), e.g. (8).

> (8) CAT(C) := GNM -U- GVB -U- CAT(A)

The opening and closing of dictionaries as appropriate is controlled in this part of an ATEF rule by means of the tactical variable DICT. The assignment of values (representing the available dictionaries) to this variable takes the same form as any assignment to a non-exclusive variable, except that the codes of origin on the RHS of the assignment may not include P1...P4, as in (9), where O1, O2 and O5 refer to source dictionaries. (The value of DICT(C) on the RHS may have been assigned during analysis of the previous form, i.e. to the variable DICT(S).)

> (9) DICT (C) : = DICT (C) -U- O1 -U- O2 -I- -N- O5

In order to avoid lengthy enumeration of variables in certain systematic transfers of values from one mask to another, groups of variables may be referenced by means of reserved identifiers predeclared by the system, as in (10), where VARES and VAREM refer to exclusive variables (syntactic and morphological, respectively), and VARNS and VARNM to non-exclusive variables (syntactic and morphological, respectively).

> (10) VARES(C) := VARES(A)
>   VAREM(C) := VAREM(A)
>   VARNS(C) := VARNS(A) -U- VARNS(C)
>   VARNM(C) := VARNM(A) -U- VARNM(C)

Standard functions

Several of the standard functions available enable the user to intervene in the segmentation algorithm (i.e. to cut the branches of the solution tree) as follows:

-ARRET- blocks any further segmentation or processing of the current argument segment, but retains valid solutions discovered previously, and allows analysis of the form as a whole to continue.

-FINAL- rejects any valid solutions found previously, and blocks any further segmentation of the current segment, continuing the treatment of subsequent segments only until the first valid solution is found.

-STOP- retains valid solutions discovered prior to its invocation, but otherwise has the same effect as -FINAL-.

-ARD- blocks further processing of the current segment, and blocks access to the same dictionary with subsegments of the current segment.

-ARF- as -ARD- but blocks access to *any* dictionary with subsegments of the current segment.

Other standard functions are used for the creation or suppression of lexical units or nodes in the analysis tree:

-SOL- creates a ULMCP node under the current ULOCC node, i.e. it is applied whenever a compound form is recognized.

-TRANS- applies when a valid segmentation cannot be found, creating a UL value identical to the entire current form, thus permitting treatment of numerals, and proper nouns whenever these are not inflected.

-TRANSA- creates a UL value from the current segment when the latter cannot be analyzed, but retains analyses for other segments of the same form. This is used for treatment of unknown words with recognizable inflections.

-INIT- creates a new ULFRA node, subsuming under this the analyses of all forms encountered until the next call of -INIT-. This function is associated with the rule for processing full stops, and has the effect of dividing the text into a series of coherent sentence units.

ELIM(x) eliminates the form x (= S, C, P1...P4).

ELIT(x) eliminates all forms between x and C inclusively. This and the previous function are used for the treatment of idioms.

Conditions

A simple condition is a boolean expression consisting of LHS and RHS connected by one of four types of relator:

-E- equality

-NE- non-equality

-DANS- set membership (non-exclusive variables only)

-INC- set inclusion (non-exclusive variables only)

The LHS of a relation always contains as its first element a "situated" variable. In the case of an exclusive variable, this is the unique component of the LHS, e.g. (11).

(11) TMP(P2) -NE- FUT TMP(S) -E- TMP(C)

In the case of a non-exclusive variable the LHS and RHS may be compound expressions involving the binary set operators -U- and —I-, e.g. (12).

    (12) CAT(P2) -U- CAT(P1) -INC- PRN GEN(S) -DANS- GEN(C)
        -I- GEN(P1)

Relations may involve literal values of type character string. The predefined function SCHAINE(X, Y, Z) returns a string value calculated from the values of its parameters, as follows:

X The code of origin of the form containing the string, i.e. S, C, P1...P4, or A, where A refers to the remainder (unanalyzed segment) of the current form C.

Y The origin of the substring in that form. This parameter is an integer between 0 and 31 inclusive (from the left if segmentation is from left to right, or from the right if it is the other way, and vice versa if the number is preceded by $).

Z The length of the substring, again an integer, or * which represents the remainder of the form string, from the specified origin.

For example, SCHAINE(P1,0,2) designates the substring consisting of the first two characters of the form P1. String literals are represented by enclosing them with single apostrophes. Literal relations take a form analogous to that of relations involving exclusive variables, e.g. (13).

    (13) SCHAINE(S,0,*) -E- 'IN'

Conditions may be compounded from basic relations by means of the logical operators, -ET- (conjunction), -OU- (disjunction) and -N- (negation), e.g. (14).

    (14) GNR(C) -I- GNR(S) -NE- GNRO -ET- NBR(C) -I- NBR(S)
        -NE- NBRO -ET- CAT(S) -E- NOM

The special boolean function TOURN takes a form code as parameter and evaluates "true" if the idiom dictionary contains a sequence of forms corresponding to a text sequence commencing with the parameter, e.g. (15)

    (15) SCHAINE(P2,0,2) -E- 'DE' -ET- TOURN(P2)

Modifications of entry

The third component of the RHS of an ATEF rule permits, like the standard functions, interference in the algorithm, in this case by transformation of the current form. This is effected by calling the pre-defined procedure TCHAINE(P, Q, R) and specifying:

P The origin in the current form of the substring to be transformed (the same as the second parameter of SCHAINE).

Q The length of the substring, or a string literal with which the substring must coincide for the modification to take effect.

R A string literal representing the result of the modification.

For example, TCHAINE(0,'','ll') might be called during the processing of a stem with an inflectional suffix, and will have the effect of prefixing the suffix with the string *ll*. TCHAINE is used principally to convert morphs to a canonical form, thus eliminating allomorphic variation, and it is also used tactically, to reduce the possible readings of an affix by using syntactic characteristics of the stem to condition different forms of the affix.

Subrules

The subrule part of the RHS is an ordered list of rule names. The first of these whose condition evaluates "true" is applied. The calling formats of these subrules are usually empty. This facility allows the common parts of several rules to be factored out.

9.4.4 Unknown words

MOTINC is a special, obligatory rule, which applies automatically when no other rules do. It may be used to effect the assignment of a set of values to any word not found in the dictionary.

9.4.5 Example ATEF rule

The following rule (16) is taken from an ATEF grammar for German. Its function is the interpretation of nonterminal morphemes found in verbal conjugations, or morphemes of comparison in adjectives, and the prefixation of the final segment. It is called by some of the dictionary entries associated with the morphemes *en*, *end*, *er*, *et*, *st*, *t*, though not all, since by the time the dictionary is accessed, these morphemes have been prefixed with various strings according to the stem with which they were found.

```
(16) RC2:  FMDVB-FMDVF-FMDA2-FMDA2X ==
           VARNM(C):=VARNM(C)-U-VARNM(A), DICT(C):=3,
           -ARD- /
           SCHAINE(A,0,1)-NE-' ' /
           TCHAINE(0,'','30').
```


9.4.6 Evaluation of ATEF

The ATEF system obviously permits expression of a wide variety of analysis techniques to the linguists concerned with morphological and preliminary syntactic analysis. Given the limitations of the tree as a data structure for representing possible ambiguous readings of sentence constituents (cf. the chart), it is obviously desirable for cases of morphosyntactic ambiguity to be resolved as early and as simply as possible.

However, the intensely procedural nature of the ATEF system, as exemplified by:

- multiple assignments to variables, particularly the widespread use of tactical variables;
- modifications of the data during the course of processing, by means of TCHAINE;
- intervention in the algorithm by means of -ARRET-, -FINAL-, etc.

results in grammatical rules whose functions in isolation are extremely difficult to ascertain, and consequently grammars which are more difficult to write, debug and extend.

9.5 Multilevel analysis

Multilevel analysis is the term used by GETA to designate the analysis stage effected by the abstract tree-transduction model ROBRA. The input to this stage is the flat labelled tree output by ATEF. The model comprises a set of transformational rules (TRs) which progressively convert the input into the desired intermediate structure by applying local transformations in the object tree. TRs are grouped into transformational grammars (TGs): each TG consists of an ordered set of TRs and in general will correspond to a specific linguistic phenomenon, e.g. relativization, infinitival complements, expressions of comparison.

The linguistic data consist of:

- declaration of variables and formats
- a transformational system comprising

    - condition functions and assignment procedures
    - transformational rules
    - transformational grammars
    - a control graph specifying the flow of control

Variables and formats are declared in a similar way to those of ATEF, except that the morphological vs. syntactic distinction is here inapplicable. For variables which have been previously defined in ATEF, the list of their values is replaced by * in the ROBRA declaration.

Condition functions and assignment procedures are used to simplify the writing of TRs. They are declared in the same file as the rules, following the reserved word -PROC-. Different types are distinguished by prefixing each rule with one of the following codes:

PCP (*procédure condition propre*) – boolean functions invoked during evaluation of conditions on individual nodes.

PCIS (*procédure condition inter-sommet*) – boolean functions invoked during evaluation of internode conditions.

PAF (*procédure d'affectation*) – assignment procedures.

The use of these will be explained at appropriate points.

9.5.1 Transformational rules

A transformational rule (TR) consists of a rule-name, an LHS (the schema) and an RHS (the image):

```
<TR> ::= <rule-name> :  <schema> == <image> .
```

A TR is thus a production rule, where the schema represents the pattern and the image represents the action.

Schema

The schema part of a rule contains all the information necessary to identify the type(s) of tree to which the rule applies. It consists of four components:

- an optional section, defining the root node of the transformation, and the restrictions on the level of the object tree at which the root of the schema tree may occur;
- a schema tree, giving the structural geometry of the subtree upon or within which the rule applies;
- an optional set of conditions on the labels of individual nodes of that subtree;
- an optional set of conditions on relations between the labels of these nodes, i.e.

```
<schema> ::= ( <root of transformation> ,
    <constraints on level of root of schema> )
    <schema tree> / <individual-node conditions> /
    <internode conditions>
```

Root of transformation   It is important to note that the schema is not necessarily limited to describing only that section of the object tree which is actually transformed by the rule; the section to be transformed (rooted in RT) may in fact be a strict subtree of the schema tree (rooted in RS). In this case the invariant (nontransformed) part of the schema acts as the context of the subtree to be transformed and so helps to constrain the number of possible subtrees that may undergo the transformation. Though invariant, nodes forming part of the context may appear on the RHS of assignments in the image part of the rule.

The element `<root of transformation>` will be empty if RT and RS are the same node. If RT does differ from (is a descendant of) RS, then its node name in the schema tree must be stated in the `<root of transformation>`. RT is the lowest node in the tree such that all transformed nodes are subsumed under it, and it is not necessarily transformed itself. If it is not transformed, its name should be preceded by `*`, so that the interpreter may safely apply several transformations each rooted on this same node (horizontal parallelism).

Constraints on level of root of schema   The tuple of levels at which RS is permitted to be located (&NIV) can be constrained by the use of the arithmetic relation operators =, >, >=, <, <= and <>, as in Table 9.1.

Table 9.1 Constraints on level of root of schema.

Expression	Levels	Comment
2 >= &NIV	1, 2	
2 <= &NIV <=5	2, 3, 4, 5	intersection
2 >= &NIV >=5	1, 2, 5, 6, 7, . . .	union

That is, if the expression contains two relations, it evaluates to the intersection of the tuples, unless this is empty, in which case it evaluates to their union.

Schema tree   The geometry of the schema tree is represented by the conventional use of bracketing, e.g. (17a) which represents (17b).

    (17) a. `1(2,3)`

       b.

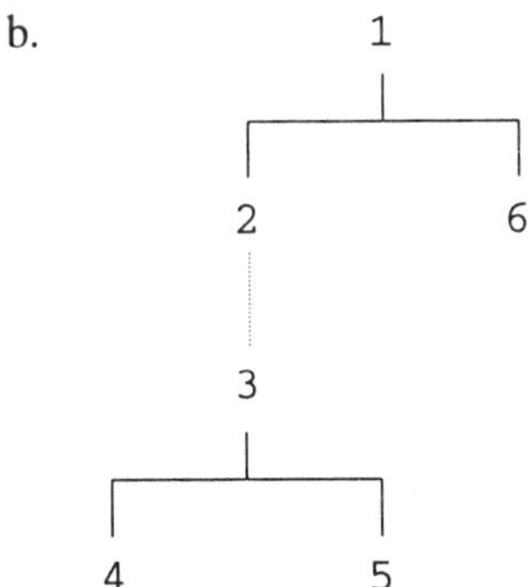

Note that the node names 1, 2, 3 etc. are arbitrary: any identifier could be used (in production system terminology, nodes are called variables).

    While the precision of the schema tree representation is obviously crucial, it must also be flexible enough to capture a variety of possible configurations of the basic structure to be transformed. For example, the formalism must allow reference to two elements (which may or may not form a "discontinuous constituent"), separated in surface structure by an unspecified number of elements (possibly none), or whose surface ordering with respect to each other may vary (e.g. noun + adjective / adjective + noun in French). To facilitate such descriptions, the following conventions have been incorporated:

    List nodes – A connected (and possibly empty) set of unspecified sister nodes is represented by a list node, designated by a node name preceded by the symbol $, e.g. (18) indicates that any number of daughter nodes of node 1 may intervene between nodes 2 and 4.

    (18) `1(2,$3,4)`

List nodes may not be placed adjacent to each other in the schema tree.

    Generalized dependent nodes – Reference may be made to a descendant of a particular node without the need to specify the (possibly empty) set of hierarchically intervening nodes. The generalized dependent node is designated by the symbol ? preceding its node name, e.g. (19a) represents (19b).

    (19) a. `1(2(?3(4,5)),6)`

       b.

    Antinodes – Constraints on the contiguity of nodes may be expressed by the antinode, designated by *, e.g.

1(2,*,3) indicates that sister nodes 2 and 3 must be contiguous
1(*,2,3) indicates that node 2 must be the left-most daughter of node 1
1(2,3,*) indicates that node 3 must be the right-most daughter of node 1

Without the antinode, the schema (20a) could apply to the tree (20b) as any of (20c–e).

(20) a. 1(2,3)

b.

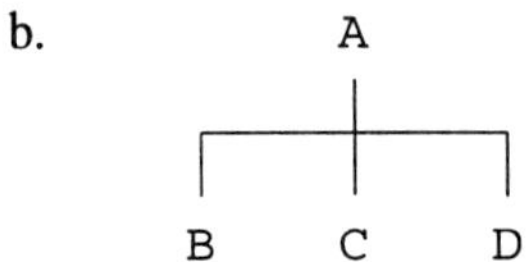

c. A(B,C)
d. A(C,D)
e. A(B,D)

Note that the list node is not thereby made redundant; a list node may figure explicitly in the individual-node and internode conditions of the schema, and in the image part of the rule.

The following codes may be used to express **constraints** on the ordering of nodes, and on the choice of nodes to which the schema applies. The codes are placed after the name-of the node to which they apply, and are immediately preceded by the symbol &:

- N – The daughters of the associated node are considered as unordered, e.g. (21a) may represent (21b) or (21c):

    (21) a. 1&N(2,3)

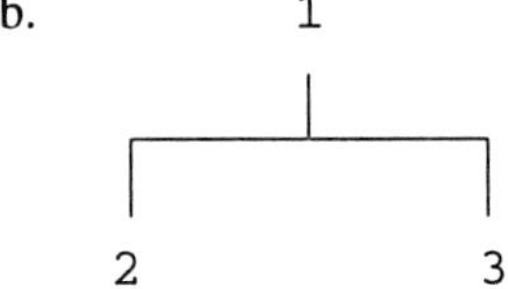 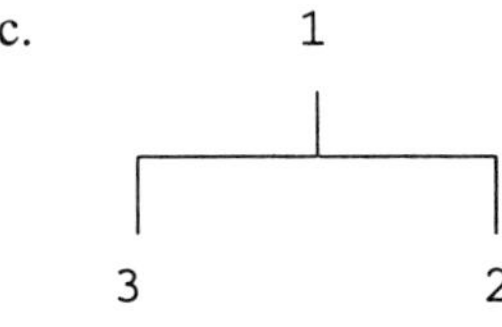

O – The daughters must respect the ordering of the schema tree as it is written.

- D – If more than one of a set of sister nodes is eligible for a particular point on the schema, priority is given to the right-most eligible node.
  G – In the same circumstances, priority is given to the left-most node.

- B – Where more than one node (with possible descendants) is eligible as a generalized dependent, the lowest node in the tree is chosen. For example, given the schema (22a) applicable to the object tree (22b), where both X and Y satisfy the conditions on node 2, Y is chosen as corresponding to node 2.

(22) a. `1(?2)`

b.
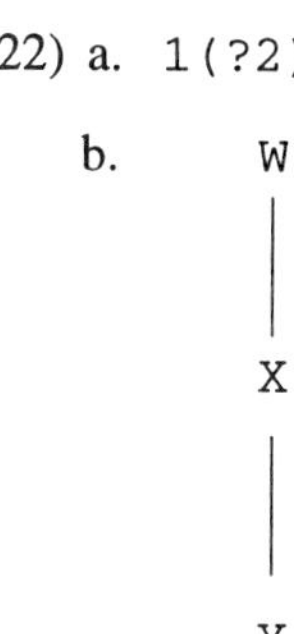

H – In the same circumstances, the highest solution is chosen.

Codes O, G and B are the default options.

Conditions   Both individual and internode conditions are stated as boolean expressions in much the same way as described for ATEF.

Individual-node conditions This component consists of a list of conditions separated one from the other by `;`. Each condition consists of the name of the node to which it applies, followed by `:`, followed by the boolean expression, e.g. (23), where NBR(*FT1) refers to the value of the variable NBR specified in the format FT1.

(23) `2 : GNR -E- MAS -ET- (CAT -NE- CATO -OU- NBR -E-`
`NBR(*FT1))`

In order to simplify the writing of conditions, predeclared functions may be invoked within a boolean expression. The function name is preceded by $, e.g. (24a), where ART might be predeclared as in (24b).

(24) a. `2 : $ART`
b. `PCP : ART == CAT -E- ART`

Note that conditions may be imposed on list nodes, in which case the condition is interpreted as applying to all the elements of the list.

Internode conditions This part of the rule consists of a single, usually complex, condition on relationships between nodes. Variables are "situated" by being followed by the name(s) of the node(s) to which they refer, enclosed in brackets. Again, functions may be called within the condition – in this case, parameters of the function – giving the nodes upon which it operates, follow the name, e.g. (25a) where CGN might be predeclared as in (25b).

(25) a. `$CGN(1,2)`
b. `PCIP : CGN(A,B) == NBR(A) -E- NBR(B)`

Note that whole subtrees of the schema may be compared as part of the condition. In this case, a subtree is specified by naming its root node, enclosed in brackets and preceded by *, e.g. (26).

(26) a. `*(1) -E- *(2)`
b. `*(1) -INC- *(2)`

Image

The image part of a rule contains all the information describing the result of the transformation. It consists of three components:

- an image tree, giving the structural geometry of the tree which is to be built
- transfer functions, giving the correspondences between nodes of the schema and image trees
- an assignment section, containing explicit assignments to the labels of the image tree, i.e.

```
<image> ::= <image tree> / <transfer functions> /
   <assignments>
```

Image tree   The image tree is expressed in a similar way to the schema tree, using arbitrarily named conventional nodes, list nodes and generalized dependent nodes, where the latter two types have been carried over from the schema. Clearly, though, the image tree does not have to capture alternative configurational patterns so that, unlike the schema tree, the image tree has fixed ordering and contiguity of nodes. Consequently, the use of the antinode ($*$) is redundant as are the codes expressing ordering and priority possibilities (cf. "Conditions" p. 127). Note that the image tree may include two or more list nodes as consecutive sisters, resulting from a reordering of (necessarily nonconsecutive) list nodes in the schema tree.

Transfer functions   These define, for each node of the transformed section of the schema, the projection of its descendants onto the image tree. For example, given the schema tree $S1(S2,S3)$, where $S1=RT$, and a corresponding image tree $T1(T2)$, the transfer functions in (27) indicate that the descendants of $S2$ and $S3$ become descendants of $T2$, and that all other descendants of $S1$ become descendants of $T1$.

   (27) T1 <-- S1, T2 <-- S2,S3

In general, each node of the transformed part of the schema tree must figure once and only once in the RHS of a transfer function; each node of the image tree must figure once as the LHS of a transfer function. However, the identity transfer function between nodes having the same name in both schema and image is assumed unless overwritten.

   Deletion of a node of the schema tree, or introduction of a totally new node in the image tree, is indicated by the antinode, e.g. (28) indicates that $S2$ and $S3$ are deleted, and $T2$ is newly created.

   (28) T1 <-- S1, * <-- S2,S3, T4 <-- S4, T2 <-- *

It is possible to specify the ordering in the image tree of non-expressed descendants of schema nodes by means of three modes of transfer. For each, assume a schema tree of the type(29a) representing the subtree (29b), where $L11\ldots L33$ represent lists of nodes which are not explicitly expressed in the schema.

(29) a. `S0(S1(S4,S5),S2(S6,S7),S3(S8,S9))`

b.
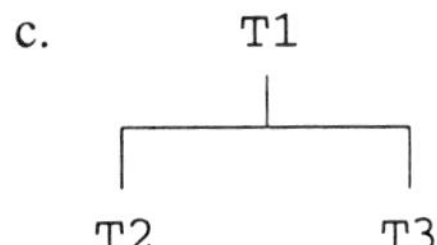

Assume further that each list is to be attached as a descendant of node `T1` in the image tree (29c).

c.

Total mode – This retains the internal ordering of each set of unexpressed sister lists, but allows the reordering of these sets with respect to each other and with respect to the explicit descendants of `T1` (30a), where `(T)` denotes total mode, and `*` represents the explicit image subtree `T1(T2,T3)`. This would result in the subtree (30b), after transformation.

(30) a. `T1 <-- (T) S3,S2,*,S1`

b.

Ordered mode – This allows for particular unexpressed descendants of `S1`, `S2` and `S3` to be extracted and placed to the right of node `T3` in the image tree. If ordered mode is specified as `(OG)`, then the rightmost descendant of each of `S1`, `S2` and `S3` is extracted; if `(OD)` is selected, then all but the leftmost descendant is extracted, e.g. (31a) would give (31b).

(31) a. `T1 <-- (OG) S2,S1,S3,*,S3,S2,S1`

b.

Projective mode – Here, one of the unexpressed lists is chosen as a cut-off point; the rightmost lists up to the cut-off point, and all except the leftmost lists after the cut-off point (including the list chosen as cut-off point) are placed to the right of `T3` in the image tree. All other unexpressed lists are placed to the left of `T2`, e.g. (32a) (where `S2(2)` designates the second unexpressed list descendant of `S2` as cut-off point) would result in (32b).

(32) a. `T1 <-- (P) S1, S2(2), S3`

b.

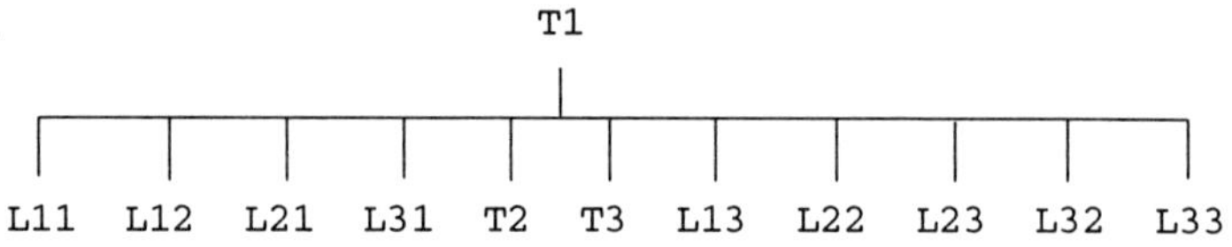
T1
L11
L12
L21
L31
T2
T3
L13
L22
L23
L32
L33

Assignments In this part of the rule, values are assigned to the variables of the nodes of the image tree. These may be transferred from the schema (with the identity assignment between nodes of the same name as default), or newly introduced, e.g. (33) assigns the complex label of node `S1` of the schema tree to node `T1` of the object tree.

(33) **`T1 : S1`**

Example (34) does likewise, and in addition assigns new values to the variables GNR and NBR, for the given label.

(34) **`T1 : S1, GNR := MAS, NBR := NBR(S1) -I- NBR(S2)`**

An assignment may include a conditional statement, as in (35) and may reference formats, e.g. (36) assigning to `T1` the values declared in format `FT1`.

(35)
```
1 : 1,-SI- ANM(O) -E- ANI
        -ALORS- UL(1) := 'QUI'
        -SINON-- UL(1) := 'LEQUEL'
        -FSI-
```

(36) **`T1 : *FT1`**

Assignments may also call predeclared procedures, e.g. (37), where AFGN might be predeclared as (38).

(37) **`T1 : $AFGN (S1,S2)`**

(38)
```
PAF : AFGN(X,Y) == GNR := GNR(X) -I- GNR(Y),
                   NBR := NBR(X) -I- NBR(Y)
```

Example ROBRA rule

The following rule is taken from a multilevel analysis grammar of Russian. It converts adjacent sister ULOCC nodes dominating a long form adjective (checked by the call to AQFOL) and a noun (call to NM) into a noun group (call to AFCGNA) with the original noun as its GOV. CGN checks that there is agreement in case, gender and number. RESEP is a conditional procedure which assigns the lexical unit `'*EPIT'` to the node which dominates the adjective. This "lexicalization" of syntactic function helps debugging, since ULs are always printed in graphic displays of trees.

```
AQN1: (*0, &NIV = 2)
      O(A(1),*,B(2)) /
      O : $ENONCE; A : $ULOCC; B : $ULOCC;
      1 : $AQFOL ; 2 : $NM / $CGN(1,2)

      == O(B(A(1),2)) /
      * <-- A,B ; A <-- * ; B <-- * /
      B : 2, $AFCGNA(1,2) ;
      A : 1 ;
      1 : *F, $AFGOV(1) ;
      2 : *F, $AFGOV(2), $$RESEP(A;1).
```

The rule is illustrated in (39).

(39)

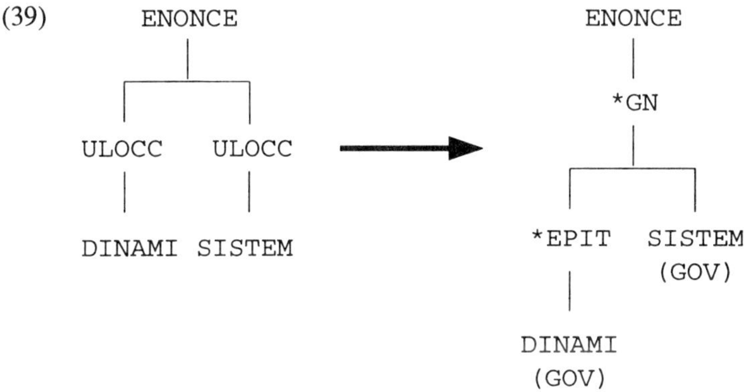

9.5.2 Transformational grammars

A transformational grammar (TG) consists of an ordered set of transformational rules (TRs). TRs are grouped into TGs according to two main criteria:

- They correspond to related linguistic phenomena.
- They share the same execution modes (see "Execution modes").

TGs are declared in a file of application in the form:

```
<TG> ::= <TG name> ( <execution modes> ):
         <list of rule names> ; <control graph> .
```

Execution modes

One of the most important characteristics of the ROBRA model, which is intimately linked to the use of a single tree as a database, is that it updates the database by substitution rather than addition. In other words, the image tree replaces the schema tree on application of a rule. This has important consequences for the interpreter. First, the structure built by application of several rules will be dependent upon the order in which they are applied. Therefore it is essential that a means is provided to enable the interpreter to resolve conflicts between applicable rules. Secondly, since a text may be locally or globally ambiguous, a facility must be provided to permit backtracking in the event that a particular sequence of rule application turns out to be incorrect. Execution modes are provided for conflict resolution and control of backtracking, as well as for control on the iteration of TGs.

The execution modes are specified in brackets following the name of the TG. They number seven, and each involves a binary choice between two values, one of which is a default, and any combination is valid (though not necessarily sensible), as shown in Table 9.2.

Table 9.2 Execution modes in TGs.

	Default		Other
U	*unitaire*	E	*exhaustif*
B	*bas*	H	*haut*
C	*coupé*	T	*total*
D	*dessous*	P	*ponctuel*
G	*contrôlé*	L	*libre*
F	*facultatif*	I	*impératif*
N	*normal*	Z	*zéro*

Elementary application of a TG

An elementary application of a TG is effected by the selection of a maximal subset of all potential applications on the database of all rules in the grammar, such that no two applications share a common active node. This is done in accordance with the following criteria:

If the TG is in mode B (*bas* 'low'), priority is given to those rule applications whose RT (see p. 124) is at a lower level in the object tree; whereas in mode H (*haut* 'high'), priority is given to the applications with RTs at the highest level. If the grammar is in mode C (*coupé* 'cut') no transformation may be applied if its root node is dominated by that of another transformation, even if the transformed subtrees are disjoint; in contrast, mode T (*total*) allows simultaneous application of such rules, thus exploiting vertical parallelism. Note that mode E (*exhaustif*) is not equivalent to modes U (*unitaire*) plus T, since the application of rules sequentially may alter the context of subsequent rules so that they are no longer applicable.

Conflicts resulting from different rules applicable at the same level (hence with the same RT, otherwise there would be no conflict) are resolved in favour of those rules which appear earlier in the TG. If, however, the schemata specifying each transformation indicate that RT remains invariant (see p. 124), and the transfer functions of the images do not include a reordering of unexpressed descendants, then all such rules may be applied, thus exploiting horizontal parallelism.

The only conflicts remaining will be the result of a single rule being applicable to different subtrees rooted in the same RT, and these may be resolved by reference to the code (D or G) of that rule (see p. 126). Again, given the appropriate conditions, horizontal parallelism may be exploited.

Iteration

The execution mode U (*unitaire*) specifies that the grammar is subject to a single elementary application only. In contrast, mode E (*exhaustif*) causes elementary applications of the TG to be iterated until no rule is applicable.

Control over the iteration is effected by two pairs of execution modes (P/D and G/L). In mode P (*ponctuel*), any rule which has applied is marked on the RT node, while in mode D (*dessous* 'below') the node is marked not only for that rule, but also for all previous rules in the grammar.

Given this marking, mode G (*contrôlé*) prevents any rule(s) marked on a particular node from being used on or below that node in subsequent iterations. A mark is thus equivalent to a tactical variable. In this way, the number of potential rule applications diminishes with each iteration of the TG (at a faster rate in mode D than in mode P); consequently, termination of iteration is ensured. In contrast, in mode L (*libre* 'free') no such invalidation of rules is effected, so that iteration may, in principle, fail to terminate.

Re-entrancy

A rule of a TG may call one or more rules (a subgrammar) of the same or a previous TG, or a transformational subsystem consisting of one or more TGs forming a section of the control graph with a single entry edge. For instance, if a rule R_i calls rules R_m to R_n ($m < n$) of a grammar G_j, this is indicated by following R_i with (40):

(40) (G_j /R_m ... R_n/ validated nodes)

The rule names may be replaced by $*$ if all rules of G_j are called. If G_j is prefixed with $*$, this indicates a call to the transformational subsystem with initial node G_j, e.g. (41).

(41) (G_j / $*$ / validated nodes)

The re-entrant call is effected by cutting out the subtree dominated by the RT specified by the rule, which is then handled as a new object tree. Only those nodes of the image tree of the rule which are listed as validated nodes may take part in any transformation during the re-entrant call. Since the validated nodes must be a strict subset of the nodes in the image tree, a recursive call is guaranteed to terminate. The result of a re-entrant call replaces the input subtree in the original object tree.

Control on grammars

The order in which TGs are applied is specified in an implicit acyclic directed graph; together the grammars and control graph constitute a transformational system (TS). The vertices of the graph are the TGs themselves, and the edges are labelled with conditions on the data structure which must hold for them to be traversed.

The graph is realized by an ordered list of transitions, separated by ;, written at the end of each TG, thus:

```
<transition> ::= <pattern> <-- <grammar name>
```

The last element of this list should have an empty pattern. The patterns are very similar to the schema parts of rules, i.e. they comprise a structure, plus individual and inter-node conditions on that structure. <pattern> may in fact be a list of patterns, separated by |.

Control is transferred to the named grammar if any of the associated patterns is verified. If the empty grammar &NUL is specified, then verification of the associated pattern indicates that the object tree is the final result of the application of the TS.

Two pairs of execution modes (I/F and N/Z) have an effect on the traversal of the control graph. If a TG is in mode I (*impératif*) then an execution of this grammar in which no rules are found to be applicable will initiate backtracking through the control graph. However, if such a grammar is in mode F (*facultatif* 'optional'), forward traversal of the control graph will continue.

A grammar in mode Z (*zéro*) indicates that backtracking is prohibited past this grammar (so that any transformations it has effected may not be undone), while one in mode N (*normal*) is not subject to any such prohibition.

Example ROBRA grammar

The following grammar is taken from a structural transfer from English to French. The grammar treats relative clauses by iterative (E) application of the rules CB2, REL1, etc. (declared elsewhere) in punctual (P) mode, and then transfers control to grammar C2P if an adverb has been found or certain other conditions obtain, or to C2R if not:

```
C2N (EP) : CB2, REL1, REL2, REL3;
           0(1) / O : K1-E-PH -OU- K1-E-MD -OU-
                      UL-E-'*ADVERBE';
           1 : K-E-B /
           <-- C2P : <-- C2R.
```


9.5.3 Evaluation of ROBRA

The facilities provided by the ROBRA formalism appear to be adequate for any task a grammar writer might wish to perform, though it is difficult to see the value of transfer functions as described (p. 128). The node variables and associated codes (p. 130) are very useful.

Because a single tree is used as a data structure, and hence update is by substitution rather than addition, ROBRA provides mechanisms for expressing precise control over the order of rule application, backtracking, etc. The use of certain execution modes with their interactions for this purpose makes it a little complicated to ascertain the precise behaviour of grammars.

However, given the general tree transduction approach to building complex structures, the facilities for collecting rules into grammars and chaining the application of grammars appear to be a useful way of achieving a perspicuous organization.

9.6 Lexical transfer

Transfer is effected in two separate stages: lexical transfer and structural transfer. Lexical transfer rules are expressed in the metalanguage TRANSF and are applied by the corresponding automaton.

TRANSF uses the following external data:

- declaration of variables
- condition formats
- assignment formats
- condition functions and assignment procedures
- dictionary

Variable and format declarations take the same form as for ATEF and ROBRA. Condition formats employ only those source-language (SL) variables and values declared in the previous phase (multilevel analysis). Assignment formats employ target-language (TL) variables and values, either newly declared or SL variables which have been carried over from the previous phase.

Condition functions and assignment procedures are used to simplify the writing of dictionary rules. As with formats, condition functions refer to SL variables only, assignment procedures refer to TL variables. Both are declared on a single file, condition functions following the reserved word -PCP-, and assignment procedures following -PAF-, the file being terminated with -FIN-. For example:

```
-PCP-
7S == PG -E- 7S -ET- ABS -INC- PP.
-PAF-
ACC == MPP:=ACC, RF:=N.
-FIN-
```

Here the function 7S is a condition on the type of prepositional group occurring as complement of certain verbs in Russian (as SL). ABS -INC- PP specifies that the verb must have a PP as one of its arguments; PG -E- 7S specifies that this PP must be of the form S + instrumental (7). The procedure ACC assigns the value ACC (direct object) in transferring certain types of Russian PPs into French, and assigns the value N (active) to the variable RF (voice).

9.6.1 Transfer dictionary

A single dictionary suffices for lexical transfer as stems (including compounds) have been reduced to a canonical form, and inflections have been incorporated as values in the node labels.

The form of a TRANSF dictionary entry is:

```
<dictionary entry> ::= <lexical unit> == <list of
    triples> <last triple> .
```

The list of triples is optional, but the last triple must be present. A triple specifies the following information:

- a boolean condition on the variables associated with the lexical unit, which must evaluate "true" for the other components of the triple to apply; this part must be empty in the last triple;
- an image subtree, which will be constructed if the triple applies;
- a set of assignments to the nodes of the image subtree, i.e.

```
<triple> ::= <condition> / <image subtree> /
      <assignments>
```

The automaton traverses the input tree in preorder, and accesses the dictionary with the value of UL in the label associated with each node thus visited. On locating the entry, the algorithm searches for the first triple whose condition is verified by the current node of the input tree. Since the last triple of each entry is always stated with an empty condition, a TRANSF rule, once accessed, will always apply. The image subtree in the second part of the triple is then substituted for the current node. Usually the image subtree will consist of only one node, so effecting no change in the input tree geometry. In certain cases however, e.g. TL compound words or idioms, a single node of the input tree may correspond to an image subtree of more than one node. In such cases, descendants of the root node of the image subtree are ordered before any descendants of the original node which it replaces. Finally, the last part of the triple is used to assign a TL lexical unit to the variable UL of each node in the image subtree, and, optionally, other values to the other variables in the label(s).

The condition part, if not empty, contains either a conditional expression, e.g. PG -E- 5K, or a call to a condition function, e.g. $7S.

The geometry of the image subtree is expressed in the same way as that of the ROBRA image tree, e.g. 0(1,2).

Generalized dependants and list nodes are prohibited.

If the subtree consists of a single node only, it need not be specified.

The assignment part contains, for each node of the image subtree:

- The name of the node followed by the symbol :. If the image subtree has not been specified, then this part is obviously empty.
- The TL lexical unit (i.e. a string literal) that is to be assigned to UL.
- An optional list of assignments to the other variables of the node label, separated by ,.

An assignment may include names of assignment formats, possibly prefixed by + or * (see below), one or more assignments to expressions, and calls to assignment procedures, e.g. (42).

```
(42) O : 'METTRE', +FVB11, $IFA;
     1 : 'A', *PP1, PG:=2ZA.
```

If the name of an assignment format is prefixed with +, this indicates that only the variables declared in this phase (i.e. not carried over from analysis) are to be assigned values as specified in the format. Thus, even if the format contains values for "transferred" variables, these values are not taken into account for the purposes of the particular assignment in question. Alternatively, the prefix * indicates that all variables listed in the format, regardless of the phase at which they originated, are to be assigned the values specified. + is the default.

(Note that the variable UL is unaffected by these restrictions: formats are prohibited from containing either source or target values for UL.)

9.6.2 Linguistic content of TRANSF entries

The context in which a given triple of a TRANSF rule applies is limited to the mask of variables immediately associated with the UL acting as entry to the rule. It is thus the responsibility of multilevel analysis to ensure that this label contains all the information necessary for lexical transfer.

In many cases, this poses no problems, and a single TL lexical unit may be conditionally or unconditionally assigned, e.g. (43) where P2A evaluates "true" if the input node is negative:

```
(43) 'MUST' == //'DEVOIR',+VB.
     'KAKOJ' == $P2A//'AUCUN'/
                        //'QUEL'.
```

Fixed SL idioms will normally have been reduced to a single node before this phase, and may thus be treated with rules such as (44).

```
(44) 'CARRY-OUT' == //'EXECUTER', +VB.
```

More complex image subtrees will be added in the following cases (examples are Russian–French and English–French, but such considerations are really language-pair independent).

Verbal government

In those cases where a particular verb conditions a "nonliteral" translation of a following preposition, the correct translation is given as the UL of a supplementary node under that of the verb, e.g. (45)

```
(45) 'ZAMENITQ' == / 0(1) / 0: 'REMPLACER';
                            1: 'PAR', PG=2NA.
```

Structural transfer will then use the information that *par* and not *sur* is the translation for *na* + accusative (which is held as the value of PG) to substitute *par* for *sur* at the appropriate point in the sentence.

Fixed idioms in TL

If an SL lexical unit requires a translation consisting of a fixed phrase, the elements of the latter are subsumed under a node with the tactical UL '*LOCF' (*locution figée* fixed phrase), e.g. (46).

```
(46) 'AS-A-RULE' == / 1(2,3,4) / 1: '*LOCF', +VIDE;
                                 2: 'EN', *VIDE;
                                 3: 'REGLER', *ACTFS;
                                 4: 'GENERAL', AQFS.
```

This is the construction of the fixed idiom *en règle générale* 'as a rule'. Note that the elements of a fixed SL idiom must have the canonical form in which they are entered in the morphological synthesis dictionary, with the label giving the information needed to generate the form in the idiom.

Variable idioms in TL

There appear to be two principal ways of representing these. Nonverbal idioms are subsumed under a node with the tactical UL `'*LOCV'` (*locution variable*), e.g. (47).

```
(47) 'CAN' == $KEs / 0(1,2(3,4)) /
                    0:  '*LOCV', +NMF;
                    1:  'BOITE', *NMF, $GOV;
                    2:  '*LOCF', *VIDE;
                    3:  'DE', *IVPP;
                    4:  'CONSERVER', *ACTF5, $SIN.
```

BOITE is subsumed directly under `'*LOCV'` since it must be inflected for number. `'*LOCV'` appears to be used in those cases where other words may intervene in the idiom (e.g. an adjective modifying *boîte*).

Verbal idioms are represented with the head as a father node dominating the remainder of the idiom, e.g. (48).

```
(48) 'TEND' == / 0(1) / 0: 'AVOIR', TRAVF =GPA;
                        1: 'TENDENCE'.
```

The value assigned to TRAVF will be recognized during the subsequent treatment of this subtree, and will initiate the generation of *à* to complete the idiom *avoir tendance à*.

Source idioms

Variable idioms in the source language may appear as subtrees in the output from multilevel analysis. As only a single source node may be considered by the TRANSF algorithm at any one time, the presence or absence of the idiom cannot be ascertained. Hence the target subtrees for each element of the idiom are constructed with tactical ULs and other variables whose values embody predictions which may or may not be substantiated during structural transfer.

For example, the three rules in (49) indicate the possible occurrence of the idiom *koyefficient poleznogo dejstviya* (*rendement* in French).

```
(49) a. 'KOYEFFICIENT' == / 0(A)        /
                        0: 'COEFFICIENT';
                        A: '+KOYEFFICIENT'.


     b. 'POLEZEN'      == / 0(X(A(1))) /
                        0: 'UTILE';
                        X: '*RLX3';
                        A: '+KOYEFFICIENT';
                        1: 'RENDRE'.
```

```
c. 'DEJSTVOVATQ'  == / O(X(A)) /
                     O: 'AGIR';
                     X: '*RLX3';
                     A: '+KOYEFFICIENT'.
```

The tactical UL `'*RLX3'` will call the rule RLX3 during structural transfer. This rule will ascertain whether the other components (i.e. those bearing the UL value `'+KOYEFFICIENT'`) are present, and if so, will replace all three by `'RENDRE'` plus the values giving the appropriate derivation (i.e. *rendement*).

It is difficult to see why this sort of complexity has not been obviated by reducing variable (but contiguous) idioms to a single node in morphological analysis, since ATEF obviously provides the facilities to do so.

Polysemy

Analysis may have been unable to resolve certain cases of polysemy (i.e. to have provided the information in the associated label to enable the condition component of the appropriate TRANSF rule to resolve it). In these cases, the alternative translations will be retained, and a tactical variable is used to indicate to morphological generation that these alternatives must be marked as such in the final output, for example (50).

```
(50)   'ZAPUSTITQ' == / 1(2) / 1: 'LANCER';
                              2: 'NEGLIGER', $HOM.
```

The procedure $HOM makes the assignment to the tactical variable.

9.6.3 Evaluation of TRANSF

Most of the above complexities could be much reduced if the TRANSF formalism allowed the dictionary writer to interrogate and/or change labels on nodes other than that bearing the UL currently being considered.

In this way, for instance, the correct preposition could be inserted in place in the tree (cf. "Verbal government", p. 137), or the presence of a variable idiom in the SL tree could be verified (cf. "Source idioms", p. 138), thus obviating the need to carry tactical information into the structural transfer stage.

This would, of course, necessitate an increase in the power of the TRANSF automaton, both to deal with generalized tree transduction and to provide user-defined general-purpose tree traversal procedures. However, this would be more than offset by the resulting increase in perspicuity of the linguistic operations.

9.7 Structural transfer and syntactic generation

The rules which effect the phases of structural transfer and syntactic generation use the ROBRA formalism described in Section 9.5.

Since the different groups who have written rules for these phases have partitioned the treatment of various linguistic phenomena differently between them, they are discussed together.

The sort of linguistic phenomena handled in these phases may be exemplified as follows:

- the rearrangement of the text into basic TL word order
- the distribution or elimination of constituents from co-ordinated phrases according to TL norms
- the generation of TL articles
- the computation of correct tenses and moods, and generation of auxiliary verb structures to realize them
- distribution of agreement information (from nonterminals onto leaves)
- the use of the tactical information added by lexical transfer to initiate various actions (e.g. recognition of SL idioms).

9.8 Morphological generation

Morphological generation is the final stage of the translation process, and has the function of converting the labelled trees output by the syntactic generation phase into character strings (i.e. words and punctuation of the output text). Rules for this phase are written in a formalism called SYGMOR, which realizes a finite-state deterministic (cf. ATEF) automaton, thus reflecting the lesser complexity of the synthesis process. The model is composed of two transducers: the first of these is "tree-to-string", the output being a string of masks of variables; the second transforms this string into a string of characters.

The tree-to-string transducer is realized by a traversal algorithm on the data structure. Obviously this algorithm will vary according to the linguistic representation in the tree, e.g. if the tree is structured according to immediate constituents, the traversal algorithm must enumerate only the leaves, while if it is a dependency tree, internal nodes must also feature in the transducer's output. The documentation claims that the traversal is user defined, but does not indicate the facilities provided to permit this definition.

The second, string-to-string, transducer makes use of the following linguistic data:

- declaration of variables, formats, condition functions and assignment procedures (similar to previous phases);
- dictionaries;
- a grammar.

9.8.1 Dictionaries

A maximum of eight dictionaries may be used during this phase, each being addressed by the values of variables. The first dictionary is of TL lexical units, and is addressed by values of UL. Other dictionaries may be addressed using the values of other variables, e.g. a dictionary of verbal inflections accessed by means of the values of the variables indicating person, number or tense.

The form of a SYGMOR dictionary entry is:

```
<dictionary entry> ::= <entry value> == <list of
    triples> <last triple> .
```

The list of triples is optional, but the last triple must be present. A triple specifies the following information, as exemplified in (51):

- the name of a boolean function, i.e. a condition on the values of other variables in the current label, which must evaluate "true" for the remaining components of the triple to apply; this part must be empty in the last triple;
- the name of an assignment format;
- a character string.

```
<triple> ::= <condition> / <assignment format> /
    <string>
```

(51) **LEQUEL == NIB / VID / LAQUELLE,**
== NID / VID / 'LESQUELLES,
== PLU / VID / 'LESQUELS,
== / VID / 'LEQUEL.

An apostrophe appearing in a string, e.g. ' LEQUEL, will be used by the grammar to make contractions.

9.8.2 The SYGMOR grammar: rules and operations

Certain special symbols appear in the grammar rules. These are interpreted in the following way:

C and P – These designate respectively the current and preceding masks of variables in the string of masks which constitute the input to the transducer.

T and S – These designate respectively the current and preceding character strings in the string of strings which constitute the output of the transducer.

G, D and M – These are codes of origin referring to positions in the character string T. The first two designate respectively the leftmost and rightmost positions. M is the position equivalent to the leftmost position in the character string most recently inserted into T, if that string was inserted to the right, or the rightmost position if it was inserted to the left.

A grammar rule has the form:

```
<grammar rule> ::= <rule name> :   <condition> ==
    <rhs> .
```

A condition is a boolean function on the values of the two masks C and P, e.g. (52):

```
(52) DD(C) -NE- DDO -ET- DD(P) -E- DD4
```

This condition must evaluate "true" for the rule to be applied. The empty condition, signified by NIL, always evaluates "true".

The RHS of a rule consists of several parts, any of which may be empty, i.e.

```
<rhs> ::= <dictionary access part> / <assignments>
    / <string transformations> / <sequence of
    transitions>
```

Dictionary access

This part of the RHS of a rule has the form:

```
<dictionary access part> ::= EC<insertion code> (
    <dictionary number> )
```

The dictionary specified (from 1 to 8) is accessed and the first entry value corresponding to a value in the mask C which has not already been treated is located. The first triple associated with this entry value whose condition is fulfilled provides the character string to be inserted into T according to the insertion code. For example ECG(2) inserts the character string obtained as a result of accessing dictionary 2 on the left (G) of T.

The dictionary number may be replaced by a string literal which will be directly inserted into T according to the specified code.

Assignments

In this part, any number of assignments (separated by ;) may be made to the character strings T and S, and to the variables of the masks C and P. An assignment to S may only be (53), which concatenates 'T' to the right of 'S'. Similarly, an assignment to T is (54), which concatenates 'S' to the left of 'T', eliminating 'S' as a separate entity. After this assignment, M will be the position in T corresponding to the point of concatenation.

```
(53) 'S' := 'T'
(54) 'T' := 'S'
```

A value assigned to a variable of C or P is either the value of the same variable in the other mask, or the value of this variable declared in the format associated with an entry in a specified dictionary accessed by means of the old value. In the case of a non-exclusive variable, a set of such values may be assigned, as in (55) for example.

```
(55) GNR(P) := GNR(C) -U- GNR(2)
```

String transformations

Transformations may be effected on T by calling the pre-defined procedure TCHAINE(*W, X, Y, Z*) and specifying:

W – the code of origin within T for the offset specified as the *X* parameter, i.e. G, D or M.

X – an integer, between −128 and +126 if the *W* parameter was M or between 0 and 254 if it was G or D.

Y – a string literal (enclosed in double quotes), which must occur in T starting at the point specified by the *W* and *X* parameters in order for the transformation to take place; or an integer.

Z – a string literal, which will replace either the character string, or the number of characters specified in the Y parameter.

The parameter X may alternatively be *, in which case parameter Y must be a literal, and the latter will be replaced if it occurs anywhere to the left of M if parameter W is G, or anywhere to the right if W is D.

For example (56a) will occur after the assignment (56b) and will apply if the value of S was previously "SI'" and that of T was "'IL". M will be situated between the two strings.

     (56) a. TCHAINE (M, -4, "SI' 'TL", "S'IL")
         b. T := S

Sequence of transitions

This part of the RHS of a SYGMOR rule includes an ordered list of the names of other rules, separated by , , each optionally bracketed. The function of this part is described below.

9.8.3 The SYGMOR algorithm

A SYGMOR grammar is an ordered list of named rules as already described. Each mask of variables, as enumerated by the traversal algorithm, becomes in turn the value of C. For each such value, the automaton searches for the first rule whose LHS conditions are fulfilled. The string T, initially empty, is given a value by means of the actions in the RHS of the rule. The automaton then steps through the rules specified in the "sequence of transitions" (taking no account of the sequence of transitions associated with any of these). For each rule, the condition is evaluated, and if "true", T is updated accordingly. If the condition is "false", and that rule was bracketed in the original list, then the next rule is tried. If the condition of an unbracketed rule is "false" then the automaton stops and indicates an error. A final (accept) state of the automaton will be reached if the condition on the last obligatory (unbracketed) rule named on the original list is "true". Whether or not the automaton reaches a final state, C will then become P and T will become S, and the algorithm will be repeated until the final mask of the input has been processed.

As in ATEF, the potential transitions that the automaton could undergo may be characterized as a tree, which in this case branches as a result of:

- the conditions on rule application
- the choice of dictionary to be accessed
- the triple of the dictionary entry chosen

However, because rules and dictionary triples are strictly ordered, and a single dictionary only may be accessed from one rule, and since the automaton does not have the facility to backtrack, the transducer realized is deterministic, and the solution generated corresponds to a single path from root to leaf in the solution tree.

9.8.4 Evaluation of SYGMOR

SYGMOR provides facilities which appear adequate for the treatment of any linguistic phenomena appropriate to this phase, e.g. contraction, elision, stem modification with particular inflectional or rectional morphemes.

It is difficult to see the value of some facilities, such as assignments to masks C and P, which are supposed to be inputs to the automaton. Certainly such assignments must detract from the perspicuity of SYGMOR grammars. The fact that the conditions on the input masks (which are the realization of the transitions) are partitioned between dictionaries and grammar must also have adverse effects on perspicuity.

The algorithm by which the dictionaries are accessed is not made clear in the documentation. It appears that it is the values in C which are accessed by means of a sequential scan of the entries in the specified dictionary, which renders the order of dictionary entries significant. The dictionary scan must continue until a corresponding value is found for a variable which has not already been treated, which means a list of treated variables must be maintained by the algorithm. It would seem more efficient and more perspicuous if a specified dictionary were accessed by means of the values of named variables, as in the assignment part of a rule; the grammar writer must have a notion of what is expected in the chosen dictionary, and could reasonably ask for it by (variable) name.

9.9 Software environment and implementation

The components of the system as described above are embedded within a conversational monitor, which makes available to the user facilities for the following tasks:

- the creation, editing, compilation and listing of the linguistic data for any phase of the translation chain;
- the preparation of texts in any of the source languages of the system;
- the execution of one or more phases of translation for any language or language pair, and examination of the results.

The monitor is hierarchically structured, with four levels of treatment corresponding to:

0 Entry to the system, giving access to general commands.

1 General commands for specifying which of the tasks described above is to be carried out, and on which phase of the translation chain.

2 Commands giving access to a particular data file associated with the phase specified at level 1, e.g. variables, grammar.

3 Specific operations on the file chosen in level 2, e.g. modify, list, compile.

In any of the levels, the user has the option of being questioned by the system in detailed or simplified mode, and of obtaining a very detailed explanation of the possible answers and their effects.

In addition to the facilities for listing provided by the monitor (including provision for various listings of files sorted according to different fields of the entries), the ROBRA system itself allows specifications within its grammars of various outputs, e.g. rules applied, rules marked on nodes of the object tree, the object tree itself in various forms.

The ARIANE system is implemented on an IBM-360 series compatible minicomputer under the CP/CMS operating system. The conversational monitor is written in the command language of the operating system. Interpreters and compilers for each algorithmic model are written in 360-Assembler, except for those of SYGMOR, which are in PL/1.

9.10 Final comments

Most of the criticisms which have been levelled at the ARIANE translation system in this work are recognized as valid by its designers themselves. Work continued at GETA aimed at improving many aspects of the system, including:

* the development of a unified, high-level formalism for the metalanguages of all components
* the introduction of a single data structure, the chart, to replace the two currently used, i.e. the tree and the string of forms
* the provision of facilities currently unavailable to various components of the translation chain, e.g. dictionary access during multilevel analysis, generalised tree manipulations during lexical transfer
* the improvement of system portability, i.e. its implementation in one or more widely available high-level languages, e.g. PASCAL and LISP.

A machine translation system with these features could be considered as very close to the state of the art, but it remains to be seen whether GETA will be the first to achieve such a system.

9.11 Documentation

Boitet, Ch. 1977. *Nouveau système: étude de définition.* Rapports de recherche nos. NS-PQ-1 et NS-PQ-2, GETA, Grenoble.
Boitet, Ch. 1978. *Bases pour l'élaboration d'un logiciel de traduction automatisée multilingue.* Rapport de recherche, GETA, Grenoble.

Boitet, Ch., P. Guillaume & M. Quézel-Ambrunaz 1978. Manipulations d'arbor-escences et parallélisme: le système ROBRA. Paper presented at 7th International Conference on Computational Linguistics, Bergen, Norway.

Boitet, Ch., P. Guillaume & M. Quézel-Ambrunaz 1982. Implementation and conversational environment of ARIANE 78.4, an integrated system for automated translation and human revision. In *COLING 82: Proceedings of the Ninth International Conference on Computational Linguistics*, J. Horecký (ed.), 19–27. Amsterdam: North-Holland.

Boitet, Ch. & N. Nédobejkine 1980. Russian–French at GETA: Outline of the method and detailed example. In *Proceedings of the Eighth International Conference on Computational Linguistics*, Tokyo.

Chauché, J. 1975. *Présentation du système CETA*. Rapport de recherche no. G–3100–A, GETA, Grenoble.

Chauché, J. 1975. Les systèmes ATEF et CETA. *TA Informations* **16**, 2.27–38.

Chauché, J., P. Guillaume & M. Quézel-Ambrunaz 1972. *Le système ATEF*. Rapport de recherche no. G–2600–A, GETA, Grenoble.

Euvrard, A. & J. Lecomte 1979. *Elaboration d'une chaîne de traduction automatique d'anglais en français: bilan d'une expérience*. Rapport de recherche CRAL no. 36, Centre de Recherches et d'Applications Linguistiques, Université de Nancy.

Guilbaud, J.-P. 1980. *Analyse morphologique de l'allemand en vue de la traduction par ordinateur de textes techniques specialisés*. Thèse de 3e cycle, l'Université de la Sorbonne Nouvelle, Paris.

Guillaume, P. 1978. *Le modèle de transformations d'arbres: ROBRA*. Rapport de recherche, GETA, Grenoble.

Jaeger, D. 1978. *SYGMOR*. Rapport de recherche, GETA, Grenoble.

Quézel-Ambrunaz, M. 1978. *ARIANE–78: Système interactif pour la traduction automatique multilingue (Version II)*. Rapport de recherche, GETA, Grenoble.

Thouin, B. 1976. Système informatique pour la génération morphologique de langues naturelles en états finis. Paper presented at 6th International Conference on Computational Linguistics, Ottawa.

Vauquois, B. 1977. *L'évolution des logiciels et des modèles linguistiques pour la traduction automatisée*. Rapport de recherche, GETA, Grenoble.

Vauquois, B. 1979. Aspects of mechanical translation in 1979. Conference for Japan IBM Scientific Program, July 1979. Reprinted in *Bernard Vauquois et la TAO: vingt-cinq ans de traduction automatique – analectes*, Ch. Boitet (ed.), 351–407. Gières (1989): Association Champollion.

10

Wilks's PS system

10.1 Introduction

The Preference Semantics (PS) system for treatment of natural language texts was conceived, designed and (partially) implemented by Yorick Wilks at Stanford Artificial Intelligence Laboratory and Systems Development Corporation in the late 1960s and early 1970s. It differs significantly from other systems described in this book, both in its origins and in its aims. Wilks's background is philosophy, and his aim is to explore in detail certain aspects of language which are not treated (or at least not stressed) within the mainstream of generative linguistics. The system can thus be located within the AI research paradigm, in that much emphasis is placed on semantics; the translation of texts from English to French that it effects constitutes a test bed for the system's facilities, rather than the *raison d'être* for the system. In no sense, therefore, is PS intended as an operational MT system.

However, this is not to deny that PS embodies ideas of relevance to the design of operational MT systems. Criticisms that are made in this chapter thus serve the purpose of highlighting those aspects of PS which would not be appropriate in an operational system.

The notion of *preference* embodies the theoretical position that utterances are more or less acceptable in a particular context, rather than "grammatical" (or otherwise), and therefore that ambiguity resolution (hence, *a fortiori*, understanding) is a matter of preferring one reading of an utterance to another. The notion appears in various forms throughout the system.

147

10.2 Basic nature of the system

Wilks refers to the structure that the system assigns to a text as an "interlingua", on the basis that "it contains sufficient information to admit of the formal manipulations, adequate for producing translations in natural or formal languages". He justifies the fact that not all information which would be necessary for translation is explicit in this structure by stating that such information "cannot be well-defined with respect to any coding scheme". Although his justification is correct, his use of "interlingua" is misleading. What is usually meant by the term in the context of MT is a particular form of system organization. That is, the result of an analysis is an interlingua if it is not subject to processing using *language-pair-specific* information.

In PS, at the point at which target-language-specific information is first used, the text has not been assigned an unambiguous representation, even in terms of the SL. The final stages of disambiguation are driven by procedures associated with TL lexemes, which in turn are accessed via the SL lexemes. The structure built using monolingual, SL information is "adequate for producing translations" only in the sense that it contains procedures to effect disambiguation and TL text generation.

The result of analysis, a *semantic block*, is a linear sequence of text fragments (usually subsentential), to each of which has been assigned one (or more) of a finite inventory of basic message forms, called *bare templates*, which are triples of the form actor–action–object.

Restrictions imposed by a particular class of action on the associated classes of actor and object are specified as the inventory of bare templates. These are the first means whereby disambiguation is effected in the system. A bare template corresponds to the notion of the "gist" of an utterance, e.g. "some human possesses some physical object", "some human experiences some internal state".

Each role in a bare template is filled either by one of the words in the fragment or by a dummy item. Each word in the fragment which does not fill a role in the bare template is incorporated into a full template as a dependant of one of the words which does. This *template extension* effects further disambiguation.

There is no morphological analysis phase, each word form being entered directly in the dictionary. The latter associates with each word a *formula* and a list of *stereotypes*. The formula is a representation of an English word sense as a tree of semantic primitives. Stereotypes are the procedures which are used to determine the case-like relationships (*ties*) between fragments and to generate the French output.

Some anaphors may be resolved at the same time as ties are determined. If unresolved ones remain after this, the system enters *extended mode*, which uses rules expressing plausible inferences for resolution.

Thus the system comprises the following phases:

1. fragmentation (subsuming dictionary lookup)
2. bare template matching
3. template extension
4. determination of ties

5. extended mode

6. generation

Phases 4, 5 and 6 are, as mentioned above, interleaved.

10.3 Dictionary entries

A dictionary entry comprises a formula and a list of stereotypes. The latter are discussed in Section 10.6. Formulae are constructed from an inventory of semantic primitives called *elements*. The elements are no more than an empirically useful subset of natural language words and are therefore ambiguous in isolation. Within a formula they will be structured so as to give an unambiguous representation of a word sense. This approach is convincingly justified by Wilks:

> Except in those special cases when people do actually draw attention to the external world in connection with a written or spoken statement, "meaning" is always *other words*, and talk about "the senses of words" is only a disguised restatement of that fact. [emphasis original]

10.3.1 Elements

There are about 70 elements, the precise number varying in different versions of the system. For explanation, they may be grouped into several classes. The rightmost element in each formula, the *head*, will be a member of the class which corresponds to the traditional syntactic category (noun, verb, adjective or adverb) of the word-sense indicated by that formula. In the rest of a formula, though, the meaning of an element does not necessarily correspond to its class, e.g. a nominal element may be used adjectivally.

In addition, there are classes which do not correspond to categories. The elements in these may not be the heads of formulae. One such class is that which comprises the case elements: these are used within formulae to indicate expected arguments. A miscellaneous class is provided for other elements which also occur only within formulae.

**-classes*, designated *<mnemonic>, are used in various places in the system as a shorthand for a set of elements.

Nouns

Certain *-classes are of particular importance in categorization of nominal elements, since they are used in the rules which define the repertoire of bare templates (see Section 10.4.1). The relevant categorization is as follows:

*AN (animate)	MAN	human being
	FOLK	human group
	BEAST	animal
	GRAIN	structure or organization
*PO (animate)	ACT	act
	STATE	state of existence
	THING	physical object
	STUFF	substance
	PART	part of thing
	THIS	a particular instance
	*AN	
*EN (entities)	SPREAD	spatial extension
	*PO excluding ACT, STATE	
*SO (soft)	STUFF	
	WHOLE	
	PART	
	GRAIN	
	SPREAD	
*MA (mark, i.e. that can	ACT	
designate items that	STATE	
themselves designate)	SIGN	
*AL (all)	*EN	
	*MA	

DTHIS is a pseudo-element which is used to fill an otherwise empty agent or object role in a bare template, i.e. it acts as the dummy nominal. It is treated as a member of *PO.

Verbs

Elements denoting actions, i.e. verbs, are the heads of formulae which will fill the middle (action) role in a bare template. They are:

BE	equality or existence	PAIR	
WRAP	enclose	PLEASE	
HAVE	possess	MOVE	intransitive only
TELL	inform with words	DO	
CAUSE		CHANGE	
SENSE	physically, e.g. *touch*	WANT	
USE		DROP	give up
FORCE	compel	GIVE	any ditransitive
PICK	choose	MAKE	
FEEL	experience internally	THINK	
FLOW	move as a fluid		

The criteria for assigning one of these elements as the head of a verbal word-sense are primarily semantic, though in certain cases these are overridden by syntactic considerations. For instance, *tell* is assigned the head GIVE, as it may feature in a ditransitive construction like *John tells me a story*. The remainder of the formula for *tell* is constructed so as to capture the "real" meaning of the word. The element TELL is assigned as the head of the formula for verbs like *say*.

DBE will fill the action role in the template assigned to a fragment without a finite verb, i.e. it is the dummy verb.

The elements PDO and PBE occur as the heads of formulae for prepositions, which fill the action roles in the templates assigned to prepositional phrases (with DTHIS as the agent).

Qualifiers

KIND: this element is the head of any noun qualifier, i.e. adjectival word-sense formula.

HOW: this element is the head of any verb qualifier i.e. adverbial word-sense formula.

Cases

These elements do not occur as heads, but are used within formulae to indicate the various arguments that are expected, either directly, in the formula for a verbal word-sense, or in a verbal subformula in a noun formula which expresses typical actions of the head as actor (see Section 10.3.2):

SUBJ	subject	
OBJE	object	
TO FROM	direction	subsumed under *DIRE
SOUR	source	
GOAL	purpose	
FOR	recipient	
LOCA	spatial or temporal location	
IN	containment	
POSS	possessed by	
INST	instrumental	
WITH	accompaniment	

The same set of cases also serves the function of labelling the ties (i.e. case relations) between fragments.

Modals

It is not apparent what element auxiliaries have as their heads (HOW?), but where necessary, modality may be incorporated into any formula by means of the elements CAN, MAY, MUST, WILL and LET.

Miscellaneous elements

This class comprises elements which are provided to enable various aspects of meaning to be captured, and which may not be used as formula heads. Included are GOOD (morally acceptable), TRUE (valid or correct), COUNT (numerical), LINE,

MORE, MUCH, WHERE, WHEN, SAME and SELF (co-referential with the actor in the formula).

10.3.2 Formulae

A formula is a binarily bracketed string of formulae, elements or elements preceded by NOT. A formula is well-formed if:

(a)   it has a legal element as its head (a nominal, verbal or qualifier element),

(b)   the left-hand member of each bracketed pair of formulae can be interpreted as a dependent on the right-hand member, and

(c)   each bracketed pair can be interpreted as being one of the following types:

   i.   adverbial, e.g. (DO HOW) = manner in which
   ii.   prepositional, e.g. (MAN SUBJ) = human is preferred agent
   iii.   adjectival, e.g. (NOTCHANGE KIND) = *fixed*
   iv.   nominal, e.g. (SENSE SIGN) = some abstract sensory property
   v.   verbal, e.g. (DONE HAVE) = *had* (past of *have*)
   vi.   sentential, e.g. (THING USE) = *apply*

Only certain elements may occur as immediate constituents of each bracket type. Certain bracket types may be nested within others consistent with the notion of dependency, e.g. the left-hand side of a prepositional pair may itself be a nominal pair. In this way, formulae may be built up to an arbitrary depth in order to provide an unambiguous representation of the sense of a word.

10.3.3 Example formulae

Nouns

policeman ((FOLK SOUR) ((((NOTGOOD MAN) OBJE) PICK) (SUBJ MAN)))

   Gloss: a *policeman* is a human (MAN), the typical subject of the action of selecting (PICK) bad (NOTGOOD) persons (MAN) from (SOUR) the body of people (FOLK).

crook ((((NOTGOOD ACT) OBJE) DO) ((SUBJ MAN)))

   Gloss: a *crook* is a human (MAN), the typical subject of the action of doing (DO) bad (NOTGOOD) acts (ACT).

crook ((((((THIS BEAST) OBJE) FORCE) (SUBJ MAN)) POSS) (LINE THING))

   Gloss: a *crook* is a long straight object (LINE THING) possessed by a man (MAN) who controls (FORCE) a particular kind of animal (THIS BEAST).

Verbs

interrogate ((MAN SUBJ) ((MAN OBJE) (TELL FORCE)))

> Gloss: *interrogate* is an action in which typically a human (MAN SUBJ) compels (FORCE) another human (MAN OBJE) to speak (TELL).

grasp ((*AN SUBJ ? ((*PHYSOB OBJE) (((THIS (MAN PART)) INST) (TOUCH SENSE)))))

> Gloss: *grasp* is an action in which an animate subject (*AN SUBJ) makes physical contact (TOUCH SENSE) with a physical object (*PHYSOB OBJE) by means of (INST) a particular part of the subject (THIS (MAN PART), i.e. the hand.

grasp ((MAN SUBJ) ((SIGN OBJE) (TRUE THINK)))

> Gloss: *grasp* is an action in which a human (MAN SUBJ) realizes the validity (TRUE THINK) of an idea (SIGN OBJE).

drink ((*AN SUBJ) (((FLOW STUFF) OBJE) ((SELF IN) (((WRAP THING) FROM) ((((*AN (THRU PART)) TO) (MOVE CAUSE))))))

> Gloss: *drink* is an action in which an animate subject (*AN SUBJ) causes a liquid (FLOW STUFF) to move from a container (WRAP THING) to an aperture (THRU PART) of the specified animate entity, with the result that the liquid is in it (SELF IN).

Note the use of the conventional pairs to represent such concepts as 'liquid','aperture' (in this case, the mouth) and 'container'.

The subformula type closed by each right bracket in the formula for *drink* is as follows:

    2 4 2 2 4 2 4 4 2 5 6 6 6 6 6

10.4 Fragmentation

The first phase of processing is the fragmentation of a text into elementary sentences, complex noun phrases, and clauses introduced by marker words, with obliteration of the original sentence boundaries. The fragmentation function PARA has access to four lists of marker words, i.e. prepositions, subjunctions, conjunctions and punctuation, with which fragments may start. PARA may also access the dictionary and refer to the heads of formulae for the words of the text, which information it uses to define the endings of fragments.

Wilks consistently stresses the minimal importance of the fragmentation process, claiming that it would be possible to reassign fragment boundaries if the results of subsequent analysis were unacceptable, or that fragmentation could be dispensed with altogether. However, it is clear that it performs tasks of linguistic interest, by means which are not always apparent, and whose general applicability is not always obvious. Among these, we may cite the following.

10.4.1 Relatives

Relative clauses are located and isolated as separate fragments, e.g. (1a) becomes
(1b).

> (1) a. The dog that bit the man has been shot
>
> b. (THE DOG HAS BEEN SHOT) (THAT BIT THE MAN)

Relatives without explicit relative pronouns, e.g. (2) are presumably treated by
recognizing adjacent noun phrases, though this is not stated.

> (2) The man the dog bit is ill.

It is not clear what action is taken in those cases where isolation of a relative as
described would introduce an ambiguity, e.g. (3).

> (3) a. The dog that killed the rat chased the cat.
>
> b. (THE DOG CHASED THE CAT) (THAT KILLED THE RAT)

Fragmentation is able to distinguish between the use of *that* as relative pronoun
and as demonstrative, so that (4) for example is not fragmented. No mention is made
of how an ambiguous use of *that*, as in (5) would be treated.

> (4) I like that wine.

> (5) I believe that man is foolish.

10.4.2 Conjunctions and scope

Conjunctions are not treated in a consistent manner. For instance, (6a) becomes
(6b), while (7) is not fragmented.

> (6) a. Britain's transport system and with it the travelling public's habits are
> changing.
>
> b. (BRITAINS TRANSPORT SYSTEM ARE CHANGING) (AND)
> (WITH IT THE TRAVELLING PUBLICS HABITS)

> (7) President and Congress are elected separately.

The reason for the latter is given as the necessity of locating the triple (CONGRESS
ARE ELECTED) during subsequent processing, but the same consideration could
equally apply to (HABITS ARE CHANGING).

There is a function REORDER, which follows PARA and has the task of delimiting
OF phrases by marking their ends with FO. This is done to exclude them from
consideration by the bare template matching routines. The marked phrases are then
moved in front of the nouns they qualify. Adverbs and infinitives are also moved
before the verbs they qualify, so that the template extension routines need only look
to the left of each word to find dependents of these types.

The means by which REORDER determines scope of *of*-constructions, and how
this interacts with the scope of conjunctions is very unclear. For instance, (8a)
becomes (8b). This is almost certainly the correct reading, but the motivation for
choosing this rather than, e.g. (8c) is not specified.

(8) a. The pattern of commuter movement and dormitory area congestion could be changed.

b. (THE OF COMMUTER MOVEMENT AND DORMITORY AREA CONGESTION FO PATTERN COULD BE CHANGED)

c. (THE OF COMMUTER MOVEMENT FO PATTERN AND DORMITORY AREA CONGESTION COULD BE CHANGED)

10.4.3 Clausal objects

Certain cases where the normal fragmentation procedure would give unacceptable results are recognized, e.g. (9a), if partitioned between *him* and *to*, would give the semantically spurious fragment (9b). Therefore, an occurrence of a verb like *want* indicates special action to produce a fragmentation of the form (9c).

(9) a. I want him to go.

b. (I WANT HIM)

c. (I WANT) (HIM TO GO)

Verbs which take participial clauses as objects also cause the insertion of a fragment boundary immediately following, so that the fragmentation has the same form as for infinitival clause objects. Thus, just as (10a) becomes (10b) by the normal fragmentation procedure, so (11a) becomes (11b).

(10) a. John likes to eat fish.

b. (JOHN LIKES) (TO EAT FISH)

(11) a. John likes eating fish.

b. (JOHN LIKES) (EATING FISH)

Presumably, subsequent processing will recognize and treat the participial/adjectival ambiguity in such cases as (12).

(12) John likes eating apples.

10.5 Bare template matching

Each sentence fragment is passed to the PICKUP routines, which attempt to match bare templates onto the heads of the formulae for the words in the fragment. Each sequence of three heads (not necessarily contiguous) is compared with the inventory of bare templates as given below. The only exceptions to this exhaustive matching process are:

* The heads of those formulae delimited by OF and FO are not considered.
* Conjoined formulae may not fill two roles in the same template, e.g. in (7) (in Section 10.4.2), *President* and *Congress* will not be considered as actor and object respectively within any given template.

10.5.1 Inventory of bare templates

The inventory of bare templates is empirically rather than theoretically motivated, and is realized by the substitution of all members of the appropriate *-class into the following:

```
*AL  BE   *AL¹        *PO  CHANGE  *EN        *PO  SESNE  *EN
*AL  PAIR  *EN        *PO  WANT   *EN        *PO  USE   *EN
*AL  PLEASE *AN       *PO  DROP   *EN        *PO  FORCE  *EN
*AL  WRAP  *EN        *PO  GIVE   *EN        *PO  PICK  *EN
*EN  MOVE  DTHIS      *PO  MAKE   *EN        *AN  FEEL  *MA
*EN  HAVE  *EN        *PO  TELL   *MA        *AN  THINK  *MA
*PO  DO   *EN         *PO  CAUSE  *EN        *SO  FLOW  DTHIS
```

Two possible types of word-sense ambiguity may be resolved during this stage. The first of these is noun–verb homography, e.g. *father* meaning 'male parent' or 'to cause to have life'. Thus two alternative strings of formulae heads may be considered for a sentence such as (13).

(13) a. Small men father small sons.

b. KIND MAN MAN KIND MAN

c. KIND MAN CAUSE KIND MAN

Bare template matching will eliminate the first of these, since no sequence of three heads is derivable from the inventory, but the second reading, based on MAN CAUSE MAN, is retained, MAN being a member of both the classes *PO and *EN.

The second type of ambiguity resolved includes certain cases of noun–noun polysemy, since a given verb imposes restrictions on the semantic classes of nouns with which it may occur. For example, *sport* may mean 'an organized activity' or 'a certain type of man', giving two readings for (14).

(14) a. My brother is a good sport.

b. THIS MAN BE KIND MAN

c. THIS MAN BE KIND GRAIN

The template associated with BE specifies that the formulae filling the actor and object roles of the triple must have the same head, so that it will be unable to match onto the second (MAN BE GRAIN) reading, and only the 'type of man' reading for *sport* will remain. Whether a given instance of noun–noun homography will be resolved at this stage depends upon the verb involved. For example, given the two senses of *crook*, i.e. 'criminal' and 'shepherd's staff', there will be two readings for the sentence (15).

(15) a. The policeman interrogated the crook.

b. MAN FORCE MAN

c. MAN FORCE THING

However, both MAN and THING occur in *EN, the class of legal objects of FORCE, so these two senses will not be resolved at this stage.

The bare templates are the only well-formedness rules in the system, i.e. the only ones specifying absolute restrictions on co-occurrence. The restrictions are

---

1. The two occurrences of *AL must be the same.

very weak, being stated in terms of formulae heads only. This ensures that even fairly "deviant" utterances will be assigned some sort of "meaning", and provides the raw material for the application of preference considerations in the next phase (see Section 10.6).

10.5.2 Template rankings

A fragment does not necessarily feature the actor–act–object roles in this canonical order, nor need each role be present. Therefore, various nonstandard and debilitated forms of templates are also considered during the matching process. These forms are ordered into four ranks, so that the forms in one rank are considered only if there was no match with a form in the previous rank. When a match with a nonstandard form is found, the equivalent standard form is assigned as the actual template of the fragment. The ranks are shown in Table 10.1.

Table 10.1 Template rankings.

Rank	"Text-items"	Standard form
1	N1 + V + N2	N1 + V + N2
	V + N1 + N2	N1 + V + N2
	N1 + N2 + V	N1 + V + N2
	N1 + V	N1 + V + DTHIS
	V + N1	DTHIS + V + N1
	N1 + V + KIND	N1 + V + KIND
	KIND + N1	N1 + DBE + KIND
2	N1 + KIND + V	N1 + V + KIND
	V + N1 + KIND	N1 + V + KIND
	N1 + KIND	N1 + DBE + KIND
	N1 + N2	N1 + DBE + N2
3	V + KIND	DTHIS + V + KIND
4	V	DTHIS + V + DTHIS
	N1	DTHIS + DBE + N1
	KIND	DTHIS + DBE + KIND

Thus a role which is missing in the fragment is filled in the standard template by the dummy verb DBE or the dummy noun DTHIS as appropriate.

The reasons for various patterns of text-items can be illustrated by considering some typical results of fragmentation, e.g. (16)–(18).

(16) **(JOHN IS) (IN THE HOUSE)**
     N1 V   **V**   **N1**

(17) **(THE MAN) (IN THE CORNER) (LEFT)**
     N1   **V**   **N1**   **V**

(18) **(THE OLD COMMA) (FRAIL MAN)**
     KIND   **KIND N1**

10.6 Template extension

It is in this phase that the notion of preference is first invoked in order to effect more extensive disambiguation. What distinguishes the preference approach from other treatments of ambiguity is its active nature. Wilks is committed to the view that it is impossible to develop a single set of well-formedness constraints that would be both:

- strong enough to eliminate all but one analysis of a text fragment that is ambiguous except in a global context, and
- weak enough to provide an analysis for a fragment that is grammatically "deviant" in some sense, but whose meaning is "obvious".

During template extension, a score is computed which indicates the degree to which preferences are satisfied, and then an active choice is made between competing analyses on the basis of this score. Thus "grammaticality" is viewed as a scale of acceptability in context, rather than an "all-or-nothing" phenomenon.

In this way, (19) would be accepted, since there is no animate entity present to fulfil the preference of *drink* for such a subject:

(19) My car drinks petrol.

The EXTEND routine seeks to set up dependencies between the formulae associated with a fragment, adding one to the score for a particular reading of the fragment for each dependency compatible with the bare template corresponding to that reading. The dependencies are of two types, i.e. dependencies between the formulae associated with the bare template (type A) and dependencies of the other formulae on those of the bare template (type B).

10.6.1 Type A extension

The formulae for verbal word-senses indicate the preferred characteristics of their associated agents and objects as prepositional (type 2) subformulae (see Section 10.3.2). Thus, of the two interpretations of (15a) above, (15b) will be preferred (its score will be higher), since the formula for *interrogate* has the subformula (MAN OBJE).

10.6.2 Type B extension

The permissible forms of dependencies of other formulae on the noun and verb formulae of the bare template are expressed as a series of context-free rewrite rules (20a) or (20b), where y is a permissible dependant on an item of type x.

(20) a. $x \rightarrow x\ y$

   b. $x \rightarrow y\ x$

The ordering of the items on the right-hand side is important. The full list is as follows (items are given in terms of conventional syntactic categories, though it should be remembered that, e.g. ADJECTIVE actually means a formula with the head KIND).

NOUN $\rightarrow$ ADJECTIVE NOUN (e.g. *red book*)

VERB → ADVERB VERB (e.g. *opened slowly*, after REORDERing)

NOUN → ARTICLE NOUN (e.g. *the book*)

NOUN → OF NOUN FO NOUN (e.g. *the house of my father*, after
  REORDERing)

ADJECTIVE → ADVERB ADJECTIVE (e.g. *very much*)

VERB → VERB PARTICLE (e.g. *give up*)

GIVE → GIVE NOUN (where GIVE is the head of a ditransitive verb,
  e.g. *tell him*)

VERB → AUXILIARY VERB (e.g. *was going*)

VERB → *to* VERB (e.g. *to relax*)

When a tense auxiliary is accepted, its meaning is incorporated as a tense marker (PRES, IMPE, PAST or FUTU) into the formula of the main verb, and does not contribute to the score.

10.6.3 Examples and discussion

The rule for extending ditransitive verbs is best illustrated by example. Bare template matching will result in the alternative assignment of the roles in the *PO GIVE *EN template, as in (21).

> (21) John gave Mary the book.
> MAN GIVE MAN MAN GIVE THING

No rule applies to extend the first of these, but a GIVE type verb may be extended by a NOUN type formula immediately to the right which is not already incorporated in the bare template. The second bare template also permits the incorporation of *the* into a full template, giving the dependency structure in (22)

> (22) John ⟷ gave ⟷ book
>   ↓   ↓
>   Mary   the

Each of the ↓ dependencies contributes one point to the score, so the second (MAN GIVE THING) reading has a score of 2, and is thus chosen in preference to the first reading, with a score of 0.

Another example may serve to illustrate some problems of this approach to disambiguation. The fragment *the old transport system* will be immediately recognized by the human reader as a noun phrase. Bare template matching will have assigned the three alternatives in (23).

> (23) a. the old transport system
>   b. FOLK DO GRAIN
>   c. KIND GRAIN
>   d. KIND GRAIN

The first reading takes *old* as a noun, as in (24a), and *transport* as an active verb, as in (24b).

> (24) a. The old are often poor.
>   b. Planes transport people.

The latter two readings will be converted to standard form (see Section 10.5.2) by incorporation of the dummy verb DBE, giving in both cases the template GRAIN DBE KIND, and corresponding to the readings 'system is old' and 'system is transport' respectively. Leaving aside consideration of *the*, the only one of the three templates that may be extended is the second, by the rule which incorporates an adjective to the left of a noun. This corresponds to the intuitively correct reading, i.e. 'the transport system is old'.

Notice that this reading has been preferred largely because the bare template was packed with a dummy symbol, thus leaving more words to be considered by template extension, thereby contributing to the score for the reading. But the number of dummies that may be incorporated into a bare template is strictly limited by the ranking of templates given in Section 10.5.2, for which there appears to be little theoretical motivation. It is far from obvious that this sort of approach is going to contribute to the assignment of correct interpretations to fragments in all cases. For instance, consider a fragment such as (25), which will probably be treated as a complex noun phrase, but which is more likely to be a complete sentence.

(25) The poor burnt charcoal.

The obliteration of sentence boundaries by fragmentation will seriously hinder resolution of what is a simple syntactic problem.

In addition, it is unclear whether the internal structure of complex noun phrases can be correctly assigned by such means. For instance, consider the fragment (26).

(26) a. wooden toy manufacturers
     b. KIND THING MAN

This will be assigned the two alternative readings of the rank template KIND + N1, i.e. 'toy be wooden', 'manufacturers be wooden'. The former is a correct reading as far as it goes, but does not include the nucleus of the noun phrase, and is therefore an inadequate parse. It is difficult to see how this could be parsed successfully within the present PS framework.

In early documentation, an extra disambiguation routine is described. This is called when two readings for a given fragment have the same score, and attempts to establish additional "semantic overlap", between actor and object formulae. The example given is the resolution of the ambiguity in (27), where *leg* could be read as a part of the body of a man, or as the support of an inanimate object.

(27) The man lost his leg.

The (MAN PART) subformula which appears in the formula for the former sense has the requisite overlap with the formula of the actor role, and thus it is this reading which is chosen.

Although this sort of consideration would appear to have great potential, the routine is not mentioned in later system descriptions. It may have been too difficult to formulate such criteria to make them generally applicable (but see the use of "semantic overlap" predicates such as PRMKOB and 2OBCAS in Section 10.7.4).

10.7 Generation

Determination of the case relations between fragments, which constitutes the final stage of disambiguation (in the basic mode of the system), is effected during the generation of the French output. In order not to mislead the reader over the interdependence of analysis and generation, we choose to describe the operation of the generation routines first.

10.7.1 Simple stereotypes

In the description of the system's operation, we talked about disambiguation between word senses represented as formulae. However, as mentioned in Section 10.2, the dictionary associates a list of stereotypes with each formula. Therefore, in selecting a particular formula, its associated stereotypes have also been selected. In the simplest case, there will be a single stereotype which will provide a unique translation equivalent for the word sense. For example, the analysis routines will have chosen the correct sense of *red* as indicated by the formula–stereotype pairs in (28).

 (28) a. (((WHERE SPREAD) KIND) (RED (ROUGE)))

   b. ((((WORLD CHANGE) WANT) MAN) (RED (SOCIALISTE)))

Thus the basic stereotype evaluation routine $MAP will simply return the French equivalent when called with whichever of these sense pairs remains in the semantic block.

10.7.2 More complex stereotypes

In the more general case, there may be more than one French equivalent for a given English word-sense. There will then be a list of stereotypes, one for each equivalent, and each (except perhaps the last) incorporating a function over the context in which the word occurs. The routine $SELECT takes the list as its value and passes each stereotype in turn to $MAP for evaluation. The first stereotype whose function evaluates to a non-NIL value will be concatenated by $MAP to the end of the text-string generated so far, and no subsequent stereotypes will then be evaluated.

For example, the stereotype for *advise* has the following form (29).

 (29) (ADVISE (CONSEILLER (PREOB A MAN)) (CONSEILLER))

PREOB is a function which returns its first parameter, a French preposition (here *à*) followed by the translation of the object (by recursive call) if that object has as its head the second parameter (here MAN). Thus if the object were *children*, as in (30a), the value of the stereotype would be (30b). If the sentence was (31), PREOB would evaluate to NIL, so the first stereotype would fail.

 (30) a. I advised my children.

   b. *conseiller à mes enfants*

 (31) I advised patience.

The second would then be evaluated, giving *conseiller*. The higher level generation function from which ($SELECT ADVISE) was called would then take care of the generation of *patience*, for which no special action would be needed.

10.7.3 Control of generation

The top-level control function for generation examines each fragment in turn. Its action depends on the form of the template associated with the fragment, as follows, where: V is any verb except BE, DBE, PBE or PDO; *REAL is any noun head or KIND; and *ANY is *REAL or DTHIS.

> 1. N1 + V + *ANY   simple active sentence
>   N1 + BE + KIND   simple active sentence
> 2. DTHIS + V + *ANY   action without subject, or infinitive
> 3. N1 + DBE + DTHIS   subject without action
> 4. DTHIS + PDO + *REAL   prepositional phrase
>   DTHIS + PBE + *REAL   prepositional phrase

Each template type is associated with a (high-level) stereotype. In the case of a type 1 template, the stereotype is INDCL, which calls the function CLAUSE-GROUP. The latter merely calls $SELECT for each word of the fragment in turn.

Notice that in the case of the stereotype for *advise* (29) PREOB effected the translation of the object by a recursive call to $SELECT. The generation routines maintain housekeeping information to indicate what has already been translated. In general, the stereotype for almost any word can take control over the translation of other words, even those in different fragments, so that the whole process of generation involves a complex control passing back and forth between stereotypes.

If the full sentence to be translated was (32), then the fragment *to leave* would be translated correctly as *de partir* by the default stereotype associated with an infinitive (type 2) template, i.e. (DE (INFVP)).

> (32) I advised my children to leave.

However, the sentence (33) would require the translation *à partir*. In this case, the stereotype for *urge* would take over the generation for the infinitival fragment as in (34).

> (33) I urged my children to leave.
> (34) (URGE (EXHORTER (DIROB MAN) (FIND-LINK VP) @ (A
>   (INFVP))))

DIROB will translate *my children* as a direct object. FIND-LINK then searches through the text representation for a fragment of type VP. If this is found, *urge* becomes the mark of the VP fragment, i.e. the word on which the VP has a dependency. The *urge* stereotype then halts (indicated by @). When control arrives at this fragment – which may not be contiguous, cf. (35) – a check is made to see if the stereotype for its mark, i.e. *urge*, has been halted. If so, then control returns to (A (INFVP)), generating *à partir*, and the actual stereotype for *to leave* will never be consulted.

> (35) I urged my children, who(m) I love, to leave.

Translation of the sentence (36a) as (36b) is achieved by a halting stereotype for *drink* as in (36c), where PROBJE is a function which returns the translation of its object only if its argument is found in the object formula.

(36) a. I drink wine out of a glass.

    b. *Je bois du vin dans une verre.*

    c. (DRINK (BOIRE (PROBJE (FLOW STUFF)) (FIND-LTNK PR)

        @ (PREOB DANS THING)))

Since wine is a liquid, (FLOW STUFF) occurs, and PROBJE evaluates to *vin*.[2] FIND-LINK searches for a fragment having a prepositional (type 4) template, and *drink* becomes the mark of this fragment. The subsequent pattern of control is then analogous to that for *urge* above.

Wilks claims that this treatment is necessary because the translation of *out of* or *from* as *dans* is "specific to the occurrence of certain French words, such as *boire*, rather than to the application of certain concepts". But this would appear to be an over-simplification, given the plausible translations in (37) and (38).

(37) a. I drink water out of the well.

    b. *Je bois de l'eau du puit.*

(38) a. I steal the book from the room.

    b. *Je vole le livre dans la chambre.*

10.7.4 Paraplates

Usually, the translation of a preposition will not be dictated by the stereotype for its mark, but by paraplates associated with the preposition. In general, by the time control arrives at the prepositional fragment, its mark will not have been determined. It is the function of a paraplate to locate it in a previous fragment, to ascertain the case relationship of the prepositional fragment to the mark, and to generate the appropriate translation for the preposition. Thus a paraplate is merely a stereotype which specifies, in addition to the generation functions, predicates on the items in the fragment containing the possible mark, and the case tie to be assigned if these predicates evaluate to T (true).

For example, the list of paraplates for *with* is as in (39).

(39) a. ((PRMKOB *ENT) (POSS) (PREOB A *ENT))

    b. ((PRMARK *DO) (INST) (PREOB AVEC THING))

    c. ((PRMARK *ENT) (POSS) (PREOB A *REAL))

The predicate PRMKOB in (39a) searches for a mark in the previous two fragments, examining only those formulae whose heads are in the class of its argument *ENT, i.e. THING, MAN, FOLK, BEAST, or WORLD. It returns T only if the formula for the object of the preposition can be a part of the entity which is the candidate mark. The case relation between the fragments has been resolved as POSS. PREOB then generates the correct translation (*à* for *with*) for a sentence such as (40) since the formula for *leg* contains the subformula (MAN PART).

(40) He hit the boy with the wooden leg.

If PRMKOB fails, as in the case of (41), the second paraplate (39b) is tried. The predicate PRMARK searches for a mark with its argument as head (here any verb,

---

2. Concord routines applied later will take care of generating *du vin*.

indicated by *DO). If it succeeds, and the object of the preposition is a physical object (PREOB THING), then the case relation is INST, and *avec* is correctly generated.

(41) He hit the boy with a stick.

In the case of failure of both of these, the third paraplate (39c) specifies weaker conditions, that the object of the preposition is in *REAL, i.e. any nominal, and assumes the latter is related by case POSS. This will cope with sentences such as (42).

(42) He hit the boy with the blue shirt.

Paraplates may also help to resolve outstanding word-sense ambiguity. For example, the paraplates for *in* are shown in (43) (the French equivalents have been omitted for ease of explanation).

(43) a. ((PRMARK (MOVE CAUSE)) (2OBCAS INST GOAL) (TO)
     (PROBJE CONT THING))

   b. ((PRMARK *DO) (2OBHEAD) (LOCA))

   c. ((PRMARK (MOVE CAUSE)) (TO) (PROBJE CONT THING))

2OBCAS and 2OBHEAD are predicates that compare the formulae which occupy the object role in the templates assigned to the current (prepositional) fragment and the mark fragment. 2OBCAS is T if they contain the same subformulae indicated by the arguments, in this case, the same INSTrument or GOAL. 2OBHEAD is T if they have the same head. The first stereotype (43a) would succeed for the *in* of (44) given the 'door fastener' sense of *lock*, since *key* and *lock* both have a subformula indicating their GOAL is to close something. Therefore the 'canal' reading of *lock*, which may still be present in the text representation at this point, will now be eliminated.

(44) I put the key in the lock.

The ambiguity of *table* ('list' or 'flat object') in (45) will be resolved successfully by the second paraplate (43b), as the 'flat object' reading will have the same head, THING, as the formula for *fork*.

(45) He put the fork in the table.

Similarly, (46) will be resolved correctly, as the 'list' reading has the head SIGN, the same as that for *number*. The third paraplate (43c) is a weaker version of (43a), i.e. without the 2OBCAS predicate, which will cope with more general examples of *in* as the direction case marker.

(46) I put the number in the table.

Note that the ordering of paraplates is crucial, in that the earlier ones specify stronger conditions, i.e. more preferred case relations, and only if these conditions are not filled are less preferred relations accepted (i.e. the later paraplates evaluated).

10.8 Anaphora resolution

10.8.1 Basic mode resolution

The stereotype for a pronoun initiates a search for possible antecedents in the preceding fragments. Alternative antecedents represent alternative readings for the fragment containing the pronoun. This ambiguity may be resolvable from simple preference considerations such as those described in Section 10.6.1. For example, given the sentence (47), there will be two readings for each fragment containing an occurrence of *they*, corresponding to the bare templates (48) and (49).

(47) Give the bananas to the monkeys although they are not ripe because they are very hungry.

(48) a. BANANAS ARE RIPE
    b. MONKEYS ARE RIPE

(49) a. BANANAS ARE HUNGRY
    b. MONKEYS ARE HUNGRY

The formulae for *ripe* and *hungry* contain an indication that they prefer to be applied to plant-like and animate things respectively, and thus the correct resolutions (48a) and (49b) will be chosen.

10.8.2 Extended mode resolution

If the "superficial" conceptual information contained in the relevant formulae is inadequate to resolve anaphora, the system enters extended mode. This proceeds by an extraction of various template-like forms from the relevant text templates (i.e. those containing possible antecedents and that containing the pronoun itself), followed by an attempt to relate the extracted forms by means of common-sense inference rules (CSIRs).

Extractions

Extractions are obtained by:

(i) Unpacking the case ties from the formulae involved. For instance, the formula for *drink* specifies ((MAN PART) TO) as the destination of the object of *drink*, and (SELF IN) as a result of the action. Therefore, the fragment (X DRINK Y) give the extractions [Y DIRE (to) X-PART] and [Y IN (in) X].

(ii) Insertions of the mark of a preposition into the prepositional fragment, e.g. (X DRINK Y) (DTHIS DIRE (from) Z) gives the extraction [Y DIRE (from) Z], consistent with the case determined by paraplate application.

Thus, from the text (50), which will have the basic template structure as in (51) (lexical items are given rather than formula heads for clarity), will be derived the extractions in (52).

(50) John drank whisky from a glass and it felt warm in his stomach.

(51) a. JOHN DRINK WHISKY
    b. DTHIS DIRE (from) GLASS
    c. ?IT FEEL WARM
    d. DTHIS IN (in) STOMACH

(52) a. WHISKY DIRE (to) JOHN + PART　　from (51a) by (i)
　　 b. WHISKY IN (in) JOHN　　　　　　　from (51a) by (i)
　　 c. WHISKY DIRE (from) GLASS　　　　from (51a) and (51b) by (ii)
　　 d. ?IT IN (in) JOHN + STOMACH　　　from (51c) and (51d) by (ii)

From this pool of template forms, Wilks claims that (52d) may be fuzzy matched directly onto (52b), thus resolving *it* as *whisky* (this assumes that *his* has already been resolved as *John's*). Since this is the shortest possible chain between a template form containing the anaphor and one containing a possible antecedent, it will be preferred. Only if this "zero-point" strategy fails will inferences be employed.

Inferences will be needed for resolving *it* in the text (53) which will have the templates in (54) and give rise to the extractions in (55).

(53) John drank the whisky on the table and it was good.

(54) a. JOHN DRINK WHISKY
　　 b. DTHIS LOCA (on) TABLE
　　 c. ?IT BE GOOD

(55) a. WHISKY DIRE (to) JOHN + PART　　from (54a) by (i)
　　 b. WHISKY IN (in) JOHN　　　　　　　from (52a) by (i)
　　 c. WHISKY LOCA (on) TABLE　　　　　from (52a) and (52b) by (ii)

Common-sense inference rules

CSIRs are rules relating two templates by a one ($\rightarrow$) or two ($\leftrightarrow$) way inference. They are intended only to correspond to likely sequences of cause and effect, rather than deductions that are necessarily true.

CSIRs may contain variables (expressed as integers), and restrictions on these (the restrictions need be stated on one side of the rule only).

The common-sense notion that if some thing is good, some animate creature wants it, and vice versa, is expressed by (56).

(56) (1 BE (GOOD KIND)) $\leftrightarrow$ ((*AN 2) (WANT) 1)

While if some animate creature causes some real thing to be in itself, then it will judge that thing (57).

(57) (((*AN 1) (SELF IN) (MOVE CAUSE)) (*REAL 2)) $\rightarrow$
　　　(1 (*JUDGE) 2)

The class *JUDGE includes WANT, FEEL, etc.

Inferencing

The process of inferencing proceeds from both ends of the chain, i.e. from the template containing the anaphor, and from those containing the possible antecedents. All inference rules containing an action subformula which appears in these templates are applied, and the shortest chain is considered to have resolved the anaphor correctly.

In the case of (58), the inference chain will proceed as shown.

(58) John drank the whisky on the table and it was good.

```
1 JOHN  DRINK  WHISKY                              (52a)
2 JOHN  CAUSE-TO-MOVE-IN-SELF  WHISKY   eq. to (52a) ↓
3 JOHN  *JUDGE  WHISKY by (57)                 from 2 ↓
4 JOHN  WANT  WHISKY by *JUDGE  →  WANT         from 3 ↓
                                     and by (57) from 5 ↑
5 WHISKY  BE  GOOD            substitution for ?IT in 6 ↑
6 ?IT  BE  GOOD                                    (52c)
```

At step 4 the forward and backward inference chains converge, confirming the hypothesis of step 5, that *it* refers to the *whisky*. Were other CSIRs present, alternative chains might be derivable, but the one given will almost certainly be the shortest.

10.9 Evaluation of PS

Wilks pre-empts much of the criticism that could be levelled at the PS system by repeatedly stating that he would not defend various aspects of it, such as the detailed contents of dictionaries and rules, or the particular control structure of the programs. However, in order to give an idea of the system's strong and weak points, we discuss in turn each component of the system in which the knowledge used for translation resides, attempting to evaluate the form in which it occurs.

10.9.1 Dictionary

Wilks claims that his is essentially a dictionary-based system, and it is true that the form of the dictionary entries is one of its significant innovative aspects. Their significance lies, as Wilks point out, not in the particular set of primitives from which they are constructed, but in the way these may be structured within formulae to give as much information about a word sense as could be considered useful for understanding. The primitive vocabulary is not intended to be capable of representing the differences between any two or more lexical items in any language, e.g. between *hammer* and *mallet*. There is no unique mapping from formula to lexeme for a given language.

10.9.2 *-classes

The *-classes of nouns and verbs (*ENT, *JUDGE, etc.) are used throughout the system, i.e. in dictionary entries, bare templates, stereotypes, CSIRs. They appear to be introduced whenever convenient, on an *ad hoc* basis. Since they perform the important role of structuring the set of primitives in a useful and very justifiable way, it is surprising that they are not given a more formal basis.

10.9.3 Fragmentation

Since the fragmentation procedure is barely described, it is difficult to assess. It is in this that the majority of the purely syntactic knowledge which the system uses is concentrated, and one of Wilks's strong claims is that such knowledge is not really important. What is obvious is that the representational facilities used in later stages of the system would not be capable of expressing syntactic distinctions of subtlety, and therefore there would be little point in computing them. Whether PS is really capable of handling such phenomena as co-ordination accurately is not apparent.

10.9.4 Bare templates

The inventory of bare templates is not intended to be other than a very coarse means of disambiguation. If it were possible to define new subclasses of primitives, its role could be refined. However, it is the coarseness of the subclasses which provides the weak constraints on grammaticality that are necessary for the preference approach to be effective. Therefore there would be little point in improving the level of detail of linguistic knowledge that is expressed in the form of bare templates

10.9.5 Extension rules/template rankings

The rather unclear manner in which the extension rules interact with the rankings of template forms has already been mentioned in Section 10.6.3. In fact, since the rankings are crucial to the disambiguation process, it would be helpful if they were given a stronger theoretical basis. It is not obvious that a table of rankings would be applicable in describing other languages with more free word order, since one would have to distinguish between nonstandard forms resulting from fragmentation and those with significant semantic content.

The fact that the syntactic information about the SL which has been found necessary for translation is represented in diverse ways, i.e. in fragmentation, formula heads, template rankings and type B extension rules, would make adding to it very difficult.

In addition, this *ad hoc* approach to syntax must exaggerate the problems of ambiguity, since, after all, it is the role of syntax to distinguish between utterances which may make reference to identical lexical concepts and yet have totally different meanings.

10.9.6 Stereotypes and paraplates

In generation, the pervasive notion of preference is realized as a linear ordering on stereotypes. Thus the choice of the appropriate one is intimately bound up with the others which are present. Add to this the highly procedural nature of individual stereotypes and the fact that determination of case ties is also interleaved with stereotype application, and it becomes obvious that the linguistic knowledge in this part of the system would be very difficult to refine and extend.

10.9.7 CSIRs

The extended mode and the use of CSIRs represents an interesting and extensible approach to the problem of real-world knowledge. The fact that the text is represented as a sequence of messages having a very similar structure – that of the template – and with the relevant information easily accessible (in terms of the *-classes) enables the causal relationships expressed as CSIRs to be stated simply and applied in a chained fashion.

Wilks conjectures that the maximum number of CSIRs which would need to be applied to resolve anaphora is two. However, this would almost certainly be inadequate for other understanding tasks such as question-answering. If it were necessary to deal with long chains and many inference rules, the problems of imposing an organization on the rules so that heuristics could be defined would have to be faced.

10.10 Software and hardware details

PS is programmed in LISP 1.6 (the fragmentation, bare template matching and extension routines) and MLISP 2 (the generation and extended mode routines). The program swaps in two large core images of 46K and 50K and two small ones of 5K each.

The dictionary comprises 500 entries. A paragraph of text takes about 6 CPU-seconds to process, but if inferencing is required, a quite simple sentence may take as long.

10.11 Final comments

If Wilks's ideas on dictionary organization and common-sense knowledge, plus an implementation of preference which does not depend on enumeration of alternatives, could be combined with a more theoretically based treatment of syntactic phenomena and a less procedural approach to TL generation, it would represent a significant advance in the state of the art in MT. However, it is not immediately apparent that increasing the power of the representation to include syntactic details would not have an adverse effect on the complexity of expression of semantic and real-world knowledge.

10.12 Documentation

The PS system was developed over several years, and the literature reflects this. The dictionary, fragmentation routines, bare templates and extension are introduced in

Wilks (1972). Wilks (1973a,b) (essentially the same paper) discusses these in more detail and introduce the notions of stereotype and paraplate. Wilks & Herskovits (1973) discuss the generation component (written by Annette Herskovits) in greater detail. Two papers (Wilks, 1975a,b) start to address the problems of incorporating real-world knowledge, and Wilks (1975c) describes a solution in the form of CSIRs. Wilks (1978) discusses the imposition of a thesaurus-like organization over dictionary entries, and the use of frame-like knowledge structures. These ideas are not implemented, so we have not considered them here.

Wilks, Y. A. 1972. *Grammar, meaning, and the machine analysis of language.* London: Routledge & Kegan Paul.

Wilks, Y. A. 1973a. The Stanford Machine Translation project. In *Natural language processing*, R. Rustin (ed.), 243–90.. New York: Algorithmics Press.

Wilks, Y. A. 1973b. An Artificial Intelligence approach to Machine Translation. In *Computer models of thought and language*, R. Schank & K. M. Colby (eds), 114–51. San Francisco: Freeman.

Wilks, Y. A. 1975a. An intelligent analyzer and understander of English. *Communications of the ACM* **18**, 264–74.

Wilks, Y. A. 1975b. Preference semantics. In *The formal semantics of natural language*, E. L. Keenan (ed.), 329–50. Cambridge: Cambridge University Press.

Wilks, Y. A. 1975c. A preferential pattern-seeking semantics for natural language inference. *Artificial Intelligence* **6**, 53–74.

Wilks, Y. A. 1978. Making preferences more active. *Artificial Intelligence* **11**, 197–223.

Wilks, Y. A. & A. Herskovits 1973. An intelligent analyzer and generator for natural language. In *Computational and mathematical linguistics*, A. Zampolli & N. Calzolari (eds), 741–68. Amsterdam: North-Holland.

11
METAL

11.1 Introduction

METAL is the translation component of a total software package for the definition and application of linguistic data, developed by the Linguistics Research Center (LRC) of the University of Texas, Austin. The LRC began working on MT in 1961, though its early research was largely theoretical. Like that of other groups at this time, the LRC's conception of MT was founded on the interlingua philosophy and was also influenced by the then current theories of Transformational Grammar. A system for German–English translation based on these ideas was implemented during the years 1972–1975. However, the complexities of transformational parsing and the inadequacies of the syntactic interlingua eventually led the LRC to redesign their system according to different principles.

Of all the systems described in this collection[1], METAL has undergone the most development since the original text of this book was written. Notably, METAL has completed the full cycle from basic research system, through R&D prototype to full commercial release in 1989. Further language pairs have been treated, including Spanish, French, Dutch and Danish at research laboratories in Barcelona, Leuven (Belgium) and Kolding (Denmark). Along with commercialization has come the registering of the name METAL as a trademark, which is hereby acknowledged. Most of the changes have involved either the software environment surrounding

---

1. This paragraph has been added for this edition — HLS

the linguistic modules described in this chapter, or else fine details of the linguistic implementation. As far as we know, the underlying computational and linguistic approach has remained intact, and is as described here. Because the developments in METAL are so wide-ranging, we have added several footnotes indicating the main developments, and an extensive bibliography of more recent articles.

11.2 Basic nature of the system

In 1977, the Rome Air Development Corporation made funding available to the LRC for the development of an operational MT system based on state-of-the-art principles, METAL. By 1980, funding had been taken over by Siemens[2]. The main application of the system to date[3] has been the translation of telecommunications texts from German into English, though other applications (e.g. English analysis) are currently[4] the subject of experimentation. METAL is constructed in a modular fashion that enables it to be interfaced with application-specific routines tailoring it to the needs of a particular language, text type, translation type, linguistic theory, etc.

Like its predecessor, METAL owes a large debt to mainstream theoretical linguistics, with different algorithmic components dedicated to the treatment of such phenomena as context-free PS rules, transformations, and case frames.[5] However, in the new system, the PS rules define a surface grammar, and the transformations convert structures built by these into deeper-level structures, so that the problems associated with classical transformational parsing (i.e. applying deep-to-surface transformations in reverse) are obviated. The structures built are not intended to be language independent representations, but are passed to a bilingual transfer phase. However, transfer subsumes operations normally performed during structural generation and even morphological generation; and control over transfer is effected solely by transfer procedures attached by the analysis rules which built the representation, the two sets of rules being conceived as a single entity. Hence METAL is far from being a transfer system in the conventional sense.[6]

METAL is implemented in (a dialect of) LISP and the linguistic data which it uses for translation are expressed in one of two ways; certain linguistic phenomena are described in a form suitable for direct execution by the system functions, others are LISP functions themselves, which are passed as parameters to system functions. Since

---

2. Now Siemens-Nixdorf. — HLS

3. That is, at the time of writing of the 1st edition. — HLS

4. See footnote 3.

5. Recent publications concentrate on various aspects of METAL's linguistic approach: Gebruers (1988) describes the use of valency; Thurmair (1990b) mentions the influence of X-bar theory, and gives some details of the coverage of the system; Thurmair (1991) discusses the treatment of anaphora. — HLS

6. With the development of further language pairs, it was found that a stricter separation of analysis, transfer and generation was desirable, cf. Thurmair (1990a: p. 91), and to the design of a common intermediate representation MIR (METAL Interface Representation) for true multilinguality (cf. Alonso 1990). — HLS

LISP functions may be executed according to a strictly data-driven model, and since the permitted form of the data functions is highly restricted, the fact that data may actually be algorithmic does not contravene the principle of strict separation of the two components. In fact, such an organization confers real advantages. As well as reducing the total software, the linguistic data may be interpreted directly by the LISP interpreter, without the need for compilation into a form suitable for execution by an interpreter. This provides the means for data to be written and tested with minimum delay. However, once tested, the data may be compiled for greater efficiency.

The three principle phases of the translation chain are realised by the three LISP functions, PARSE, TRANSFER and GENERATE, which are called in order by the top-level drive function TRANSLATE. The latter expects a sentence in the source language (SL) and returns as its value the equivalent sentence in the target language (TL). PARSE and TRANSFER call other functions. Functions are of two types: core functions, which are permanent in the sense that they do not vary with the SL/TL languages being treated, nor with the type of linguistic theory being implemented; and application-specific functions as described above, which are user defined, although the system provides appropriate defaults.

The core functions are:

```
TRANSLATE
PARSE
DO-TXFORM
DO-TXFORMS
FIND-FRAME
TRANSFER
TLX
XLX
GENERATE
```

The application-specific functions are:

```
USER-PREPROCESSOR
USER-WORD
USER-ADD
USER-IDIOM
USER-RULE
USER-ERROR
USER-POSTPROCESSOR
```

11.3 Data structure

The data structure of METAL may be divided into two components, computational and linguistic. The parser itself manipulates only a chart, whose properties have been discussed extensively elsewhere, and has access only to the roots of the structures which label the edges, and to certain other limited information. The complete form of the labels, i.e. the linguistic structure of well-formed phrases in the input, is determined by the application-specific module USER-RULE (see Section 11.5). These may be syntax trees, database queries or whatever else the user chooses.

11.4 Monolingual dictionaries

METAL dictionaries are either monolingual or bilingual.[7] The latter are used for lexical transfer. SL and TL (monolingual) dictionary entries are essentially of the same form, though they are accessed differently – via ALO values in the case of SL dictionaries, and via CAN values in the case of TL dictionaries.

Monolingual dictionaries contain lexical entries for all elements analyzed by the system, including word stems, idioms, affixes, punctuation, symbols, etc.

Each entry is essentially a list of feature + value pairs. The first item on the list is reserved for values of the feature "canonical form", whose feature name (CAN) is in fact omitted. This item is followed on the same line by the feature CAT(egory), and on the next line by the feature ALO (allomorph). These first three items are the only obligatory ones. The format is:

```
(<canonical form> CAT (<category>)
   ALO (<allomorph>)
   <feature 1> (<list of values>)
   <feature 2> (<list of values>)
   .
   .
   .
   <feature n> (<list of values>)
```

At one time, the dictionary entries for each ALO corresponding to a particular CAN were conflated, that is, a list of different ALO values would appear in the ALO line of the entry, and subsequent lines would give a list of the corresponding ALO-dependent feature values. These lines were separated from the rest of the entry (i.e. ALO-independent features and values) by $, e.g.

---

7. Much is made in later publications of the fact that METAL's dictionaries are highly structured, forming a hierarchical structure with function word dictionary, general vocabulary and "common technical vocabulary" at the top, through general and then specific subject-oriented terminological dictionaries down to customer- or product-specific dictionaries (see Schneider 1987: p. 125). The *size* of the dictionaries developed so far depends on the language pair, but ranges from 20 000 to 90 000 words according to Thurmair (1990b). Schneider (1991, 1992) is evasive on this topic, while Little (1990: p. 102) mentions a dictionary with 30 000 entries delivered by Siemens. — HLS

```
(THIS  CAT (DET)
      ALO (this) (these)
      NU (SG) (PL) $
      PLC (WI WF)
      .

      .

      .

)
```

It now appears that a different entry corresponds to each ALO value, which is presumably intended to improve the efficiency of dictionary organization.

Any feature may have zero or more values. The same value may appear in the value list of different features, and the values of any features are formally compatible, i.e. there is no strong typing of values according to feature. Features used in dictionary entries are of two kinds, system features and specific features.

11.4.1 System features

System features are those to which the core functions may make reference, or those which are considered applicable to any lexical entry in any language, although the possible values that are defined for each may vary with the application (e.g. language pair, text type, etc.). The system features currently used are:

- CAN (canonical form). The values of this feature are character strings, corresponding to "morphemes", unique forms representative of possible paradigmatic variants. When two different morphemes have identical canonical forms, e.g. *table* (verb) vs. *table* (noun), these may be distinguished by means of an integer added to the end of the character string, e.g. TABLE1 vs. TABLE2. The values of CAN are used as entries to access the bilingual transfer dictionary.

- CAT (lexical category). Values of this feature correspond to morphological and syntactic classes, and include:

AST	adjective stem	CONJ	conjunction
NST	noun stem	PREP	preposition
VST	verb stem	PRN	pronoun
DET	determiner	N-FLEX	noun inflection
LOC	locative adverb	A-FLEX	adjective inflection
MAN	manner adverb	D-FLEX	determiner inflection
TMP	temporal adverb	V-FLEX	verb inflection
DEG	degree adverb	PNCT	punctuation

These values are used by PARSE in performing pattern-matching against the context-free rules: CAT is the principal component of the label on a chart edge which is accessible to PARSE, i.e. the root node. The nonterminal categories which are introduced by the context-free rules may thus also be considered as values of CAT.

- ALO (allomorph). Values represent the actual surface strings in which canonical forms may be realized. There may be several allomorphs corresponding to a single canonical form, when there exist, for instance, spelling variations or forms not recognizable by a regular morphological analysis. ALO is the key by which the analysis dictionaries are accessed.

- PLC (placement). This indicates the possible positions of the morph with respect to other morphs with which it may occur in a word. PLC values are used to limit the application of morphological level context-free rules; the possible values are:

WF	word final
WI	word initial
NI	noninitial
NF	nonfinal

These values often occur in clusters. For example, an inflection ending must occur word-finally, and never word-initially, i.e. (WF NI); a pronoun in English occurs only as an unbounded form, i.e. (WI WF).

- PRF (preference). Values of PRF are numeric: 1 indicates no preference, 2 indicates "twice as good", 0.5 indicates "half as good", etc. Such values are introduced in the dictionary so that a numerical ordering may be defined on all analyses discovered by PARSE, affording a means for choosing between alternatives. For example, a compound noun or fixed idiom may be entered as such in the dictionary with an indication of whether it is to be preferred to a reading derived by analyzing its components individually. During application of context-free rules the PRF values associated with the daughters are multiplied together and then by a PRF value provided by the rule being applied, to give a new value for the root of the phrase. At the end of analysis, the structure with the highest PRF value will usually be chosen by USER-POSTPROCESSER as the final output from PARSE and hence the input to TRANSFER.

- LEX (lexical collocation). This boolean-valued (T or NIL) feature is used to indicate whether a word may be a constituent of a variable (i.e. inflected) and discontinuous collocation. A T value will indicate to PARSE that special action must be taken. The documentation is unclear as to the precise action taken, the relationships between fixed and variable idioms, continuous and discontinuous idioms, context-free rule and dictionary representations of idioms, and the role of the function USER-IDIOM.

- SNS (sense number). It appears that this feature, whose values are integers, was originally used to distinguish between homographs, i.e. different lexemes realized by the same string; in later documentation it is used to distinguish different allomorphs of the same morpheme, i.e. different strings realizing the same lexeme.

- CNO (concept number). This feature may be used to assign a common index (an integer) to semantically related words. For example, *compute, computer, computation, computational* and *computable* would share the same concept number.

- TAG (area of provenience tag). This indicates the subject area(s) in which a particular word or word-sense is most likely to be used. Where multiple translations of a word are possible, the TAG value may be used to select the appropriate translation according to the subject area of the source text.

11.4.2 Specific features

Specific features are those which are particular to individual lexical items and/or to individual languages. They carry the additional morphological, syntactic and semantic information proper to an item and necessary for accurate translation. They include the more obvious morphosyntactic features like:

NU   grammatical number
GD   grammatical gender
PS   person
TN   tense
MD   mood
VC   voice
CL   inflectional class

These features may have their values assigned in the dictionary for certain items, such as GD for nouns, while the values for other items, such as GD for adjectives, will be assigned during analysis.

The feature TY (semantic type of noun) has as values a matrix of semantic attributes which may be used to characterize any given noun, e.g.

ENT   entity
MAT   material
LIV   living
TMP   temporal
COM   commodity
VOL   volitional

In the entry for a particular noun, each attribute is marked for "polarity", in one of the following ways:

+ <attribute>   The noun has the attribute.
− <attribute>   The noun does not have the attribute.
+/− <attribute>   The noun may or may not have the attribute, or it has certain subattributes but not others.
NIL   The attribute is irrelevant.

Semantic attributes are hierarchically structured, and in describing the set of attributes particular to a given noun, certain optional choices of values, e.g. −LIV, will automatically generate appropriate values for others, e.g. NIL for VOL.

TY values are used in imposing semantic co-occurrence restrictions between constituents. This is achieved by the use of what may be called "contextual features".

For example, the dictionary entries for verbs include the following contextual features:

- RA (role of argument(s)). Expresses functional relations between a verb and its arguments. Values are based on the "deep case" relations of case grammar theory, and include:

AGT	agent
TAR	target
BEN	benefactive
REC	recipient
INS	instrument
LOC	locative

  RAs are therefore case-frame features, representing all the possible central (i.e. verb specific) arguments that a particular verb may take. Peripheral roles, which are not verb-specific, are not specified. RAs serve an identificatory purpose, labelling potential arguments for further specification by other contextual features. Like TY values, RAs may be hierarchically structured. For instance, LOC, which occurs as a central argument of verbs of motion, subsumes STA (static location) and MOT (motion), and both of these in turn have more specific RAs as daughters. The reason for such a hierarchy is that certain prepositions will dictate that their phrases fill a certain argument role, and this role must be dominated in the hierarchy by the role specified for a particular verb in order for the phrases to be recognized as central arguments to that verb. There does not appear to be a facility for specifying that the optional arguments for a particular verb must not have certain RA values, though such a facility would appear to be of some use.

- TA (semantic type of argument(s)). Imposes semantic constraints on the arguments listed as RA values. TA values are identical to the TY values for nouns. For example, the verb *murder* requires that its AGT be +RSP (responsible); in the entry for *kill*, however, the AGT argument would be marked as +/-RSP, indicating that this verb may take an AGT marked +RSP, -RSP or +/-RSP.

- FA (constituent-type of argument(s)). Usual values are:

NP	noun phrase
PP	prepositional phrase
CP	clausal argument
ADV	adverbial phrase

- MA (syntactic marker of argument(s)). This indicates the surface case markers which help to identify argument roles. Common values for English are particular prepositions or U (unmarked case). Others include:

S	subject case
O	object case
TH	*that* complement
FT	infinitival complement
WH	complement initiated by *wh*-word

(S and O are used in English for pronouns).

- TT (transitivity type). Summarizes the main valency patterns in which central arguments may occur, e.g.

> I1A   intransitive verb with one argument, an AGT
> I2AL   intransitive verb with two arguments, AGT and LOC
> T2AT   transitive verb with two arguments, AGT and TAR

A single verb may be specified for more than one TT value, e.g. *eat* may be either I1A (*John ate*) or T2AT (*John ate the cake*). For each TT value there is a corresponding user-defined LISP function which uses voice and mood features to instantiate case frames for particular verbs during analysis and transfer (see Section 11.5.2).

11.5 Linguistic content of grammar

The METAL grammar consists of an unordered set of context-free phrase structure rules augmented (and effectively made context sensitive) by rule body expressions. These expressions, which are passed to USER-RULE by PARSE for evaluation, impose conditions on rule application and determine the linguistic structure built by each rule.

11.5.1 Grammar rules

Each rule of the grammar consists of:

(a) the context-free rewrite rule, defining a constituent in terms of its component constituents;

(b) the rule body, comprising:

   (i)   column tests, stating conditions on each component constituent individually;

   (ii)   an interconstituent test part (TEST), stating conditions on agreement between component constituents;

   (iii) a phrase constructor (CONSTR), formulating an interpretation of the phrase;

   (iv) a transfer part (TRANSF), specifying functions to be performed during the transfer stage of translation (see Section 11.7).

The TEST, CONSTR and TRANSF parts may include transformations and calls to case frames (see below). Before describing each part in more detail, the example (1) of a word-level rule will illustrate the overall form of rules.

```
(1)  NN         NST          N-FLEX
     0          1            2
     --         (REQ WI)  (REQ WF)

     TEST      (INT 1 CL 2 CL)


     CONSTR  (CPX 1 ALO CL)
             (CPY 2 NU CA)
             (CPY 1 WI )

     TRANSF  (XFR 1)
             (ADF 1 ON)
             (CPY 1 MC DR)
```

Context-free rules

The first line of each grammar rule specifies the context-free rewrite rule on which the grammar rule as a whole is based, with daughters on the RHS and father on the LHS, but including no explicit rewrite symbol. Thus the first line of the example rule (1) indicates that a noun may consist of a noun stem followed by a noun ending.

The LHS always consists of a single element, a major morphosyntactic category (value of CAT), defining the word or phrase of which the RHS elements are constituents. The RHS consists of one or more elements. These may be major morphosyntactic categories, or string literals representing a particular word, symbol or punctuation mark (with the pseudo-category LITERAL). String literals are enclosed between double quotation marks, e.g. " , " for a comma. For reference purposes, first-line elements are numbered from 0 to n, for an RHS of n constituents, the single LHS element corresponding to 0.

The context-free rules may be recursive; this is essential if a finite number of rules is to be capable of describing a theoretically infinite number of sentences. For example, the rule (2) indicates that a nominal (NO) may consist of an adjective followed by a nominal. It will apply recursively to a sequence of any number of adjectives, followed by a nominal:

```
(2)  NO            ADJ          NO
     0             1            2
```

Column tests

In many cases, specifications of the values of features of the RHS elements other than LITERAL or CAT are essential to prevent the context-free rules applying over-generally. To this end, the third and subsequent lines of a grammar rule may include column tests, i.e. boolean expressions on the presence or values of features on the RHS element in whose column they occur. USER-RULE must evaluate these expressions as T for the rule to be applied. The forms of expressions used in column tests and their semantics are as follows:

(REQ <feature name>): T if the named feature is present, regardless of its value(s).

(REQ <feature name> <list of values>): T if the named feature has a value in the list (hence NIL if the feature is absent).

(REQ <feature name> * <list of values>): T if the named feature has at least one value not in the list.

(NREQ <feature name>): T if the named feature is not present.

(OPT <feature name> <list of values>): T if the named feature is absent, or present with at least one of the values in the list.

(OPT <feature name> * <list of values>): T if the named feature is absent, or present with at least one value not in the list.

These expressions may be compounded by means of the standard LISP functions *OR* and *AND*. *AND* is in fact redundant except when used within an *OR* expression, since the overall value of all column tests is the *AND* of each of their values.

Note that the "placement" values WI, WF, NI and NF are used in this and other parts of the rule body as features in their own right, and so occur without the feature name PLC.

The examples (3) and (4), from German analysis rules, illustrate column tests.

```
(3)  VB        GE-VB       VST              V-FLEX
     0         1           2                3
               (REQ WI)    (NRQ WI)         (NRQ WI)
               --          (OPT PX NIL)     (REQ PF PAPL)
```

Example (3) can be glossed as follows: a verb (VB) may consist of a past-participle marker (GE-VB) followed by a verb stem (VST) followed by a verb ending (V-FLEX). The GE-VB element must be word-initial, the VST and V-FLEX must not be word-initial. The VST may optionally have the feature prefix (PX), but if so it must have the value NIL. The V-FLEX must have the paradigmatic form (PF) past participle (PAPL).

```
(4)  NP        NO
     0         1
               (REQ IN ST)
               (OR (REQ GEN) (REQ UNK) (REQ NUM)
               (REQ CA * G))
```

A noun phrase (NP) may consist of a NO(minal). The latter must have the IN(flection) feature with a ST(rong) value, and at least one of the following features: GEN(itive), UNK(nown), NUM(ber) or CA(se), with at least one value other than genitive (G).

TEST

The TEST part of a grammar rule, like the column test part, has the purpose of limiting rule application by imposing conditions on features and values associated with RHS elements. Unlike column tests, TEST expressions relate the features and values of one constituent to those of a sister constituent. Any one TEST expression may refer to a maximum of two RHS elements, designated by the reference numbers given in the second line of the rule.

TEST expressions are based on the two set functions: INT(ersection) and SUM (set union). In certain expressions, the result of these operations, i.e. a set of (featureless) values, may be assigned to a rule-internal variable for use in other TEST expressions or in the CONSTR part of the rule. The basic expression types are listed below as described in the documentation. The INT expressions appear to evaluate T if the specified set-intersection is not NIL. It is not clear how SUM expressions are used to return boolean values, since no examples are given.

(INT <integer *i*> <feature *A*> <integer *j*> <feature *B*>): Intersect the values of feature *A* on constituent *i* with those of feature *B* on constituent *j*. Also succeeds if constituent *i* is not marked for feature *A*, or if the set of values for feature *A* is empty.

(INT <integer *i*> <feature *A*> <integer *j*> <feature *B*> = <variable *Xk*>): Intersect the values of feature *A* on constituent *i* with those of feature *B* on constituent *j*. Both features are assumed to be present. The result of the intersection is assigned to the variable X_k.

(INT <variable *Xi*> <integer *j*> <feature *A*> = <variable *Xk*>): Intersect the values of the variable X_i with those of feature *A* on constituent *j*. Assigns the result to variable X_k.

(INT <integer *i*> <feature *A*> <list of values>): Used within COND expressions, to intersect the values of feature *A* on node *i* with the specified list of values.

(SUM <integer *i*> <feature *A*> <integer *j*> <feature *B*> = <variable *Xk*>): Create the union of values of feature *A* on constituent *i* with values of feature *B* on constituent *j*. Both features are assumed to be present. Assigns the result to variable X_k.

(SUM <variable *Xi*> <integer *j*> <feature *A*> = <variable *Xk*>): Create the union of values of variable X_i with values of feature *A* on constituent *j*. Assign the result to variable X_k. X_i can only be the result of a previous SUM.

The above expressions may be compounded by means of the standard LISP functions *AND*, *OR*, *COND* and *NOT*.

The function RET(rieve) may also be used within compound expressions to test for the presence of a particular feature on a specified constituent. RET expressions take the form:

(RFT <integer *i*> <feature *A*>): T if feature *A* occurs on constituent.

In addition, the functions FRM and FRT are used in TEST to invoke the case-frame processor – see Section 11.5.2.

Examples (5) and (6) show complex TEST expressions (only the TEST parts are glossed):

```
(5)  ADJ         ADJ              PP
     0           1                2
                 (NRQ COMP PP)  --


     TEST  (COND ((INT 1 FC PP) (INT 1 MC 2 PR = X1))
           (T NIL))
```

If the ADJ has the FC (form of complement) feature with a PP (prepositional phrase) value, then intersect the values of the MC (marker of complement) feature marked on the ADJ with values of the preposition feature marked on the PP, and assign the result to variable X1, else (i.e. if FC for ADJ does not include PP) return NIL.

```
(6)  PP          PREP             NP
     0           1                2
                 --               (OPT KP * DEM)


     TEST  (INT 1 GC 2 CA = X1)
           (OR (RET 1 WF)
               (AND (RET 2 BF) (INT 1 CN 2 BF = X2)))
```

Intersect the values of the feature GC (governing case) marked on the PREP with the values of the feature CA(se) marked on the NP and assign the result to variable X1. Then, either ensure that the PREP is marked for the value WF (word final), or ensure that the NP is marked for the feature BF (bound form) and intersect with its values the values of the feature CN (contraction) marked on the PREP, assigning the result to variable X2.

CONSTR

If all the conditions on rule application succeed, USER-RULE builds a structure in which the LHS element of the rule is the root, with RHS elements as its daughters. The CONSTR part of the rule specifies which features and values are to be assigned to the father node; it may modify the tree by applying transformational rules (see Section 11.5.3). CONSTR also includes the area-of-provenience tag (TAG) specifying the subject area(s) in which the rule applies, though it is difficult to see why this should be here and not in the TEST section.

The basic functions and expressions used in CONSTR are as follows (addition or copying of features and values is in all cases to the newly created father node):

(ADD <feature *A*>): Add feature *A* to the father node.

(ADD <feature *A*> <list of values>): Add feature *A* with the specified list of values.

(ADF <integer *i*> <feature *A*>): Add feature *A*, assigning to it the values of the same feature marked on constituent *i*. The function operates only if feature *A* is marked on *i*.

(ADF <integer *i*> <feature *A*> <feature *B*>): Add feature *B*, assigning to it the values of feature *A* marked on constituent *i*.

(ADX <variable *Xi*>): Add the values of variable X_i, using the feature-name given as second argument of the TEST function which originally assigned the values to X_i.

(ADX <variable *Xi*> <feature *A*>): Add the values of variable X_i, using feature name A.

(CPX <integer *i*> <list of features>): Copy all the features and values from constituent i, except system features and those listed.

(CPY <integer *i*> <list of features>): Copy from constituent i the listed features (with their values).

(PRF <integer *i*>): Assign preference factor i to the father node. This factor will be multiplied by that calculated from the preference values of the other components to determine this node's final weight. If the result falls below CUTOFF-WT, this node will be pruned from further analysis.

These assignments may be compounded by means of the standard LISP functions *AND*, *OR*, *COND* and *NOT*, and the set function INT.

The examples (7) and (8) illustrate the CONSTR part of rules (only the CONSTR parts are glossed).

```
(7)  PRED              WERDEN                PREDEF
     0                 1                     2
     (REQ PF FIN)      (REQ PK PAPL INF MDX)


     TEST


     CONSTR (CPX 2 PK)
            (CPY 1 PS NU MD)
            (COND ((INT 2 PK PAPL)
                          (ADF 1 TN)  (ADD VC P))
                   (T (ADD TN FU)  (ADF 2 VC)))
            (TAG ALL)
```

Copy from the PREDEF (defective predicate) all features (with their values) except PK (kind of predicate). Copy from WERDEN (passive auxiliary) the features PS (person), NU(mber) and MD (mood), with their values. If the PK feature marked on the PREDEF has the value PAPL (past participle), then add the feature TN (tense) with its values from WERDEN, and add the feature VC (voice) with value P(assive); else add the feature TN with value FU(ture), and the feature VC with its values from the PREDEF. The rule is general (TAG ALL).

```
(8)  NO            ADJ             NO
     0             1               2
                   (REQ PO ATR)    --


     TEST  (INT 1 NU 2 NU = X1)
           (INT 1 CA 2 CA = X2)
           (INT 1 GD 2 GD = X3)
```

```
CONSTR    (ADX X1)
          (ADX X2)
          (ADX X3)
          (CPX 2 IN NU CA GD)
          (CPY 1 IN DG WI)
          (ADD PNM)
          (AND (INT O CA G) (ADD GEN))
          (TAG ALL)
```

Add the values for variables X1, X2 and X3 assigned during TEST. Copy from the daughter NO(minal) node features with their values, except the features IN(flection), NU(mber), CA(se), GD (gender) and system-features. Copy from the ADJ the features IN, DG (degree) and the placement value WI. Add the feature PNM (prenominal modifier). If the values of the feature CA marked on the father node include the value G(enitive), then add the feature GEN to the father node. The rule is general (TAG ALL).

11.5.2 Case frames

As stated in Section 11.4.2, the dictionary entry for each verb stem includes a feature TT (transitivity type). The values (e.g. T3ATR, T2AT, I1A etc.) of TT correspond to case-frame functions[8], written in LISP, which are part of the linguistic data available to the system. They may be called as part of the TEST in a rule-body expression to check for well-formedness of clauses, and to assign case-labels to the arguments of predicates. Case frames may also be invoked by transformations within any part of the rule body, and must apply for the transformation to apply.

A clause is well-formed if:

- the central arguments to its predicate match the specifications stated in one of the case-frame functions called for that predicate, given the values for mood and voice marked on the predicate;
- any remaining arguments not so matched are valid as peripheral arguments, i.e. arguments which may occur with any predicate.

Any clause analysis whose result is not a well-formed clause is rejected.

Application of case frames

The case-frame processor (FIND-FRAME) is responsible for calling the relevant case-frame functions for the predicate in question. FIND-FRAME itself is called by the function FRM, included in the TEST part of grammar rules which build clauses; or by the function FRT, used within a transformation rule. The possible expression types are as follows:

---

8. See more recently Gebruers (1988). — HLS

```
(FRM (<integer i>)
(FRM (<integer i> <integer j>)
(FRT (<integer i>)
```

In all three, the first or only parameter (*i*) to the function is a clause, i.e. any structure containing a finite verb, designated by the reference number of its root node in the RHS of the context-free rule. The second parameter (*j*) may be any other argument to the verb which has not yet been included within the clause, e.g. an initial subject argument.

On being called, the case-frame processor accesses the TT feature associated with the verb in the specified clause and, for each TT value in turn, applies the corresponding function, until a successful application is achieved. Possible TT values are listed in descending order according to the number of central arguments specified, e.g. T3ATR before T2AT. In this way, the valid interpretation that uses the greatest number of central arguments will be selected. Upon successful application of a case-frame function, the processor checks that any remaining arguments (i.e. ones not accounted for by the case frame) are legal peripheral arguments. If they are, it reorders the daughters of the clause, placing the predicate first followed by all the arguments in the order in which they appeared in the clause. The feature RO(le of argument), with values given by the case frame, is assigned to each central argument, and the prepositions of central PP arguments are deleted. If all case-frame functions fail, FRM/FRT fails, causing the clause rule to fail.

Form of case-frame functions

Each case-frame function consists of two main parts, used respectively for analysis and transfer. The function SYNTAX, which succeeds during analysis and fails during transfer, determines which part is applicable at each phase. Within SYNTAX the nested conditional (*COND*) tests for values of the features VC (voice) and MD (mood) marked on the predicate, and these values determine the selection of one of several subframes. For example, the function I1A (i.e. an intransitive verb with one central argument, an AGT) for English will specify that the imperative form of the verb occurs without central arguments. Each subframe consists of a list of central arguments, with each argument being specified in the following way:

```
(FRAME <marker of argument> <form of argument>
       <role of argument>)
```

FRAME is a function which determines which of the arguments of the clause being analyzed is eligible for the given argument role. Constituents are processed left-to-right until one is found which matches the specifications given in the first two parameters of FRAME. The parameters are specified as follows:

<marker of argument>: a value of the feature MA, denoting the surface grammatical case, preposition, or complementizer by which the argument is marked (see Section 11.4.2)

<form of argument>: a value of the feature FA, denoting the constituent type (e.g. NP, PP) of the argument

`<role of argument>`: the case role to be assigned to the argument

If either of the first two parameters is specified as NIL, then the lexical entry for the verb in question is accessed to provide the relevant information.

Example (9) shows the analysis part of the I2AL case frame for German verbs such as *gehen* ('go').

```
(9) (DEXPR I2AL (VC MD)
        (COND ((SYNTAX)
                  (COND ((AND (ACTIVE)
                              (NON-COMMAND)
                              (FRAME N NP AGT)
                              (FRAME NIL NIL LOC))
                           T)
                         ((AND (ACTIVE)
                               (COMMAND)
                               (FRAME NIL NIL LOC))
                           T))
        )    )
        (* transfer part of case-frame *))
```

The first subframe is instantiated if the verb is active and declarative (NON-COMMAND). This frame consists of two central arguments, AGT and LOC. The AGT must be an NP in the nominative case; the surface form and marking of the LOC is specific to each particular verb. If the verb is active and imperative (COMMAND), the only central argument is a LOC, again with a verb-specific surface realization.

11.5.3 Transformations

Transformation rules are invoked by the rule bodies associated with phrase-structure rules. They are used:

- To modify syntactic structure by adding, deleting or reordering nodes in the object tree.
- To copy, add or delete features and values to/from descendants of the nodes specified in individual context-free rules. For this purpose, the functions and expressions described above for CONSTR – ADD, ADF, ADX, CPY, etc. – may be incorporated in transformations.
- To impose conditions on descendants of the nodes specified in individual context-free rules. For this purpose, the functions and expressions described above for column tests and TEST, REQ, INT, SUM, etc. may also be incorporated.

The use of transformations provides a powerful means of attaining the deeper, more abstract structural descriptors output by PARSE.

Application of transformations

Transformations are invoked in a grammar rule by the function XFM. There are three different forms for doing so:

(XFM <pattern> <action>): Here the transformation is specified directly in the rule-body. XFM calls the system function DO-TXFORM, which matches the pattern against the structures which are active in the current context-free rule.

(XFM <transformation name>): Once again, DO-TXFORM is accessed, in order to apply, if possible, the named transformation, which will have been predefined in a special file so that it may be invoked from several rules, thus:

(DT <pattern> <action> <transformation name>

(XFM): In this case, DO-TXFORMS is called, which will call DO-TXFORM for each transformation in a predefined set of general transformations. When invoked, each member of the set whose pattern matches against any of the active structures will be applied. Although the system allows for such transformations, they have not been used.

Form of transformations

Both the pattern and action of a transformation are based on tree structures, which are represented in the conventional way, using nested bracketing. The nodes of the trees may be of three types; in each case <integer> is a reference number used to equate nodes in the pattern with those in the action. The numbering is specific to the particular transformation rule, and need not correspond to the numbering of nodes of the context-free rule in whose rule body it occurs:

<category name or literal> <integer>: The node thus specified must be of the named category or have a CAN value equal to the literal.

& : <integer>: Such a node will match against any single node, regardless of its category, i.e. in the terminology of production systems, & is a node variable.

-- : <integer>: -- will match against any number (including zero) of contiguous sister nodes, i.e. -- is a list variable.

Note the absence of a variable which may be used to match nodes of an unspecified depth in the tree (generalized dependant variable).

An expression may be associated with any node, by bracketing the expression as though it was a daughter of the node to which it refers. Expressions in the pattern must be of type boolean, e.g. using the functions described for column tests (see p. 180) and TEST (see p. 181). Those in the action will generally be structure-changing expressions as in CONSTR (see p. 183).

The following rules (10)–(12) drawn from a German analysis grammar are used to exemplify transformations:

(10) **RCL**	**PRED**	**","**	**CLS-SUB**
0	**1**	**2**	**3**
	--	**--**	**(REQ MK TH)**
TEST			

```
CONSTR (CPY 1 TT MD SPX PX)
       (XFM (RCL:1 (PRED:2 &:3 CLS-SUB:4))
            (RCL:1 (PRED:2 CLS-SUB:4)))
       (PRF 3)
       (TAG ALL)
```

The transformation performed in (10) is straightforward. It has the effect of deleting any single unspecified node (in this case, a comma) intervening between a PRED(icate) node and a CLS-SUB (subordinate clause) node, when these constitute an RCL (right-branching clause).

The transformation in (11a) transforms the subtree (11b) into (11c). In addition, the feature CAN(onical form) is copied from the PRFX (prefix) to PRED, and the feature VC (voice) with value A(ctive) is added to PRED; the features CLF (clause-final) and SPX (separable prefix) are added to RCL:2.

```
(11) a.  RCL          RCL          PRFX
         0            1            2
                      (NRQ SPX)    (REQ WI)


         TEST    (INT 1 PX 2 CAN = X1)


         CONSTR (XFM (RCL:1 ((RCL:2 ((PRED:3 (--:4))
                                        --:5))
                             PRFX:6))
                     (RCL:2 ((PRED:3 (--:4) (CPY 6 CAN)
                                            (ADD VC A))
                      -- :5) (ADD CLF) (ADD SPX)))
                (TAG ALL)
```

```
b.          RCL:1                c.          RCL:2
           /     \                          /      \
       RCL:2     PRFX:6                 PRED:3      --:5
      /     \                             |
  PRED:3    --:5                         --:4
    |
   --:4
```

The transformation in (12) does not alter the subtree defined by the context-free rule, but applies the case-frame processor to the daughters of the LCL and adds to the `CLS-SUB` node a function which during transfer will transfer and reorder the daughters `--:4`.

```
(12) CLS-SUB          CONJ            LCL
     0                1               2
                      (REQ CU SUB)  (REQ MD + IMP)


TEST  (XFM (CLS-SUB:1 (CONJ:2 (LCL:3 (--:4)
                                       (FRT 4))))
           (CLS-SUB:1 (CONJ:2 (LCL:3 (--:4)
           (ADD EXPR TRANSF (XFR) (ORO))))))))
```

11.6 The parsing algorithm

The context-free grammar specified by the first lines of the analysis rules is compiled into two forms, a grammar indexed according to the leftmost constituent for bottom-up determination of possible applicable rules, and a discrimination net which will be used to realize a top-down filter to limit the rules applied to those which will actually form part of a sentential analysis. The top-down filter may be turned on or off by USER-PREPROCESSOR, since its use has been found to be advantageous only for sentences above a length of about eight words.

METAL actually provides alternative bottom-up parsers[9], one implementing the Cocke–Kasami–Younger algorithm and the other, a left-corner algorithm.

Both of the parsing algorithms are chart based but make no commitment to the sort of structures with which the chart edges are labelled. The structures are built by the user-defined routine USER-RULE which is called by PARSE when the latter finds a possible applicable rule. The two functions communicate by means of a linguistically neutral interface, through which are passed the structures corresponding to the RHS components of the context-free rule, and the expression (i.e. column tests, TEST, CONSTR and TRANSF) included in that rule. USER-RULE returns either a structure that it has built, for addition to the chart, or an indication that the rule was not applicable. By this means, the algorithm for building the structure can be tailored to fit both the style of analysis that has been included in the grammar and the purpose for which the structure is to be used.

The system provides a default for USER-RULE which realises a conventional *n*-ary immediate-constituent syntax tree by means of attribute-value pairs (structural attributes with values generated by the function itself and user- and system-defined features with their values).

The organization of the calls by PARSE to the user-defined functions is as follows:

---

9. Later sources only mention the latter, e.g. "an active chart parser which works middle out, left corner, some paths" (Thurmair 1990b). — HLS

1. USER-PREPROCESSOR is called with the sentence to be translated, and may turn the top-down filter off or on according to the length of the sentence, as well as making other initializations for the purpose of keeping performance statistics etc. This function then returns the sentence, as a LISP list, to PARSE.

2. USER-WORD is called with each word of the sentence, which returns a structured list of possible alternative segmentations of the word, or NIL if there are none. The elements of the list are added to the chart.

3. USER-ADD is called if the word is a literal of a type found on the list ADD-INTRINSICS (a number in one of various forms), and will assign a syntactic category to the word, NUMBER being the default.

4. USER-ERROR will be called if both USER-WORD and USER-ADD have failed to provide an interpretation of a word, and the global variable ADD-UNKNOWNS does not indicate (i.e. has not been assigned a value corresponding to) a grammatical category to which unknown words should be assigned, e.g. PROPN (proper noun). USER-ERROR must take some action, such as calling an automatic spelling-correction routine, initiating an interactive request for the word's definition, or returning *ERROR*, thus terminating the parse and initiating a call to USER-POSTPROCESSOR to print an error message.

5. As each new edge is added to the chart, all context-free rules which are rendered applicable by this addition are determined, and for each, USER-RULE is called with the component symbols of the rule, the structures from the chart corresponding to the daughter components, and the rule-body expression. USER-RULE evaluates the rule-body expression, expanding the macros FRM, FRT and XFM into calls to the system functions FIND-FRAME, DO-TXFORM and DO-TXFORMS as appropriate. USER-RULE returns either a structure for PARSE to associate with the new edge corresponding to the root (LHS) symbol from the rule, or the value *ERROR*, in which case no new edge will be built. A new edge may cause further context-free rules to apply, so PARSE continues recursively until no more rules are applicable. Stages 2, 3, 4 and 5 are repeated until all morphs for all words have been treated.

6. PARSE determines the categories associated with those edges spanning the chart from entry to exit vertices and checks these against the list ROOTCATEGORIES to see if they correspond to sentential analyses. Depending on the values in ROOTCATEGORIES, sentential analyses may be sentences, or some other constituent if, for instance, the input text derives from a table. Acceptable analyses are passed to USER-POSTPROCESSOR, which may choose between alternatives by means of the preference values associated with them, and may also print out processing statistics. If no sentential analyses have been found, PARSE passes the chart to USER-POSTPROCESSOR. The latter may then specify a phrasal analysis by subsuming the edges of the shortest, highest-scoring path through the chart

under a "dummy" S(entence) edge. Such a phrasal analysis may actually lead to a quite acceptable translation, and will also be useful in determining why the grammar failed to find a sentential analysis.[10]

11.7 Transfer

After SL analysis has been completed, the driver routine TRANSLATE invokes the function TRANSFER on the highest weighted interpretation output by PARSE. In current applications, the purpose of the transfer phase is to convert the deep, semi-abstract representations resulting from analysis into surface syntactic structures in the TL. In this sense, transfer assumes most of the task of structural generation, leaving relatively little for the final GENERATE phase to do.

There is no centralized control procedure for transfer: control is exercised by the TRANSF part of grammatical rules. During analysis the rule-body interpreter USER-RULE automatically associates the rule-body expressions (including TRANSF) of each successful rule applied, with the new father node created by that rule. The transfer phase begins with TRANSFER evaluating the TRANSF part of the rule body associated with the root node of the analysis tree. By means of the function XFR contained in the TRANSF part of nonterminal nodes, TRANSFER may be recursively called on daughters of the current node, i.e. TRANSFER will descend one level in the tree to evaluate the TRANSF expressions associated with one or more daughter nodes. When a terminal node is reached the function XLX or TLX specified in TRANSF will effect lexical transfer on that node. In addition to these functions, TRANSF expressions may modify tree structure by invoking transformations and case frames, and may propagate features and values upwards or downwards in the tree. These operations may be performed either before or after invoking XFR, depending on the ordering of expressions in any particular TRANSF section. Thus, for example, TRANSFER may be invoked on a particular daughter, and features or values (which may be those of the TL if the daughter has been lexically transferred) may then be returned from that daughter to the father node in order to be used in, or to initiate, further TRANSF operations specified on the father node.

11.7.1 Transfer functions

The forms of the functions used in the TRANSF parts of rule bodies are as follows (unlike their counterparts in CONSTR, in which all operations change the father node, these functions add or copy features to a specified daughter):

(SEV <integer *i*> <feature *A*>): Add the feature *A* to the daughter *i*.

---

10. Mention should also be made of the "preference and scoring" mechanisms introduced to give a further element of control over the grammars. These are described by Caeyers & Adriaens (1990). — HLS

(SEV <integer *i*> <feature *A*> <list of values>): Add feature *A* to daughter *i* with the specified list of values.

(SEF <integer *i*> <feature *A*>): Add feature *A* to daughter *i* with the values of *A* from the father.

(SEF <integer *i*> <feature *A*> <feature *B*>): Add the feature *B* on daughter *i* with the values of feature *A* on the father.

(XFR): Invoke the system function TRANSFER on all the daughters of the current node in order.

(XFR <list of integers>): Invoke TRANSFER on the daughters of the current node whose reference numbers appear in the list.

(XLX <integer *i*>): Lexically transfer the daughter node *i*.

(XLX <integer *i*> (<list of features>)): Lexically transfer the daughter node *i* using the features listed to select the correct entry in the transfer dictionary.

(XLX <integer *i*> (<list of features 11>) (<inflection category> <list of features 12>)): Lexically transfer the daughter node *i*, using the list of features 11 to select the correct entry in the transfer dictionary. Inflect the stem with the appropriate allomorph in the TL dictionary entry for the specified inflection category, selected according to the list of features 12 (see Section 11.7.2).

(TLX <list of features 11>) (<inflection category> <list of features 12>)): Lexically transfer the current node, using the other information as described for XLX. This function is used within a transformation.

(ORO): This function, of zero parameters, is invoked on the father node of a clause, with the purpose of converting the canonical ordering of the predicate and its arguments into a TL ordering. ORO applies the transfer part of the same case-frame function that was successful during analysis. For example, the transfer part of the I2AL case-frame cited earlier is (13).

```
(13) (DEXPR I2AL  (VC MD)
        (COND ((SYNTAX)
                 (* analysis part of case-frame *))
              ((AND (ACTIVE) (NON-COMMAND)
                 (PRED AGT LOC))
               (ROL-ORDER (AGT) (PRED) (LOC)))
              ((AND (ACTIVE) (COMMAND) (PRED LOC))
               (ROL-ORDER (PRED) (LOC))))))
```

After checking to find which TL subframe is applicable, according to the values of VC and MD and to the central argument roles assigned during analysis, the function ROL-ORDER is called to reorder the PRED(icate) and arguments as specified in its parameters. Any peripheral arguments are placed after the last central argument, to be reordered by transformations if necessary. The central arguments are marked (e.g. by insertion of prepositions) using the specifications given in the dictionary entry for the particular TL verb (note that this requires lexical transfer to have been performed on the predicate and its arguments before ORO is invoked).

In addition to the functions just listed, TRANSF may incorporate any of the add or copy functions used in CONSTR, together with the standard functions *AND*, *OR*, *COND* and *NOT* and the TEST function INT, and may invoke transformation rules in the usual way via the function XFM. Example (14) shows a complex TRANSF section, associated with the German analysis rule corresponding to NP → DET N0.

```
(14) TRANSF (XFR 2)
            (CPY 2 MC)
            (COND ((AND (INT 2 DR NP)
                        (NOT (INT 2 DR RD)))
                   (XFM (NP:1 (DET:2 N0:3))
                        (NP:1 (N0:3))))
                  (T (ADF 2 ON) (SEF 1 ON)
                     (SEV 1 KD DET) (XLX 1 (ON NU)))))
```

11.7.2 Lexical transfer

Lexical transfer is effected in the following stages:

1. The bilingual transfer dictionary is accessed with the SL canonical form, to identify the corresponding TL canonical form. Entries are essentially equations in LISP format; example (15), from the German–English dictionary, illustrates the basic form of an entry.

   ```
   (15) (give (geben) VST (CAT VST))
   ```
   i.e. the canonical form *geben*, marked for the feature CAT with value VST, translates as the canonical form *give*, also a VST. Where multiple translations are possible, further conditions may be imposed on the feature-values of the SL form to ensure that the correct selection is made, e.g. (16).

   ```
   (16) (be-lost (gehen) VST (CAT VST) (PX VERLOREN))
        (go      (gehen) VST (CAT VST) (PX NIL)
                                       (PF FIN INF PAPL))
        (outgo   (gehen) VST (CAT VST) (PX NIL)
                                       (PF PRPL))
   ```
   i.e. *gehen* translates as *be lost* if it is marked for the feature PX (prefix) with value VERLOREN; if PX has the value NIL, then *gehen* translates as *go* if its PF (paradigmatic form) feature includes at least one of the values FIN(ite), INF(initive) or PAPL (past participle); or as *outgo* if PF has the value PRPL (present participle).

2. The TL canonical form is then used to access the TL monolingual dictionary, which provides the appropriate allomorph. Where a single TL canonical form has more than one allomorph, the second argument of the function XLX/TLX in TRANSF is used to select the correct entry. For example, the lexical transfer of a verb is initiated by the function

   ```
   (TLX (PF NU TN PS) (V-FLEX CL PF NU TN PS))
   ```

which is invoked from the named transformation VB The second argument indicates that the features PF (paradigmatic form), NU(mber), TN (tense) and PS (person), as specified for the TL allomorph in its dictionary entry, must have values which agree with the corresponding values marked on the SL verb.

3. If the TL word is inflected, this is indicated by the third argument of the function XLX/TLX. Since inflectional endings are not canonically transferred, and since the TL lexicon is accessed via CAN values, the TL lexicon includes special entries for inflectional endings, in which the canonical form is the same as the inflection category. An example English entry (17) should clarify this.

```
(17) (V-FLEX           CAT (V-FLEX)
          ALO (-es)
          SNS (61)
          CL  (PR-ES2)
          PS (3)
          NU (SG)
          TN (PR)
          MD (IND)
          PF (FIN)
     )
```

The inflection category stated as the first element of the third argument of XLX/TLX accesses all those entries with a corresponding CAN value. The remaining elements of the argument are used to select the entry for the appropriate allomorph. In the example TLX expression for verbs given above, the third argument specifies that the allomorph of V-FLEX must agree with the values of CL, PF, NU, TN and PS marked on the verb stem.

4. Once the appropriate allomorph of the TL stem has been selected as in Stage 2, the inflectional allomorph (where applicable) is added to it and the whole string, with its associated lexical information from the TL dictionary, is substituted for the SL node upon which lexical transfer was called. Note that there are no facilities for performing transductions on character strings, so phonological phenomena like elision and contraction must be realized by using phonological features on nodes to select differing allomorphs.

If there are multiple translations, as a result of unresolved lexical ambiguities, these are all marked on the same node, but are separated by slashes.

11.8 Generation

When all leaves of the tree have been assigned TL stem allomorphs with their appropriate inflectional allomorphs, the tree is passed to GENERATE, which performs a traversal, visiting all the leaves, and appending each of the associated character strings to the end of the global variable TRANSLATION.

11.9 Evaluation of METAL

The fact that the METAL grammars and system functions are directly interpreted/applied by the LISP interpreter is advantageous in two ways. First, new rules may be added without the need for compilation, and secondly, the full power of LISP is potentially available for use as necessary.

The use of a basically context-free grammar has several advantages, in terms of ease of grammar writing, perspicuity (at least of the surface grammar) and efficiency of parsing, the last being exploited to the maximum in METAL. The current number of rules is 400, and METAL's designers estimate that a total of 1000 rules[11] will be adequate for all sentence forms in all languages.

The close strategic link which exists between the rules of analysis and "transfer" must detract from the independence of the two stages[12]; and even though the system has a claim to multilinguality, this would necessitate several changes to the syntax of grammatical data, e.g. for case frames, where the data for the two phases is closely linked.

The fact that lexical transfer (including structural changes conditioned by lexical items) and structural transfer are inextricably linked, and that the order in which transfer must be effected is conditioned largely by the order in which analysis rules were applied, must give rise to difficulties in writing, debugging and extending transfer grammars, by reducing the modularity of individual rules within the transfer phase. This compounds the problems arising from the interdependence of the two phases.

In contrast to the interdependence of analysis and transfer, which from a theoretical point of view might be better separated, the processes of string segmentation with dictionary lookup (USER-WORD) and the determination of morphological coherence (PARSE) are independent, although they might be more profitably interwoven.

Despite these reservations, the facilities provided for the treatment of case-like phenomena, particularly the hierarchical structuring of features and the explicit devices for case-frame representation, are extremely useful. Other aspects of the system which appear to be of particular value include the use of the PRF feature for disambiguation between competing analyses, and the capability of continuing with translation despite a failure to derive a sentential analysis. The documentation does

---

11. Schneider (1992: p. 587) says the system should use "no more than 600 rules". — HLS

12. This problem was later recognized, and the "METAL Interface Representation" (MIR) introduced to lessen the interdependence of the two modules, especially with a view to introducing further language pairs; see Thurmair (1990a). — HLS

not mention the theory underlying the assignment of PRF values to rules, although it appears to be reasonably effective (see below).

11.10 Software environment, implementation and results

METAL is embedded within a software environment[13] that provides the following facilities:

- rule handlers dedicated to the treatment (creation, editing, etc.) of each type of grammatical data, i.e. dictionaries, context-free rules, transformations and case-frames; of particular interest is the "lexical default" program which automatically generates dictionary entries from a minimum of specified information;
- the choice of applying linguistic data in source or compiled form, depending on whether grammars are being developed, or being applied in an operational context, respectively;
- a suite of text-processing programs which, with a minimum of human intervention, format the text, dividing it into sentences and excluding material which should not be translated; this is particularly significant in the texts that are submitted to METAL, which often contain flowcharted information such that a single "sentence" must be read vertically rather than horizontally;
- facilities for human revision and reformatting the text; in those cases where METAL has failed to achieve even a phrasal analysis, the post-editor has access to translations of the technical terms in the text.

METAL was originally implemented in INTERLISP on a DEC 2060, and was found to translate at a speed of about 2 CPU-seconds per word, of which about 45 per cent was accounted for by storage management. In terms of real-time, this amounted to about 3.7 seconds per word. Transferred to a Symbolics™ LM-2 LISP machine, translation time increased to 10 to 12 seconds per word, but it is envisaged that substantial reductions in this figure will occur when the memory of the LM-2 is increased from 256K to 512K.[14]

---

13. Perhaps the most significant development in METAL since the first edition of this book is in the software environment. At the level of both developer and end user, METAL is to be admired for its sophisticated software environment. For the developers, "productivity tools" to facilitate interactive lexicon development (the INTERCODER) and grammar development (METALSHOP) were introduced. For the end-user, the translation system itself is embedded in a software package including text acquisition, deformatting, post-editing and reformatting tools. In addition, standard formats for exchange of documents and lexical data were established, to facilitate cooperation amongst METAL users and members of MAUS, the METAL users' group. For details see particularly Thurmair (1990b, 1991) and Hutchins & Somers (1992: pp. 260–2). — HLS

14. Figures in subsequent reports vary: Schneider (1987: p. 123) has the translation system running on 4 to 8 Mb. Translation speed has increased dramatically: Schneider (1989: p. 130) mentions a throughput capacity of more than 200 pages per day, equivalent to one word per second (Hutchins & Somers 1992: p. 277f). — HLS

11.10.1 Prototype evaluation

Tested on a corpus of 1103 sentences in 1980, METAL gave the following results for translation quality (discounting eight sentences with major source errors) (based on Lehmann et al. (1980: p. I-97ff)):

Analyzed sentences		90.0%
	excellent translation 83.7%	
	inadequate translation 6.2%	
Unanalyzed sentences		10.0%
	excellent phrasal 2.9%	
	inadequate phrasal 5.4%	
	no translation 1.7%	

11.10.2 Recent evaluation

A more recent survey[15] has been reported by Shah (1987). He describes the first ever test of METAL other than by its own developers: installed at a translation agency in Switzerland, after a three-month startup period (for training and tuning of the system), Shah reports (p. 152f)

- very short lead times in translation production: one week for a 1000-page document;

- reduction of 30–40 per cent of overall costs due to automatic reformatting;

- 20 per cent lower translation costs due to controlled vocabulary;

- "unsurpassed terminology consistency";

- "improved functionality due to consistent phraseology".

Of particular interest are the case studies shown in Table 11.1 showing between 29 and 45 per cent quicker translation at 60 per cent of the cost.

With savings of this magnitude, it is not surprising that METAL is doing well as a commercial system. Schneider (1991: p. 43) reports 25 installations, mostly in industry, trade or banking, primarily using the system for publication-quality documents. He adds that "cost/benefit analyses have shown that a METAL installation is cost-effective at a volume of 2000 pages per year or higher". With the appearance of a METAL users' group, and given the attention that the developers pay to their users' needs (see Schneider 1991), we can point to METAL as a success story in the development of MT and machine-aided translation.

---

15. This section has been added for this edition. — HLS

Table 11.1 Evaluation case studies.

	Manual	METAL
Case A: 16 000 pages (8 lines/page = 128 000 lines)		
Draft translation (days)[a]	400	80
Editing (days)[b]	178	178
Word processing (days)	320	0
Total (days)	898	258
Total (%)	100	29
Cost (in unspecified cost units)	320	190
Cost (%)	100	60
Case B: 6 000 pages (20 lines/page = 120 000 lines)		
Draft translation (days)[c]	500	30
Editing (days)[b]	167	334
Word processing (days)	188	20
Total (days)	855	384
Total (%)	100	45
Cost (in unspecified cost units)	450	265
Cost (%)	100	59
Savings time: 55% cost: 41%		

Key: a manual 320 lines/day/translator, system 200 pages/day
b 720 lines/day/editor
c manual 240 lines/day/translator, system 200 pages/day

Source: Shah (1987), p. 158

11.11 Documentation

Bennett, W. S. 1982. *The linguistic component of METAL.* Working paper LRC-82–2, LRC, University of Austin, Texas.

Lehmann, W. P., W. S. Bennett, J. Slocum, H. Smith, S. M. V. Pfluger & S. A. Eveland 1980. *The METAL system: final technical report.* RADC/TR-80–374, Griffiss AFB, Rome Air Development Center.

Slocum, J. 1981. *The METAL parsing system.* Working paper LRC-81–2, LRC, University of Austin, Texas.

Slocum, J. 1981. *A status report on the LRC Machine Translation system.* Working paper LRC-82–3, LRC, University of Austin, Texas.

Slocum, J. & W. S. Bennett 1982. *The LRC Machine Translation system.* Working paper LRC-82-1, LRC, University of Austin, Texas.

11.12 Further References

Alonso, J. A. 1990. Transfer InterStructure: designing an 'interlingua' for transfer-based MT systems. In *Proceedings of the Third International Conference on Theoretical and Methodological Issues in Machine Translation of Natural Language*, Austin TX, 189–201.

Caeyers, H. & G. Adriaens 1990. Efficient parsing using preferences. In *Proceedings of the Third International Conference on Theoretical and Methodological Issues in Machine Translation of Natural Language* Austin TX, 279–86.

Gebruers, R. 1988. Valency and MT: Recent developments in the METAL system. In *Proceedings of the Second Conference on Applied Natural Language Processing*, Austin, Texas, 168–75.

Hutchins, W. J. & H. L. Somers 1992. *An introduction to Machine Translation*, Chapter 15. London: Academic Press.

Little, P. 1990. METAL – Machine translation in practice. In *Translating and the Computer 11: preparing for the next decade*, C. Picken (ed.), 94–107. London: Aslib.

Schneider, T. 1987. The Metal system, status 1987. In *Machine Translation Summit*, M. Nagao (ed.), 122–7. Tokyo: Ohmsha.

Schneider, T. 1989. The METAL system. Status 1989. In [Proceedings of] *MT Summit II*, Munich, 128–36.

Schneider, T. 1991. The METAL system. Status 1991. In *Proceedings, Machine Translation Summit III*, Washington DC, 41–4.

Schneider, T. 1992. User driven development: METAL as an integrated multilingual system. *Meta* **37**, 583–94.

Shah, R. 1989. Translation of engineering documentation with METAL. In *Machine Translation Summit*, M. Nagao (ed.), 152–9. Tokyo: Ohmsha.

Thurmair, G. 1990a. Complex lexical transfer in METAL. In *Proceedings of the Third International Conference on Theoretical and Methodological Issues in Machine Translation of Natural Language*, Austin TX, 91–107.

Thurmair, G. 1990b. METAL: Computer integrated translation. In *Proceedings of a workshop on Machine Translation*, Manchester, J. McNaught (ed.), DTI/Speech and Language Technology Club.

Thurmair, G. 1991. Recent developments in machine translation. *Computers and the Humanities* **25**, 115–28.

Bibliography

This bibliography includes references from Part I and entries from the References sections in Part 2, but not entries from the Documentation lists, except where they were cited in the text. Also included are references from the new footnotes.

Alonso, J. A. 1990. Transfer InterStructure: designing an 'interlingua' for transfer-based MT systems. In *Proceedings of the Third International Conference on Theoretical and Methodological Issues in Machine Translation of Natural Language*, Austin TX, pp. 189–201.

ALPAC. 1966. *Language and machines: computers in translation and linguistics* (Report by the Automatic Language Processing Advisory Committee, Division of Behavioral Sciences, National Research Council). Publication 1416, National Academy of Sciences, Washington DC.

Barnes, A. M. N. 1983. *An investigation into the syntactic structures of abstracts and the feasibility of an 'interlingua' for their translation by machine.* MSc thesis, UMIST.

Bloomfield, L. 1933. *Language.* London: Allen & Unwin.

Caeyers, H. & G. Adriaens 1990. Efficient parsing using preferences. In *Proceedings of the Third International Conference on Theoretical and Methodological Issues in Machine Translation of Natural Language*, Austin TX, 279–86.

Catford, J. C. 1965. *A linguistic theory of translation*, London: Oxford University Press.

Chandioux, J. 1989. Météo: 100 million words later. In *American Translators Association Conference 1989: coming of age*, D. L. Hammond (ed.), 449–53. Medford, NJ: Learned Information.

Chomsky, N. 1957. *Syntactic structures.* The Hague: Mouton.

Chomsky, N. 1982. *Lectures on government and binding.* Dordrecht: Foris.

Davis, R. & J. King 1977. An overview of production systems. In *Machine Intelligence 8*, E. Elcock and D. Michie (eds), 300–32. Chichester: Ellis Horwood.

Gachot, D. A. 1989. The SYSTRAN renaissance. In *MT Summit II*, Munich, 60–5.

Gebruers, R. 1988. Valency and MT: recent developments in the METAL system. In *Proceedings of the Second Conference on Applied Natural Language Processing*, Austin, Texas, 168–75.

Georgeff, M. 1982. Procedural control in production systems. *Artificial Intelligence* **18**, 175–201.

Gervais, A. 1980. *Evaluation of the TAUM-AVIATION Machine Translation pilot system.* Translation Bureau, Secretary of State, Ottawa.

Gobeil, F. 1981. *Machine Translation feasibility study: final report.* Planning, Management and Technology Branch, Translation Bureau, Secretary of State Department, Ottawa.

Hutchins, W. J. & H. L. Somers 1992. *An introduction to Machine Translation,* London: Academic Press.

Isabelle, P. & L. Bourbeau 1985. TAUM-AVIATION: its technical features and some experimental results. *Computational Linguistics* **11**, 18–27.

Johnson, R., M. King & L. des Tombe 1985. EUROTRA: a multilingual system under development. *Computational Linguistics* **11**, 155–69.

Johnson, R., S. Krauwer, M. Rosner & N. Varile 1983. Controlling complex systems of linguistic rules. *American Journal of Computational Linguistics* **9**, 199–201.

Kaplan, R. 1973. A general syntactic processor. In *Natural language processing,* R. Rustin (ed.), 193–241. New York: Algorithmic Press.

Kaplan, R. & J. Bresnan 1982. Lexical-Functional Grammar: a formal system for grammatical representation, in *The mental representation of grammatical relations,* J. Bresnan (ed.), 173–281. Cambridge, Mass.: MIT Press.

Kay, M. 1977. Morphological and syntactic analysis. In *Linguistic structures processing,* A. Zampolli (ed.), 131–234. Amsterdam: North-Holland.

Lehmann, W. P., W. S. Bennett, J. Slocum, H. Smith, S. M. V. Pfluger & S. A. Eveland. 1980. *The METAL system: final technical report.* RADC/TR-80–374, Griffiss AFB, Rome Air Development Center.

Lehmann, W. P. & R. Stachowitz 1975. *Development of German–English Machine Translation system.* Final (annual) report, LRC, University of Texas, Austin.

Lehrberger, J. & L. Bourbeau 1988. *Machine Translation: linguistic characteristics of MT systems and general methodology of evaluation.* Amsterdam: John Benjamins.

Little, P. 1990. METAL – Machine Translation in practice. In *Translating and the Computer 11: preparing for the next decade,* C. Picken (ed.), 94–107. London: Aslib.

Lytinen, S. L. & R. C. Schank 1982. Representation and translation. *Text* **2**, 83–111.

Macklovitch, E. & L. Bourbeau 1981. The principle characteristics of the TAUM-AVIATION system. In *Linguistic documentation of the computerized translation chain of the TAUM-AVIATION system,* L. Bourbeau (ed.). Montréal: TAUM.

Maegaard, B. & H.-D. Maas 1985. *Definition of the Eurotra user language,* Final Report (ETS-7-DK/D), submitted to the Commission of the European Communities.

Marcus, M. P. 1980. *A theory of syntactic recognition for natural language.* Cambridge, Mass.: MIT Press.

Newmark, P. 1981. *Approaches to translation.* Oxford: Pergamon.

Pierce, C. S. 1934. *Collected papers.* Cambridge, Mass.: Harvard University Press.

Schneider, T. 1987. The Metal system, status 1987. In *Machine Translation Summit,* M. Nagao (ed.), 122–7. Tokyo: Ohmsha.

Schneider, T. 1989. The METAL system. Status 1989. In *MT Summit II*, Munich, 128–36.

Schneider, T. 1991. The METAL system. Status 1991. In *Proceedings, Machine Translation Summit III*, Washington DC, 41–4.

Schneider, T. 1992. User driven development: METAL as an integrated multilingual system. *Meta* **37**, 583–94.

Shah, R. 1987. Translation of engineering documentation with METAL. In *Machine Translation Summit*, M. Nagao (ed.), 152–9. Tokyo: Ohmsha.

Siebenaler, L. 1986. SYSTRAN for ESPRIT and ECAT Bureau service. *Terminologie et Traduction* **1**, 40–6.

Thurmair, G. 1990a. Complex lexical transfer in METAL. In *Proceedings of the Third International Conference on Theoretical and Methodological Issues in Machine Translation of Natural Language*, Austin TX, 91–107.

Thurmair, G. 1990b. METAL: computer integrated translation. In *Proceedings of a workshop on Machine Translation*, Manchester, J. M\u1d9cNaught (ed.), DTI/Speech and Language Technology Club.

Thurmair, G. 1991. Recent developments in machine translation. *Computers and the Humanities* **25**, 115–28.

Trabulsi, S. 1989. Le système SYSTRAN. In *Traduction assistée par ordinateur: perspectives technologiques, industrielles et economiques envisageables à l'horizon 1990*, A. Abbou (ed.), 15–34. Paris: Editions Daicadif.

Van Eynde, F. 1983. Two views on the translation problem. Unpublished EUROTRA trigger paper, Katholieke Universiteit Leuven.

Van Slype, G. & I. Pigott 1979. Description du système de traduction automatique SYSTRAN de la Commission des Communautées Européennes. *Documentaliste* **16**, 150–9.

Vauquois, B. 1975. *La traduction automatique à Grenoble*. Paris: Dunod.

Wheeler, P. 1987. SYSTRAN. In *Machine Translation today: the state of the art*, M. King (ed.), 192–208. Edinburgh: Edinburgh University Press.

Winograd, T. 1983. *Language as a cognitive process. Volume 1: syntax*. Reading, Mass: Addison-Wesley.

Woods, W. 1970. Transition network grammars for natural language analysis. *Communications of the ACM* **13** 591–606.

Woods, W. 1973. An experimental parsing system for transition network grammars. In *natural language processing*, R. Rustin (ed.), 111–54. New York: Algorithmic Press.

Index

Page references in italics refer to footnotes.